THE UNIVERSITY OF
WINCHESTER

Martial Rose Library
Tel: 01962 827306

To be returned on or before the day marked above, subject to recall.

Contemporary Adaptations of Greek Tragedy

Auteurship and Directorial Visions

Edited by
George Rodosthenous

Bloomsbury Methuen Drama
An imprint of Bloomsbury Publishing Plc

B L O O M S B U R Y
LONDON · OXFORD · NEW YORK · NEW DELHI · SYDNEY

Bloomsbury Methuen Drama

An imprint of Bloomsbury Publishing Plc

Imprint previously known as Methuen Drama

50 Bedford Square	1385 Broadway
London	New York
WC1B 3DP	NY 10018
UK	USA

www.bloomsbury.com

BLOOMSBURY, METHUEN DRAMA and the Diana logo are trademarks of Bloomsbury Publishing Plc

First published 2017

© George Rodosthenous and contributors, 2017

George Rodosthenous has asserted his right under the Copyright, Designs and Patents Act, 1988, to be identified as editor of this work.

British Library Cataloguing-in-Publication Data

A catalogue record for this book is available from the British Library.

ISBN: HB: 978-1-4725-9153-1
PB: 978-1-4725-9152-4
ePDF: 978-1-4725-9155-5
ePub: 978-1-4725-9154-8

Library of Congress Cataloging-in-Publication Data

A catalog record for this book is available from the Library of Congress.

Cover design: Eleanor Rose
Cover photograph © Wonge Bergmann

Typeset by Fakenham Prepress Solutions, Fakenham, Norfolk, NR21 8NN
Printed and bound in Great Britain

CONTENTS

LIST OF FIGURES

ACKNOWLEDGEMENTS

My directorial interest in Greek tragedy has been forming since 2002. I have, since then, updated and directed twelve plays. I would like to thank Mark Dudgeon at Bloomsbury Methuen Drama for his immediate interest in my research. Also many thanks to Emily Hockley and the editorial team at Bloomsbury Methuen Drama for all their help and guidance towards the final steps of the process, the anonymous reader for his or her constructive feedback and insightful suggestions, and our copy editor for their hard work.

Special thanks to the Michael Cacoyiannis Foundation, which functioned as the main inspiration for this volume, where I presented my *Antigone* in 2014 as part of the Ancient Drama: Influences and Modern Approaches initiative, included in the 'ATTICA' Regional Operational Programme of the NSRF 2007–13 funded by the European Union; Alexandra Georgopoulou, Dimitris Yolassis, Xenia Kaldara, Angeliki Poulou, Olga Gratsaniti, Stella Angeletou, Sarantis Zarganis, the technical staff of MCF, Alexander Mordoudack, Chara Petrounia and Eleni Kyprioti, as well as to both casts of *Antigone* (Leeds and Athens versions). Thanks to the International Theatre Institute (Cyprus branch), Neophytos Neophytou and the Festival of Ancient Drama for its two invitations (*Ajax* and *Hippolytus*).

I am grateful to all the contributors to this volume for their excellent contributions and hard work in ensuring its smooth publication.

Also, sincere thanks to Stergios Mavrikis for sharing his expert knowledge on the classics over the years and my mentor Arthur Pritchard for his support and guidance over the past decade and a half. Dr Avra Sidiropoulou has been a constant inspiration, Dr Andri Constantinou has provided some useful suggestions for contributors and Dr George Sampatakakis has made astute comments on my Introduction.

Thanks to Dr Scott Palmer for his encouragement in publishing my research on updating Greek tragedy, Ms Susan Daniels, Dr Kara McKechnie, Dr Fiona Bannon, Professor Alice O'Grady, Professor Alice O'Grady, Dr Anna Fenemore, Dr Tony Gardner, Dr Philip Kiszely, Dr Ben Walmsley, Dr David Shearing, Steve Ansell and all my colleagues, technical and support staff, stage@leeds and students at the School of Performance and Cultural Industries for their support. And to my colleagues at the Department of Classics for their generous feedback on our performances.

Additional thanks to Luk Van Den Dries, Michael Fentiman, Dr Eleanor OKell, Dr Angela Hadjipanteli, Georgea Solomontos, Varnavas Kyriazis, Nikos Charalambous, Professor Edith Hall, Jan Fabre, Marina Maleni, Lea Maleni, Tom Colley, Lauren Garnham, Scott Harris, Alex Clark, George Z. Georgiou, Anastasia Georgiou, Ashley Scott Layton, Patrick Bannon and all the performers I worked with for helping me develop and shape my directorial practice and vision.

I also need to thank Dr Duška Radosavljević for her feedback on the initial proposal and constructive presence in everything I do.

I owe a lot of gratitude to those who gave me permission to include their photographs in the volume, as well as all the actors and performers portrayed in them.

I would like to thank my sister Marina Rodosthenous and my brother Nektarios Rodosthenous for their continuous support of my work. And, finally my mother Aphrodite and my late father Andreas, who generously introduced me to theatre, music and culture.

This book is dedicated in loving memory to Jonathan Hudson.

Dr George Rodosthenous
Associate Professor in Theatre Directing, University of Leeds

CONTRIBUTORS

Penelope Chatzidimitriou (PhD Aristotle University of Thessaloniki, MA Royal Holloway) is Theatre Lecturer in the International Programmes of the University of London and in various acting schools in Thessaloniki, Greece. Her book *Theodoros Terzopoulos: From the Personal to the Global* (University Studio Press, Thessaloniki) is the result of her ten-year collaboration with the Greek director. Chatzidimitriou has also published in journals and collections in Greece and abroad, such as in *Theater der Zeit* (Germany), Cambridge Scholars Publishing (UK), Peter Lang (New York) and China Theatre Press (Beijing). Her research interests focus on twentieth-century performance history, (post-)modern stagings of ancient Greek tragedy, the performing body and systems of acting, amongst others.

Dominic Glynn is Lecturer in French at the Institute of Modern Languages Research (IMLR), London. Prior to his appointment in 2015, he worked in professional theatre and academia in France. Over the course of his career, he has collaborated with a number of writers and directors, including Olivier Cadiot, Ludovic Lagarde and Joël Pommerat, and has taught at Sciences Po (Paris Institute of Political Studies) and the universities Paris Ouest Nanterre La Défense and Reims Champagne-Ardenne. Glynn's research interests include French contemporary literature and theatre, adaptations of Molière on the Restoration stage and, more generally, the rituals of performance. He is the author of *(Re)telling Old Stories: Peter Brook's Mahabharata and Ariane Mnouchkine's Les Atrides* (Peter Lang) and *Lignes de fuite* (Paris: L'Harmattan).

Sue Hamstead came late to Classics after a career in computing. Having completed her doctoral thesis – a study of off-stage characters in Greek tragedy – she held a series of temporary lecturing posts, firstly at the University of Manchester, then at the University of Leeds, and is currently an Honorary Research Fellow at Leeds. Her major research interests are in ancient Greek tragedy and epic. Publications include contributions to a collected volume, *Greek Drama IV* (eds D. Rosenbloom and J. Davidson), and to an *Encyclopedia of Greek Tragedy* (ed. H. M. Roisman).

Andrew Haydon is a freelance theatre critic based in Manchester, UK. He has written for the *Guardian*, Nachtkritik.de, Frakcija, Kulturpunkt.hr and Exeunt. As theatre editor of CultureWars.org from 2005 to 2010, he discovered and commissioned a generation of new theatre critics, including Matt Trueman, Miriam Gillinson and Andy Field. His account of British theatre in the 2000s is published by Methuen's *Decades* series as *Modern British Playwriting: 2000–2009* (ed. Dan Rebellato), and forthcoming chapters include 'A Brief History of Online Theatre Criticism' in Duška Radosavljević's new collection on writing about theatre and 'Directing Stephens' in Jacqueline Bolton's book on the playwright Simon Stephens.

Sophie Klein is a lecturer in Classical Studies at Boston University. Her research focuses on the ways in which themes and devices from Greek and Roman theatre pervade and influence other ancient and modern art forms. Her recent projects have explored Horace's use of dramatic material in the *Sermones* and *Epistles*, the chorus in Sophocles' *Ajax*, mute characters in the plays of Plautus and Terence, and the striking similarities between the comedic formulas employed by Greek satyr drama and the American cartoon *Animaniacs*. In addition to her academic work, Klein has written several plays inspired by classical literature.

Marianne McDonald, a distinguished professor of Theatre and Classics at the University of California, San Diego and a member of the Royal Irish Academy, is a pioneer in the field of modern versions of the Classics. With over 250 publications, her translations and original plays include: Aeschylus' *Prometheus Bound*; Sophocles' *Antigone, Ajax, Oedipus Tyrannus* and *Oedipus at Colonus*; Euripides' *Hecuba, Trojan Women, Iphigenia at Aulis, Bacchae, Phoenician Women* and *Children of Heracles*; Seneca's *Thyestes*; Aristophanes' *Lysistrata, The Trojan Women, Medea, Queen of*

Colchester; *The Ally Way*, ... *And Then He Met a Woodcutter*, *The Last Class*, *Fires in Heaven*, *A Taste for Blood* and *Peace*. Her website is http://mariannemcdonald.net.

George Rodosthenous is Associate Professor in Theatre Directing at the School of Performance and Cultural Industries of the University of Leeds. He is an award-winning director (*Body Faded Blue*) and the Artistic Director of the theatre company Altitude North. His research interests include directing, updating Greek tragedy, the British musical, the body in performance, improvisational techniques, composed theatre and devising pieces with live musical soundscapes as an interdisciplinary process. Rodosthenous has edited the book *Theatre as Voyeurism: The Pleasures of Watching* (Palgrave) and he is currently editing *The Disney Musical on Stage and Screen: Critical Approaches from* Snow White *to* Frozen (Bloomsbury Methuen Drama).

George Sampatakakis (MPhil, Cambridge; PhD, London) is Assistant Professor of Theatre Studies at the Department of Theatre Studies, University of Patras. His areas of interest include performance studies, history and theory of theatre directing, Asian theatre, theatre theories and queer theory. He has published articles in many international journals and volumes, as well as four books in Greece. He is a former scholar of the Onassis Foundation.

Avra Sidiropoulou is Assistant Professor at the MA Programme in Theatre Studies of the Open University of Cyprus. She is the artistic director of Athens-based Persona Theatre Company. Her main areas of scholarly specialization include the theatre of the director–auteur, adaptation and the ethics of directing and theory of theatre practice. She has taught, directed and conducted theatre workshops in various parts of the world. She has also contributed articles to international peer-reviewed journals and chapters to international edited volumes. Her monograph *Authoring Performance: The Director in Contemporary Theatre* was published by Palgrave Macmillan in 2011. She was a Japan Foundation fellow in 2015–6.

Adam Strickson is a theatre director, environmental artist, poet, librettist and Teaching Fellow in Theatre and Writing at the University of Leeds, where he has taught many successful young

writers from Yorkshire and England's north west and India. His first
collection of poems, *An Indian Rug Surprised by Snow*, came out
in 2005; his second, *Tear Up the Lace*, in 2011. He was lead artist
for the imove Olympic cultural project Wingbeats. Adam has been
poet in residence for Ilkley Literature Festival, Trinity Centre Leeds,
and for the town of Boston in Lincolnshire. In 2014 he was artist in
residence in Dewsbury Country Park, creating bird sculptures and
poems to celebrate the Tour de France in Yorkshire. He completed
his AHRC-funded, practice-based PhD, 'The librettist's adaptation
of source in collaboration with the composer', in June 2014; this
was a collaboration between the University of Leeds and Opera
North, part of the DARE partnership.

Demetris Zavros is Lecturer of Drama and Musical Theatre in the
School of Performing Arts at the University of Wolverhampton
in the UK. He is an award-winning theatre composer (*Electra
and Orestes, the Trial*, dir. Hanan Snir), a member of the Persona
Theatre Company (Cyprus), and Associate Director and composer
for Altitude North. His research interests include composed
theatre, post-dramatic theatre, non-logocentric approaches to
staging 'myth' in performance, devising processes and composing
music for theatre.

Magdalena Zira is a theatre director based in Cyprus and scholar of
the reception of Greek tragedy. She is the artistic director of theatre
company Fantastico Theatro, which focuses on adaptations of the
classics as well as new work by Cypriot playwrights. Her interests
include Greek drama, traditional cultures and their contribution
to contemporary performance, re-imagining the classics in a new
political and aesthetic context and developing new work by
emerging playwrights. She is also a PhD candidate at King's College
London and her thesis focuses on the staging of the chorus in
contemporary productions of Greek drama.

Introduction:
The contemporary director in Greek tragedy

George Rodosthenous

Greek tragedy today: The year 2015

The year 2015 was a difficult one for Greeks – a very complex one indeed. But something remarkable happened. Productions of Greek tragedy suddenly appeared all over the world. And while everybody was talking about a 'Grexit', as Dan Rebellato remarks, 'in British theatre, we have the opposite. We have a Grentrance. 2015 looks likely to be the year of the Greeks' (2015). I counted four productions of the *Oresteia* in the UK, three of *Antigone* in London, and three of *Medea*, one of *Hecuba*, *The Iliad* and *The Odyssey* elsewhere. Castellucci directed a revival of his *Orestie* in the Théâtre de l'Odéon, Paris, after his *Oedipus the Tyrant* at the Schaubühne in Berlin and Robert Wilson his *Odyssey* in Milan; Ivo van Hove was on a world tour with his production of *Antigone*; and Theodoros Terzopoulos opened *Antigone* (translated by Marianne McDonald) in the Wilma Theater in Philadelphia.

Jan Fabre was on the road with his post-dramatic twenty-four-hour phantasmagoria *Mount Olympus*. *Mount Olympus*, an orgy of parading tragedies, gods and satyr plays, was:

A Marathon of Exhaustion.
A Marathon of Patience.

FIGURE 1 *Fabre's* Mount Olympus. *Photo Wonge Bergmann*

A Marathon of Stamina.
A hymn to Greek Tragedy.
An in-between state of trance and meditation.
Bodies in Exaltation
Warriors' bodies on stage ...
and ultimately – Beauty!

In his acerbic style, Jan Fabre attempted the unattainable: to present his vision in a durational performance by employing museum-looking Greek *chiton*s to add another level of ironic critique to our immediate understanding of Greek (human) tragedy. There were hints of the orginal plays here and there: a monologue about why we need women (Hippolytus), some sheep and a warrior with a sword (Ajax), a monologue about laws set by humans (Antigone), and the performance developed into a puzzle of recognition. Fragments betray fuller texts, an excavation of the past, flirting with archaeological findings – an intense hypnotic state of experience – where the moon and sun are no longer part of the equation within the performative act.

In London, the Greek season at the Almeida lasted for six months and presented *The Oresteia*, *The Bacchae* and *Medea*. Artistic Director Rupert Goold's aim was to:

FIGURE 2 *Fabre's* Mount Olympus. *Photo Wonge Bergmann*

be true to their plays – staging them in full complexity, presenting their formal iconoclasm, their humour, musicality, politics, violence and unswerving drama. These writers took society's old myths and made them new: changed them, exploded them, set them loose as contemporary stories that spoke to their city [...] We are taking the Greeks out of the Attic. (2015: 127)

Goold wanted to update Greek tragedy and try to answer some of the questions raised by these classic works.

For the director of the Theater of War project Bryan Doerries, Greek tragedy brings a sense of community; he surrounds himself 'with people who wanted to face the darkness together and tell their stories' so that 'hope can be found in tragedy'. And this is an aspect we need to develop further. The impact of Greek tragedy is crucial in today's society and its relevance has an undeniable effect on its audiences. Dorries comments on his participants' 'palpable sense of relief to discover that they are not alone: not alone in their communities, not alone across the world, and not alone across time' (2015).

Contemporary Adaptations of Greek Tragedy: Auteurship and Directorial Visions places the directorial vision at the forefront of the discussion, focusing on the process of becoming the 'author' of the performance, and on new approaches towards and fresh insights into adapting the text onto the contemporary stage. It addresses the relationship between original and modern re-workings, explores specific techniques of directors dealing with the original text and becoming the new author of the work, and provides a link between the present moment and a sense of historical authenticity/performance practice. The volume critically presents issues in directing Greek tragedy by focusing on different directorial perspectives (nationalistic/localized renderings, feminist readings, interculturalism), engagement with the community (impact on forced displacement, minorities and post-traumatic stress groups) and directorial techniques in addressing the original text (deterritorialization, cultural excavations/usurpations, colonial and post-modern readings, and re-imaginings).

The volume sets out to answer questions regarding the role of the director and, specifically, how contemporary directors approach Greek tragedy. It contains a carefully selected range of well-established contemporary directors who have addressed tragedy's global perspective, presented it in dialogue with a specific community or created new re-visions of Greek tragedy. Unavoidably, this book can only present a small, selective range of practitioners, and there is enough scope for a second volume covering the work of Peter Hall, Peter Stein, Tomaž Pandur, Romeo Castellucci, Deborah Warner, Robert Icke and Karolos Koun, amongst many others. Hence these are not omissions, but directors whose work will be revisited in future research work. Comedy is equally important as a vehicle for critiquing society and social norms, and directors working within this genre could certainly form another volume about their approaches and achievements.

The director as adaptor: Re-writing the original text as 'unearthed embodied exploration'

From a Continental theatre perspective, however, it has become utterly unimaginable that one would not break free from the authority of the text, not rethink the play afresh with every new reading and not 'make a performance' of the text with each new production. (Boenisch 2015: 3)

The role of the director in Greek tragedy will be the predominant unifying catalyst of this volume. The director is, in this case, more like an auteur rather than an interpreter. This process involves dramaturgical interventions and additions/removals, editing, translation, re-ordering and re-functioning of material. Many academics have debated the interchangeability of the terms author, auteur, auteurship and authorship (see Sidiropoulou, Radosavjlević, Hardwick etc.). For the purposes of our discussion, the author is the 'original', 'primary' creator, conventionally acknowledged as the 'writer' of a work (see Barthes), whereas the term 'auteur' applies to a director whose unique, signature style of composition grants him or her the status of a 'writer' of the text of performance (Sidiropoulou). If we made the same analogy between an auteur and an orchestral conductor, then the conductor not only is responsible for the interpretation of the work (tempo, silences, dynamic nuances) and/or its new re-orchestration, re-harmonization, re-instrumentation, but also for all the new notes – although some thematic motives and structural arches might be kept, there is, in fact, a new musical score.

Robert Icke adapted his own version of the *Oresteia* for the Almeida Theatre in 2015 and later received a West End transfer. His adaptation was clear, cold, clever, cyclical, cynical, cruel, clinical and calmingly chilling. For him, the task is not about being fully faithful to the original, but

to the impulse that motors the whole thing forward ... I think of adaptation as like using a foreign plug. You are in a country where your hairdryer won't work when you plug it straight in. You have to find the adaptor which will let the electricity of now flow into the old thing and make it function. (Icke 2015)

Icke managed to strike a chord with his contemporary audience and his dramaturg Duška Radosavljević believes that it is important to find a balance between the original and bringing it closer to its audience. Icke's processes of adaptation in working with the original text involve 'dramatising the introductory chorus, problematising the character of Electra' (Personal Correspondence, 2015). Also, it is crucial for Icke that the new work can be seen by an audience member without any pre-requisites of prior knowledge, but without having to 'lock the text into our socio-political context either. So, the new version remains timeless and geographically unspecific.' Radosavljević feels that

> whether or not they actually write the script for their show, what they are doing will inevitably result in an 'adaptation' of the original text as they will filter their reading of it through their own sensibility, their artistic vocabulary or their political views about the world they currently live in. (Personal Correspondence 2015)

For Patrice Pavis, the new director is 'the aesthete of theatrical forms' (2010: 406), 'the silent musician' (2010: 407) and 'the choreographer of silence' (2010: 408). It would be valuable to refer to the work of Shepherd (2012), Sidiropoulou (2013, 2014, 2015) and Boenisch (2015) on issues of directing, auteurship and the Regie. Sidiropoulou encourages us to think that

> [i]f we welcome the idea that any interpretative act is actually an attempt to generate a singular reading of a text by remodelling its original energies into a new work of art, then we can begin to understand why notions of 'fidelity' and 'respect', which have infiltrated the field of adaptation studies as well as the critical reception of innovative performances, could and should be replaced by more liberating terms, such as 'reimagining' and 'reinventing'. (Sidiropoulou 2014: 1)

In older scholarship, ideas about the collaborative nature of theatre dominated such discussions. Pavis believes that we have gone beyond the 'auteur–stage director' (Pavis 2010: 395) era and, thus, the director–auteur's relationship to the classics needs to be re-examined. Recently, there has been a clear shift from philology to scenology (Pavis 2003). This is supported by Erika Fischer-Lichte, who observes that

> [m]eanings come into being during the performance and are to be regarded as emergent. It is to miss the point to interpret

the text, even the version used in the performance, and use this interpretation as a yardstick for judging the meanings generated by the performance. Theatre is neither a derivative art nor a philological institution. (2010: 35)

In her article 'Reversing the Hierarchy Between Text and Performance', Fischer-Lichte refers to a ritual of sacrifice that needs to take place and makes a direct reference to *The Bacchae*. Fischer-Lichte believes that the text has to be 'sacrificed' in order for its performance to be born. She continues by asserting that

[t]he performance did not come into being by putting together the fragments and pieces of the dismembered text body of the play. Rather, something totally new was emerging that permanently reflected its relationship to a text that, remaining closed, strange, remote and, in the end, indecipherable, had to be sacrificed in order to allow the performance to take shape. (2001: 282)

This can be associated to the adaptational work carried out by the director.

This book will also explore the relationship from page to stage as discussed in Radosavljević's *Theatre Making* (2013: 26–37) and relate it to the directorial approaches. Radosavljević focuses parts of her discussion on re-defining faithfulness and writes that

Patrice Pavis points out the way in which the 'dogma of fidelity' persists in haunting the theoretical and critical discourse of performance. This is despite the fact that we seem to have arrived at a point where enough space has been made for both 'texto-centrics' and 'sceno-centrists' in contemporary theatre landscape. (Radosavljević 2013: 69)

Adaptation is not about being 'faithful' – it is about having a strong, well-researched vision of re-telling an old story for a contemporary audience and 'translating' its content in a clear and believable way. Issues of adaptation have been discussed extensively in Hutcheon and her writing on adaptation as subtraction (2006). It is useful to mention here that the 'adaptive faculty is the ability to repeat without copying to embed difference in similarity, to be at once both self and Other' (Hutcheon 2006: 174). Sanders also suggests that there is a pleasure in intertextuality's 'tension between the familiar and the new, and the recognition both of similarity and difference, between ourselves and between texts' (Sanders 2006: 13–14). Admittedly,

> text and stage are bound together, [...] they have been conceived in terms of each other: the text with a view to a future mise-en-scène, or at least a given acting style the stage envisaging what the text suggests as to how it should be performed in space. (Pavis 2003: 205)

However, this meaning needs to be unearthed through experiencing the performance, and 'the director reveals with the *mise-en-scène* meanings, nuances and allusions that can only be unearthed through embodied exploration' (Sidiropoulou 2015).

I would agree with Sidiropoulou's final thoughts in 'Mise-en-Scène as Adaptation', where she reminds us that the director's job is 'to give us the key to that world, allowing us to pick for ourselves the places we ultimately wish to visit' (Sidiropoulou 2015). Foley also mentions that '[e]very contemporary performance of a Greek tragedy must be an adaptation of sorts, since it involves translation of the language of the original and confronts a profound ignorance of the music, dance, and theatrical context that conditioned its first presentation' (Foley 1999: 4). It is noteworthy that some directors focus entirely on the visual aspect (Wilson and Castellucci), or the body (Papaioannou), by replacing the text with movement and creating a dance theatre piece. *Medea* (1993/2008) by Dimitris Papaioannou is a strong example, where the music and the body are responsible for conveying the narratives.

Much scepticism remains about modern adaptations and 'enemies of updating a classic' feel that this is a 'cheap and patronising trick'. They believe that directors need to 'accept and embrace [...] pastness – the fact that while a drama must always live in the theatrical presence of the performance, it simultaneously speaks to us from another time and place which doesn't need 'relevance to us' to validate it (Christiansen 2015). This myopic view of the adaptive process comes, according to Foley, from, mostly, some classicists who 'have objected to their 'cheap multiculturalism,'

FIGURE 3 *Dimitri Papaioannou's* Medea. *Photo René Habermacher*

lack of authenticity, and disrespect for the texts, above all for the words of the texts' (Foley 1999: 9).[1]

Adaptation is often distinguished from appropriation by defining the latter as

> a more decisive journey away from the informing source into a wholly new cultural product and domain. This may or may not involve a generic shift, and it may still require the intellectual juxtaposition of (at least) one text against another that we have suggested is central to the reading and spectating experience of adaptation. (Sanders 2006: 26)

These texts do not always mention or reference their original source and it is up to the audience to identify that. Appropriation is 'associated with abduction, adoption and theft, appropriation's central tenet is the desire for possession ... Appropriation is neither dispassionate nor disinterested; it has connotations of usurpation, of seizure for one's own uses' (Marsden 1991: 1).

Transadaptation is another term that describes a process that does not only directly translate a text to a second language, but also changes the content to accommodate any linguistic and cultural differences.[2] There have been modern trends where we have culture-specific translations: Goold's *Medea* (2015) at the Almeida worked as a transadaptation and allowed for geographical detail and accuracy. In Rachel Cusk's opening of *Medea* we have clear references to a butcher shop on Market Hill, in London, which gives its London audiences a familiar, localized setting.

Working towards the directorial vision: Updating Greek tragedy

In *How to Stage Greek Tragedy Today* Simon Goldhill focuses on six aspects of Greek tragedy: space and concept, the chorus, the actor's role, tragedy and politics, translations, gods, ghosts, and Helen of Troy (2007). It is true that the directorial vision has recently become the strongest part of the adaptation and can dominate the *mise-en-scène*. It is important to think of the director as the main driving source behind the theatrical machinery of updating the classic and as the sole new author of the production. This is different when working with companies that have a democratic/collaborative ethos and create devised adaptation work which is more decentred. *Contemporary Adaptations of Greek Tragedy: Auteurship and Directorial Visions* will contextualize the work of a range of twenty contemporary directors and focus on the ways in which they have re-written the original text with their own *mise-en-scène*. Each director brings his or her own authorial voice on the reimagining of the Greek drama with a clear focus and objective to communicate with a contemporary audience. The book focuses on seven areas of updating Greek tragedy.

Translation

The translation is a fundamental starting point for establishing the directorial vision. For Hardwick, it's about transmission, transgression and transformation: 'The translation processes involved in performances of Greek Tragedy constitute a nexus between the two main trajectories in the horizons of experience and expectation' (Hardwick 2013: 338). Audience members bring their own pre-conceptions, knowledge and expectations when watching Greek tragedy, so there is often an 'inevitable disappointment of expectations'. Audience expectations sometimes become an obstacle to the directorial vision and allow the ongoing disputes about authenticity and experimentation with form to be perpetuated. Hardwick continues by saying that

> [t]his presents considerable challenges to translators and theatre practitioners, not only in representing the verbal and non-verbal aspects of the ancient art-form but also in transposing the theatrical experience to a different kind of playing space for spectators with very different cultural knowledge and expectations from those in fifth-century Athens. (Hardwick 2013: 328)

Goldhill observes that translators are traitors, but he goes on to add that 'some traitors turn out to be liberators who let us recalibrate what matters, and see the world from a startlingly new perspective' (Goldhill 2015). Even though discussion of whether to speak in verse or free verse can be regarded as dated, this is still a consideration for the director when working on the adaptation, as well as theatrical 'spelling mistakes' that need to be avoided.

Directors have started to provide their own translations on a regular basis (Icke, Doerries) to reach their audiences in a more direct way:

> You'll hear idioms that are wholly different from the Greek. Where Ajax is described as sitting inside his tent with his mind like 'a ship on a tempestuous sea', I totally throw out the nautical metaphor. I have 1,000 marines to reach. So I say he sits 'inside the tent shellshocked, glazed over, looking into oblivion. He has a thousand-yard stare.' (Doerries in Sandhu, 2015)

Re-locating the action in a contemporary/localized setting

It is a common practice these days for directors to change the beginnings and endings of a tragedy, shorten longer monologues and give them to the chorus, present striking additional opening and closing imagery to offer some contextual background and give spoiler alerts for the future in order to create a more immediate response from the audience. This can also give some audience members another glimpse of tragedy's uncompromising and diachronic impact. *Queens of Syria* (2015/16) is a re-telling of *Women of Troy* using Syrian female refugees, making a harsh statement on forced displacement and uprooting. This might help an audience understand and acknowledge the destruction and political unrest that happens around us, the unnecessary loss of life, and give us courage and a space to grieve and continue the search for 'the light of comfort'. It can also alleviate trauma because it has 'the power of performative erasure, through which personal trauma and loss may be staged as public gain and violence as an act of grace, of national or cultural salvation' (Solga 2008: 149) (see Chatzidimitriou, Klein, Glynn).

Exploring the formal/religious elements and the chorus

By applying the *notion of musicality* (Roesner 2010), a performance can be seen as a composition for the stage and treated as such by accentuating any cyclical structure, motifs or gestures. Weiner suggests that '[t]he longer choral odes were possibly major interludes of alienation during which the audience could readjust itself, relax, watch the dancing, listen to the music, and perhaps ponder what it has just seen' (1980: 211). This is not dissimilar to the functions of the big spectacle numbers in the musical theatre genre, and Greek tragedy can be treated as a musical theatre piece with singing, dancing, text and spectacle. This can be well argued from the classical sources, both in literary and artistic references. Choruses were accompanied by a flute or *aulos* player, and there are some fragments of a form of musical notation, which scholars have tried to interpret. The choruses were written in metric form, which would have allowed the same musical passages to be repeated in strophe and antistrophe. It wasn't just the chorus that sang: there are passages where the actors (hypocrites) shared sung dialogue with part or all of the chorus. In the earlier plays, where there is more chorus, the majority of the text would have been sung. This supports the argument that is presented in the classical literature that tragedy originated in sung choruses in honour of Dionysus.

It is always exciting to observe how different directors deal with the eternal issue of the chorus. In my view, it is crucial to treat the chorus as individual human beings. Findlay's *Antigone* (2012) at the National was very successful in doing this and giving them individual voices. Ivo van Hove's *Antigone* did something different. 'If you are not interested in the chorus as a director, better take your hands off a Greek tragedy. Better not do it' (Hove in Higgins 2015). Hove started his rehearsal process by treating the chorus as archivists. This was later transformed and Radosavljević elucidates his doubling of characters as chorus and concludes that it was 'part of the dramaturgical design of the piece too. The individual vices and virtues of the protagonists are presented as being contained within all of us and, conversely, the crowd is presented as being a heterogenous collection of individuals rather than an anonymous mass' (2015).

The chorus often refers to specific myths and legends as background or parallel narratives. They are key to the character of the original plays, but are often cut, and it is worrying when they are not replaced by an equivalent story from the world of the adaptation. But choruses no longer talk, dress and move in the same way, do not wear masks and do not speak in unison. Foley seems to struggle with these aspects of the tragedy and indicates that 'although gods and the chorus can often be viewed as impediments to performing Greek drama on the modern stage, present-day playwrights often yearn for the sense of over-determination that shapes Greek tragedy' (Foley 1991: 1). In addition, there are also specific modes of ritualization, which speak directly to specific religions and cultural practices and provide a unique relationship within an audience at a specific moment in time (see Zira, Strickson, Sidiropoulou).

Domesticating the action

There can be specific focus on the more domestic aspects (Sidiropoulou 2014) of Greek tragedy: the relationship of a father and his son, brotherly love, incestuous undertones, in order to make the adaptation more contemporary. Also, introducing the secondary characters earlier and elevating their status to equal the one of the protagonists (without having to worry that these must be played by the same actor who can appear on stage at the same time as others) can add to the interest and the 'family drama'. In the *Medea* at The Gate, we had a completely different perspective. The whole story was told from the children's point of view. The children were always on stage and all the 'action' – the parental fights – happened off-stage and were just heard in a barrage of violent dialogical exchanges. And, for Claire Allfree, '[b]y placing centre stage the damage inflicted on the warring couple's children, [this] forces us into a whole new engagement with Euripides' themes of marital abuse, revenge and consequence' (2015). This reinforces a more voyeuristic approach to the Greek tragedy and its links to our voyeuristic society (see Rodosthenous 2015; Calvert 2000) and how theatre can compete with TV/media/documentaries. Whether adaptation involves changing the ending, adding/removing secondary characters or updating geographical/historical location, it should allow its audience to empathize and engage with the scenic material (see Hamstead, Haydon).

Confrontation with darker elements of human and social experience

Finding contemporary relevance is possibly the main concern of the contemporary director and this up-to-dateness can change a play's context from day to day. *The Bacchae* cannot be seen as we experienced them before the current violent extremities of terrorism. *The Persians* could not be directed without any full political acknowledgment of current developments in that specific geographical area. Contemporary adaptations of *Phaedra* (older woman in love with her younger stepson) are indisputably linked with soap operas and other intertextual manifestations of the same story (*The Wife of Bath's Tale* etc.). The eternal values of Greek tragedy still manage to talk to the audience members and allow them to co-spectate and face death, destruction, punishment and revenge. In this way, the viewers learn more about themselves and have time to think about their own moral and ethical values. According to Edith Hall, Greek tragedy 'can offer an important site, free from contemporary cultural specificity, for reflecting on metaphysical and (in the broadest sense) theological issues – the crucial "tragic" questions of right and wrong,

FIGURE 4 *Konstantinos Ntellas' production of* Electra. *Photo Andreas Skourtis*

FIGURE 5 *National Theatre of Wales*, The Persians. *Photo Toby Farrow*

humankind's place in the universe and relation to the unknowable forces that shape it' (2004: 44) (see Zavros, Sampatakakis).

Scenography

In working within the directorial vision, scenography is one of the first considerations (together with translation) which set the tone and provide the basis for the production. Rush Rehm in his excellent *The Play of Space: Spatial Transformation in Greek Tragedy* rightly observes that by focusing on spatial transformations we can keep

> the phenomenology of presence that differentiates theatrical performance from private reading, often neglected by semiotic critics who tend to ignore the 'nested environment' of the Athenian theater ... By attending to space and its transformations, we discover the peculiar vitality and complicated inclusiveness of ancient Greek drama. (Rhem 2002: 272)

In this approach, the transformative powers of the *mise-en-scène* must be allowed to work alongside the text and ensure that

FIGURE 6 *National Theatre of Wales,* The Persians. *Photo Toby Farrow*

the scenographic design performs and develops together with the performers to define and sustain the narrative. In a recent production of *Electra* (2015), Andreas Skourtis' design consisted of just a bed on a raised rake: 'The centre of all – infinite – layers of parallel spaces is a bed. Everything happens on, around, from–within it. It is the actual centre point – the core – defining all the concentric circles of dramatic actions and metaphoric spaces' (Personal Correspondence with author). In this way, the space is an organic part of the direction and provides additional layers of semiotic meanings.

Site-specific performance can provide new opportunities for interaction with the text. The site becomes a new stimulus, for example, in *The Persians* by the National Theatre of Wales (2010), which took place in a mock German village rarely seen by the public in Brecon Beacons. In *Rhesus* (2015), Katerina Evangelatos assembled a very strong all-male cast led by Argyris Pandazaras (as Ektoras, Athena/Aphrodite) and Orfeas Avgoustidis (as Rhesus) and created a striking rendition of this neglected and rarely performed work. Staged at Athens' Aristotle's Lyceum, one of the three oldest ancient gymnasia in the city, this innovative performance transformed a walk into a theatrical event.

FIGURE 7 *Katerina Evangelatos'* Rhesus. *Photo Thomas Daskalakis*

FIGURE 8 *Katerina Evangelatos'* Rhesus. *Photo Thomas Daskalakis*

The space of the Lyceum conversed with the palimpsest of the city; the words of Euripides were heard interspersed with extracts from Aristotle's *Physics* and *On Sleep and Sleeplessness* regarding *hypnos* (sleep). Evangelatos exploited all the possibilities of her site-specific location and dealt with the piece as a dream: she added an extended prologue and successfully reimagined *Rhesus* as Ektoras' dream. The endless energy, versatility and stamina of the cast and the inventiveness of the *mise-en-scène* (music, lighting, movement, costume and use of space) provided an unforgettable experience for the audience (see Hamstead, Haydon).

New [feminist] readings of text

Directors have worked on proposing new readings of the classic texts. By focusing on the feminist agenda of the tragedies (or the lack of it) and the female characters, these new productions offer new insights and interpretations by highlighting aspects of the work that have been either neglected or consciously ignored in the past (see Haydon's work on Katie Mitchell).

Goold's *Medea* at the Almeida, in association with the adaptor Rachel Cusk, provided an alternative ending – Medea did not kill her children.

> Bringing the play into the here and now would mean reconstructing its controversial heart; and Euripides was a controversial writer, whose dramas dismayed and unsettled their audiences more than those of his near-contemporaries, Aeschylus and Sophocles. Those audiences were entirely male, and Medea did not please them, for not only does she get away with murder, she is glorified for it. The final scene of the play shows her transported out of human reality in a golden chariot by the gods, the bodies of her dead sons beside her. The idea that a female attack on male power, and on the cultural institutions that define femininity itself, would go unpunished was controversial indeed. (Cusk 2015)

This came as a surprise to the audience, but was not dissimilar to what happened to the fifth-century BCE audience when they attended a new tragedy: the myth was re-imagined and re-worked for each new version.

Structure of the book

It is not always easy to get access to practitioners' processes regarding their directorial vision. The rehearsal space is a closed space, where the creative team can work with the actors in order to experiment, investigate and find the inner truth of a text. For this reason, outsiders, observers or academics are not usually invited in with great ease. Contributors to this book have managed to get access to the closed environment of the rehearsal space and a glimpse of directorial processes and other contemporary ways of working with Greek tragedy either through direct observation, personal interviews with the director or their dramaturg, or video material regarding the process. The contributors to the volume come from a range of disciplines – adaptation, classics, directing, music composition, theatre criticism and translation – and this adds to its richness.

Contemporary Adaptations of Greek Tragedy: Auteurship and Directorial Visions provides a wide-ranging analysis of the role of the director in shaping adaptations for the stage today. This edited collection of essays is arranged in three sections: Global Perspectives, Directing as Dialogue with the Community and Directorial Re-Visions, but each reader can decide his or her own preferred order of thematic exploration.

The first section – Global Perspectives – considers the work of a range of major directors from around the world who have provided new readings of Greek tragedy: Peter Sellars and Athol Fugard in the USA, Katie Mitchell in the UK, Theodoros Terzopoulos in Greece, and Tadashi Suzuki and Yukio Ninagawa in Japan. Their work on a wide range of plays is analysed, including *Electra*, *Oedipus the King*, *The Persians*, *Iphigenia at Aulis* and *Ajax*. Directing as Dialogue with the Community focuses on the impact of Greek tragedy on affected communities using *The Suppliants* (Charalambous), *The Trojan Women* (Serban), and *Ajax* and *Philoctetes* (Doerries) as the main case studies. Our final section, Directorial Re-Visions, explores *Prometheus*, *The Bacchae*, *Les Atrides* and *Antigone* and innovative treatments by a range of directors. In each, the varying approaches of different directors are analysed, together with a detailed investigation of the *mise-en-scène*. Each individual practitioner selected has a personal directorial methodology and working ethos that shapes the work – these will be discussed in detail in the respective chapters. In considering each stage production, the authors raise issues of authenticity, contemporary resonances, translation, directorial control, auteurship and transadaptation. This offers the reader a detailed study of the ways in which directors have responded to the original texts, refashioning them for different audiences, contexts and purposes.

Marianne McDonald opens the discussion with her chapter 'American directorial perspectives: Independence Day meets Greek tragedy'. Her contribution engages with productions of *Medea*, *Antigone* and *The Trojan Women* and she focuses predominantly on the work of Athol Fugard. She then goes on to discuss how justice and freedom become two important concerns of the American stage and how these themes are linked to contemporary productions of Greek tragedy in the USA. The chapter celebrates Greek tragedy's 'multi-dimensional reach' and the impact of translation in 'representing *our* lives *today*, in ways that speak to us in our natural idiom'.

Theodoros Terzopoulos' innovative work is presented in Avra Sidiropoulou's 'Greek contemporary approaches to tragedy: Terzopoulos' revisions of Aeschylus'. She considers his work on *Persians* and *Prometheus Bound* and the auteur's ways of working in an intercultural mode of directing and by exploring corporeality, visceral energy, thermocentricity lament and ecstasy. The global impact of his directorial vision and his absolute fascination with form make him unique in 'staging this damaged, disjointed, post-tragic universe, all the while anxious to expose through a deconstructed form his own religious search for a centre, for meaning, for a sense of human connection'. Here, questions of authenticity (Pavis 2008), auteurship (Sidiropoulou 2011) and faithfulness are raised and Terzopoulos' treatment of the text 'stretching its physical, rhythmic and sonar boundaries through the actor's body' is exemplified and contextualized.

In the third chapter, 'British auteurship and the Greeks: Katie Mitchell', Andrew Haydon offers a historical overview of the director's work, starting with *The Trojan Women* (1991) at London's Gate Theatre and moving to *Alles weitere kennen sie aus dem kino (The Rest Will Be Familiar to You from the Cinema)* (2013), a reworking of Euripides' *Phoenician Women*. Using material from unpublished interviews with Mitchell, he considers her different approaches to Greek tragedy in a critical way, as well as her (Eastern European) directorial influences. The auteur's journey from naturalism to Stanislavskian psychological dramas succeed in giving birth to a new aesthetic and bring 'modern, politically left, feminist thinking to bear on these ancient, plutocratic, male documents [where] her productions also serve as live critiques of the original structures'.

The final chapter of Part 1 addresses the work of the two key Japanese directors: 'Tadashi Suzuki and Yukio Ninagawa: reinventing the Greek classics, reinventing Japanese identity after Hiroshima'. Penelope Chatzidimitriou's attention is focused on the fusion of heterogeneous elements of the East and West and the new avenues presented by these underlying tensions, 'clashes and fissures'. Her argument returns to questions of escaping classical beauty and history and the analysis shifts to tragic females in resistance (*The Trojan Women*), gender (*Medea*) and the ways these directors' 'undercurrent post-Hiroshima political and social considerations find in the classical texts their perfect match. They blend to address the suffering but also the beauty of the traumatized modern human condition, playing with the verbal and non-verbal, with dark ontological depths and shimmering visual surfaces'.

Part 2, Directing as Dialogue with the Community, features Magdalena Zira's 'Directing Greek tragedy as a ritual: mystagogy, religion and ecstasy', where she presents the work of the Greek Cypriot director Nikos Charalambous and his legendary production of *The Suppliants* (1978). His use of symbolism, religious imagery and ritual are given a socio-political context and linked to the 1974 Turkish invasion of Cyprus. The author then addresses the ritual as a set of actions that belong to the communal knowledge of a collective. They exist to mark a pivotal event, they are codified and shared, and as such can create bonds among the performers but also between the performers and the on-lookers, who, through their presence and observation, become participants in the ritual itself.

Adam Strickson starts his 'La MaMa's *Trojan Women*: forty years of suffering rhythms from Edinburgh to Guatemala' by identifying this production as a 'a living piece of theatre that has a forty-two-year history'. His reading of the production is juxtaposed with an interview with the director and highlights the production's musicality, but also the ownership of this collaborative ethos, which involves form and text, music and rhythm. Towards the end of his chapter, Strickson asserts that when we move beyond adaptation/translation centred on the word in our exploration of Greek tragedy, we find a plethora of new, rich understandings in an emotional intelligence that can resonate throughout our lives.

The social impact of Greek tragedy is discussed by Sophie Klein in 'Theater of War: Ancient Greek drama as a forum for modern military dialogue'. She inspects the work of the theatre company Outside the Wire and its director Bryan Doerries, whose aim is 'to comfort the afflicted and to afflict the comfortable'. Theater of War productions are more staged readings than full-scale productions and more than 60,000 veterans and their families have seen them – 'He promised to share the ideas that we came up with that day from one community to the next.' *Philoctetes* and *Ajax* are the two projects discussed here in depth, and Klein stresses that the audience demographic is crucial in composing these projects. Doerries' work is 'a vivid illustration of how a theatrical production can derive power from a targeted understanding of its audience. Every aspect of the Theater of War project is designed with military communities in mind, with the goal of fostering communication and compassion among soldiers and civilians.'

Part 3, Directorial Re-Visions, begins with enfant terrible Jan Fabre's post-dramatic work *Prometheus Landscape II*. Demetris Zavros articulates the auteur's processes through a Deleuzian perspective. '*Prometheus Landscape II*: [de]territorialization of the tragic and transgressive acts of arson' offers an in-depth analysis of re-imagining Greek tragedy into a landscape and explains how 'Fabre conceptualizes the choral attribute of the tragedy in such a way that it permeates, floods and opens up the performance into a choral acoustic/visual landscape'. Zavros looks at excess and the continuum of reference and abstraction as well as representation and affect and thinks about the implications of Fabre's auteurship as a process that offers 'a new contemporary experience of the tragic as a new transgressive, constitutive and affirmative in-between'.

The ninth chapter deals with the most audacious tragedy figure in Greek tragedy, Dionysus, who becomes the focal point of George Sampatakakis' contribution, 'Dionysus the destroyer of traditions: *The Bacchae* on stage'. The author gives a historical overview of recent productions of the tragedy and stresses the importance of archaeological reconstructions versus the desire for authenticity. He presents Schechner's monumental performance *Dionysus in 69* and continues to bring together different thematic threads that affect subsequent productions: ritualization, unfaithfulness, colonialism and post-modernism. Sampatakakis suggests that authorial innovations are legitimate 'cultural usurpations', and the chapter finishes by reminding us of the work's 'aesthetic polyphony', which makes it so unashamedly attractive to adventurous directors.

The penultimate chapter is dedicated to Ariane Mnouchkine's *Les Atrides*. Dominic Glynn here examines Théâtre du Soleil's collective spirit and values and Mnouchkine's dramaturgical innovations. In doing so, he examines issues of translation, textual excavations, distance and mixing devices to challenge the audience's assumptions. He concludes by comparing the viewing of Greek tragedy through the lens of French cultural history and as a global artistic product.

The volume ends with 'Re-imagining *Antigone*: contemporary resonances in the directorial revisioning of character, chorus and staging' in which Sue Hamstead selects four recent productions of *Antigone* (Findlay 2012; Rodosthenous 2013; Romer 2014; van Hove 2015) and examines questions of contextualization and setting, approaches to the chorus, the (undeveloped) love romance of Antigone and Haemon, the exposition of secondary characters and decisions on staging death, and how the four directors dealt with these aspects. Her concluding thoughts revolve around variation and the different potential narrative opportunities *Antigone* can offer.

Bibliography

Allfree, C. (2015) '*Medea*, Gate Theatre, Review: Powerfully Naturalistic'. *Telegraph*, 11 November. Online at http://www. telegraph.co.uk/theatre/what-to-see/medea-gate-theatre-review/ (accessed 29 July 2016).

Billings, J., Budelmann, F. and Macintosh, F. (2013) *Choruses, Ancient and Modern*. Oxford: Oxford University Press.

Boenisch, P. (2015) *Directing Scenes and Senses: The Thinking of the Regie*. Manchester: Manchester University Press.

Bosher, K., Macintosh, F., McConnell, J. and Rankine, P. (2015) *The Oxford Handbook of Greek Drama in the Americas*. Oxford: Oxford University Press.

Calvert, Clay (2004) *Voyeur Nation: Media, Privacy, and Peering in Modern Culture* (Boulder, CO: Westview Press).

Carroll, R. (2009) *Adaptation in Contemporary Culture: Textual Infidelities*. London and New York: Continuum.

Christiansen, R. (2015) 'Modernising classic plays is a cheap and patronising trick'. *Telegraph*, 3 March. Online at http://www. telegraph.co.uk/culture/theatre/theatre-features/11447162/ Modernising-classic-plays-is-a-cheap-and-patronising-trick.html (accessed 29 July 2016).

Cole, E. (2014) 'The Method Behind the Madness: Katie Mitchell, Stanislavski, and the Classics'. *Classical Receptions Journal* 7.3: 400–21.

Cusk, R. (2015) 'Medea is Not Psychotic – She's a Realist'. *The Telegraph*, 30 September. Online at http://www.telegraph.co.uk/ theatre/actors/medea-rachel-cusk/ (accessed 27 July 2016).

Delgado, M. M. and Rebellato, D. (ed.) (2010) *Contemporary European Theatre Directors*. London: Routledge.

Doerries, B. (2015), 'When people see their own struggles reflected

in ancient stories, something powerful happens'. *The Guardian*,
26 December. Online at https://www.theguardian.com/
commentisfree/2015/dec/26/when-people-see-their-own-struggles-
reflected-in-ancient-stories-something-powerful-happens (accessed 22
August 2016).

Fischer-Lichte, E. (2014) *Dionysus Resurrected: Performance
of Euripides' 'The Bacchae' in a Globalizing World*. Bristol:
Wiley-Blackwell.

Foley, H. (1999) 'Modern Performance and Adaptation of Greek
Tragedy'. *Transactions of the American Philological Association* 129:
1–12.

Foley, H. (2001) *Female Acts in Greek Tragedy*. Princeton: Princeton
University Press.

Foley, H. (2012) *Reimagining Greek Tragedy on the American Stage*.
Berkeley; Los Angeles: University of California Press.

Gagne, R. and Govers Hopman, M. (2013) *Choral Mediations in Greek
Tragedy*. Cambridge: Cambridge University Press

Goldhill, S. (2007) *How to Stage Greek Tragedy Today*. Chicago:
University of Chicago Press.

Hall, E. and Harrop, S. (2010) *Theorising Performance*. London:
Duckworth.

Hall, E., Macintosh, F. and Wrigley, A. (2004) *Dionysus Since 69*.
Oxford: Oxford University Press.

Hardwick, L. (2013) 'Translating Greek Plays for the Theatre
Today: Transmission, Transgression, Transformation'. *Target* 25.3:
321–42.

Hare, D. (2016) 'How I Learned to Love Adaptation'. *Guardian*, 23
January. Online at http://www.theguardian.com/stage/2016/jan/23/
david-hare-adaptations-the-master-builder-chekhov-old-vic (accessed 2
August 2016).

Hutcheon, L. (2006) *A Theory of Adaptation*. New York: Routledge.

Icke, R. (2015) 'Robert Icke, Theatre Director: "Oresteia? It's Quite
Like *The Sopranos*."' *Guardian*, 23 August. Online at http://www.
theguardian.com/stage/2015/aug/23/robert-icke-director-oresteia-
1984-interview (accessed 2 August 2016).

Krebs K. (2013) *Translation and Adaptation in Theatre and Film*.
London: Routledge.

Laera, M. (2013) *Community, Democracy and Other Mythologies in
Adaptations of Greek Tragedy*. Bern: Peter Lang.

Laera, M. (2014) *Theatre and Adaptation: Return, Rewrite, Repeat*.
London: Bloomsbury Methuen Drama.

Ley, G. (2014) *Acting Greek Tragedy*. Exeter: University of Exeter
Press.

MacKinnon, K. (1986) *Greek Tragedy into Film*. Rutherford NJ: Fairleigh Dickinson University Press.

Martindale, C. and Thomas, R. (2006) *Classics and the Uses of Reception*. Malden MA: Blackwell.

Mee, E. and Foley, H. (2011) *Antigone on the Contemporary World Stage*. Oxford: Oxford University Press.

Pavis, P. (2012) *Contemporary Mise en Scène: Staging Theatre Today*. London: Routledge.

Radosavljević, D. (2013) *Theatre-Making: Interplay between Text and Performance in the 21st Century*. New York: Palgrave Macmillan.

Radosavljević, D. (2015) 'Layers of Complication'. *Exeunt*, 10 March. Online at http://exeuntmagazine.com/features/layers-of-complication/ (accessed 2 August 2016).

Rehm, R. (2002) *The Play of Space*. Princeton: Princeton University Press.

Roesner, D. (2010), 'Musicality as a paradigm for the theatre: a kind of manifesto', *Studies in Musical Theatre*, 4: 3, pp. 293–306.

Sanders, J. (2006) *Adaptation and Appropriation*. London: Routledge.

Sandhu, S. (2015) 'Sophocles and Awe: The Director Hitting War Vets with Greek Tragedy'. *The Guardian*, 6 October. Online at https://www.theguardian.com/stage/2015/oct/06/greek-tragedy-theater-of-war-bryan-doerries (accessed 22 August 2016).

Sidiropoulou, A. (2011) *Authoring Performance*. New York: Palgrave Macmillan.

Sidiropoulou, A. (2014) 'Adaptation, Re-contextualisation, and Metaphor: Auteur Directors and the Staging of Greek Tragedy'. *Adaptation* 8.1: 31–49.

Sidiropoulou, A. (2015) 'Mise-en-Scène as Adaptation'. *Critical Stages* 12.

Solga, K. (2008) 'Body Doubles, Babel's Voices: Katie Mitchell's *Iphigenia at Aulis* and the Theatre of Sacrifice'. *Contemporary Theatre Review* 18.2: 146–60.

Stalpaert, C. (2015) 'CREW's O_REX (2007) and Nicole Beutler's *Antigone* (2012)'. *Performance Research* 20.2: 18–23.

Stanford, W. (1983) *Greek Tragedy and the Emotions*. London: Routledge & Kegan Paul.

Taplin, O. (1978) *Greek Tragedy in Action*. Berkeley: University of California Press.

Weiner, A. (1980) 'The Function of the Tragic Greek Chorus'. *Theatre Journal* 32:2: 205–12.

PART ONE

Global Perspectives

1

American directorial perspectives: Independence Day meets Greek tragedy

Marianne McDonald

Theatre is a collaborative activity of creation, and so I have found it most profitable to write about those playwrights, actors and directors to whom I have either had extensive access or with whom I have worked. Of course, in any survey such as this, other names have to be mentioned: here, Martha Graham, Lee Breuer and Bob Telson's *Gospel at Colonus* and Peter Sellars' work fit. But I have saved my powder for those whom I know best and feel most secure in valuing. Pride of place belongs to Athol Fugard (though a South African by birth, an American by citizenship and outlook), with whom I have collaborated. But the stagings of Velina Hasu Houston and Peter Cirino, L. Kenneth Richardson, Ruff Yaeger, Kirsten Brandt, Delicia Turner Sonnenberg, L. L. West and Seret Scott are also discussed as fully as space permitted. The Greek plays and characters dealt with most fully are *Medea*, *Antigone* and *Trojan Women*, though Sophocles' *Oedipus* and Aeschylus' Clytemnestra also make an appearance. My approach has been to show the driving forces that have led modern American directors to the kinds of innovations that have helped revitalize American theatre as well as the ancient classics.

Directorial innovations in America today: Contexts

How a director shapes the modern presentation of a classic is vital to its meaning and resonance – as, for example, when Peter Sellars claimed that the microphones he placed under the seats in his version of the *Persians* (1993) were substitutes for the ancient masks. Sound replaced the ancient mask that transformed an actor into a character, the *persona* in the play: modern tools, tapping the responses of the viewers and even giving them voice, complemented and extended the ancient technology. Now the actors' clear voices from onstage – but only theirs – reaching to the audience seated in those acoustically stellar hillside amphitheatres were completed by what those audiences might have to say. Sellars was depicting the abuses he saw in the world, but he also found a way to make his audience's reactions part of the play, a choral commentary. The audience had become another *persona* in the play.

In spite of remarkable innovations like this, there had been for a while few books on modern versions of Greek tragedy; that has changed and, happily, such explorations have proliferated.[1] This book addresses the direction of these works. I shall be looking at the American directors with whom I am most familiar, and with whom I have spent many hours in rehearsal rooms – the most accurate way, I think, in which a director can be evaluated.

Americanizing the myths: Medea, feminism and race

Martha Graham specialized in representing powerful women like Clytemnestra and Medea.[2] Clytemnestra murdered her husband Agamemnon on his return from Troy, avenging his sacrifice of their daughter and his duplicity in bringing home his Trojan concubine, while also fulfilling an ancient curse going back to Agamemnon's father Atreus (three reasons she gives in Aeschylus' *Agamemnon*, the first of the *Oresteia* trilogy, which advocates an end to personal revenge through courts of law).

Medea, princess of Colchis, has fruitlessly demanded justice from Jason for abandoning her after she had sacrificed everything for him, including murdering her own brother to enable their escape after stealing the Golden Fleece. She leaves him, having killed their two children and his new bride, thus destroying his past, present and future. Medea is, like Clytemnestra, a woman not to be taken lightly.

Compared to many international productions, American productions often feature mixed races. Both the directors and the actors profit from the American melting pot, as Velina Hasu Houston did in *The House of Chaos* (at San Diego State University, 2007): her version of *Medea*, in which she describes the immigrant experience of the Japanese wife, displaced from one society – protected, polite – to another that assaults her sensibilities every day (a usual war-bride experience). The bride is also often abandoned, as we know from Puccini's *Madame Butterfly*, and exchanged for someone younger and more acceptable to the new society.

Hasu Houston also has a feminist approach. Her Medea shows something infinitely better than murdering a rival – what can happen when women work it out together (how much better to destroy the philandering husband!). Mina Takahashi founds a fashion house called House of Chaos and makes a deal with her husband's mistress: they both take over the business and ruin the husband, who would certainly betray his new wife as he had his old one. The director, Peter Cirino, featured runway scenes, with the women strutting their new products, exhibiting the reification of women, just objects on display. These objects strike back, as the title of the book containing the play – *The Myth Strikes Back* – suggests.

This was also the thrust of my *Medea, Queen of Colchester*. The princess has become a black drag queen abandoned by her 'husband' when he sees advancement in a profitable marriage.[3] This Jason discovers that it's far more advantageous in America not just to have a white partner, but also to 'play' it straight rather than live openly gay. Once again, these are sadly still very relevant issues.

Medea, Queen of Colchester – Colchester was a 'location' in South Africa where whites segregated the blacks, or 'coloureds'

– was directed originally by Kirsten Brandt for Sledgehammer Theatre in San Diego in a 2002 reading and a 2003 performance. The reading featured a rap chorus, with music performed by authentic African American rappers, all devised by the composer and performer George Lewis. In the full performance, Brandt had to do away with the rap music, which demanded special expertise, and added Las Vegas show songs with a female chorus, who assumed some of the text. This altered my intention of having an all-male cast and of being faithful to the original Greek tragedy. Then the neophyte African American actor George Alphonso Walker, who ended up playing Medea, regretfully admitted that this was 'the first time I've worn heels', which led to wobbling moments in which the audience gasped; the chorus had to take over some of his lines because of memory problems. The reading, however, had a Medea, played by Hiroshi McDonald Mori, who had grown up wearing heels and was graceful and bitchy. His main drawback, on the other hand, was that he never fully tapped into Medea's suffering, but concentrated on her vengeance. All this shows how directors have to adapt to the conditions and the actors they have to work with.

This American play drew on the freedom theme and protested against imperialist abuses in South Africa, drawing a parallel with Jason seducing and using Medea as long as it suited him. But there is also an African version of *Medea* by Guy Butler, from the late 1950s, which shows Jason as Jonas Barker, a former English officer who joins tyrannical white Boer racist Kroon, the leader who finally eliminates anyone of colour or mixed blood from his trek. Jonas/Jason had married a black Tembu priestess, Demea, with whom he had two boys, only to renounce her for a white bride. Kroon beats the boys to death, freeing this Medea from that responsibility of murder, but, by virtue of her alliances with fellow blacks, the Trekkers are killed. Demea's vengeance is devastating, a warning to South Africans not to persist in the abuses of apartheid, a warning that they ignored.[4]

Silas Jones wrote *American Medea* to correct the myth.[5] He found it appalling that she killed her children for the sake of the 'superhero, Jason', since, of course, 'African women are nature's mother'.[6] Kevin Wetmore, who has dealt with such racist issues[7] – as he pointed out in George Lucas's *Star Wars*, another typically American production[8] – discusses this play's particular take.

Jones bemoans that all Medeas are not black. Certainly, Medea was the 'other' or the barbarian that Jason arrogantly claims he rescued by offering her 'civilization', though, as Jones rightly points out, she actually rescued him. Jones also sees Colchis as a stand-in for Africa, and he draws parallels with American slavery. In this play, Washington is seen as 'the father of his country', who just happened to own slaves. Native Americans were the 'other' victims when the white Americans freed themselves from the 'other' ruler, the British King George III, allowing them in their turn the 'right' to oppress imported slaves as well as native inhabitants (by killing the latter and seizing their land). In Jones's play, Jason's children ask why blacks are segregated and not treated equally; he answers, ironically, 'It's Americratic – separate but equal.' Obviously a paradox, this is however still the case regarding race in the USA, a country where women are not given salaries equal to men. Ancient Athens sets the example – that democracy hardly considered women, slaves and children *equal* to their adult male masters.

In Jones's play, Washington is a Creon stand-in who distrusts Medea and wants to send her and her children back to Africa. Medea points out how many black women have suckled white children, and that their milk now flows in their veins. This Medea rewrites the text – she 'de-Greeks the myth'. Now the Egyptian god Set – a demon who curses America (slides of Reagan and Bush flash) – is unleashed. Medea then foretells the brutal crimes of black descendants. As if instantiating this, Medea's two sons kill each other, and so, once again, this variation on Medea is innocent of child-murder. She next descends into the underworld to be with her children, but first makes Jason black and condemns him to live through the entire history of slavery and crime in America. This is a true American variation on the myth, mixing history and fantasy, and encompassing a desire for freedom and justice. The director used technology for some of the effects, such as the appearance of Set as a terrifying monster.[9]

My translation of *Medea* had a first reading by Grassroots Greeks in 2004, but was first performed at 6th At Penn Theatre in 2007, directed by Ruff Yaeger. He also chose an African American actress, Monique Gaffney, to play Medea, and combined Japanese elements with African ones. He had the Tutor appear in a silk kimono, and Medea herself was an expert at flower arranging: she took bunches of roses, gave them to actors coming onstage, and, after she had made up her mind to slay the children, she ripped off the flowers and planted the headless stems in barren sand. Throughout, all the costumes were white, so the red roses contrasted as flowers of blood, and the green branches were the stems of fertility itself deprived of its fruits, as Jason would be. She put on African war paint in preparation for the killing, white over her dark skin, and performed a frenzied African war dance to drums – a truly terrifying vision.

The lines often were delivered in monotone, rather like spoken Japanese, but ominously, as if they also were deprived of life. Ruff Yaeger's direction was further stylized by his tapping into Brecht's *Verfremdungseffekt* (as described in *The Messingkauf Dialogues*). To have the audience think, rather than have the emotions overwhelm those thought processes, he showed slides of black children, sometimes deformed or disabled – in effect, Medea's children. As the act of a mother killing her children is deformed by its deviation from the natural instinct of mother love, so showing these handicapped children emphasized this deviation. Pity and fear are not just for beautiful victims, like the handsome princes we imagine Medea murders.

In some ways, I find the horror is diminished when the more direct emotional approach is avoided. In my *Medea, Queen of Colchester*, the director, Kirsten Brandt, opted for live children appearing night after night to be killed by their 'mother'. No slides could so evoke the pathos of the living presence.[10]

Athol Fugard: Playwright, actor, director – Medea, Jason and Antigone

I have spent more hours in rehearsals with Athol Fugard than any other American director[11] and have collaborated with him as a writer. My *Medea: The Beginning* and Fugard's *Jason: The End* were directed by him and performed by myself and Fugard. This diptych[12] was first staged at Bewley's in Dublin in 2006, and later in San Diego, Cape Town and Oxford. It illustrated the passionate love affair that had turned into hate and bitterness, and, eventually, competition for the children's love. The first part dramatized Medea's abandonment, her confrontation with Creon, the murder of the princes and, finally, Jason's begging for the bodies. In *Jason: The End*, the last scene took place on a beach near the wreck of the *Argo*. Medea's final sight of the children had been of their bloodied bodies, whereas now they came to Jason happily and danced with him, only running away when they saw their mother. Jason

> turned his back on her and went dancing up the beach in a grotesque parody of the way he had danced on the night when they made love for the first time. Now she watched and waited ... The laughter had been too much for him and had turned into a violent fit of coughing. This ... was too much for his weak legs and he reached out to support himself on one of the rotten beams of the old ship ... One of them came crashing down on him ... For a few seconds he lay there struggling helplessly like an upturned beetle, arms and legs flailing the air ... and then it was all over. (Fugard 2007: 146)

Fugard directed the transformation from passionate love to passionate hate, the story of many a marriage gone awry. As always in genuine theatre, the non-verbal communication was as important as the words.

Even early on, Fugard risked expressing the ideas so close to Americans, namely, a democracy advocating equality and justice for all (however selectively exercised in America). Fugard was widely recognized for his version of *Antigone* as played by two prisoners on Robben Island, that notorious South African prison under apartheid, that abuse system which declared blacks as *de facto* inferior to whites and deprived them of their rights. This was *The Island* (1973), which Athol wrote with John Kani and Winston Ntshona's help. Antigone's final speech (which Ntshona performed) was a paean to freedom and justice that indicted the prison guards watching the play. No wonder Fugard attributes his successes to the America that welcomed him and his theatre with open arms: he has American citizenship and carries an American passport,[13] and most of his recent productions have opened in America.

Having read avidly throughout his life, he has often referred to the Greek classics, particularly the myth of Sisyphus. It was natural, then, that he would turn to Oedipus in his *Exits and Entrances* (for which I translated the Oedipus speeches, wrote an afterword and conducted an interview).[14] There, Fugard commemorated the great South African actor Andre Huguenet, an Afrikaner – and a homosexual – growing up in a Dutch Reformed community, who jokingly called himself a *dopper moffie*, a 'Calvinist queer'.

Huguenet introduced classical theatre to South Africa, but his identity, isolation and suffering finally became too much for him, and he died in total poverty, perhaps of heart failure, but possibly by suicide. Oedipus' final speech applied to himself as well:

> But it is not right to speak
> Of what was not right to do;
> So for the sake of the gods, hide me away,
> As soon as possible, out of sight,
> Or kill me: throw me into the ocean
> Where you will never see me again ...
> Do it and don't be afraid.
> I alone am polluted:
> I am the only man who must bear this suffering. (*Exits and Entrances*, 19–20)

Gradually, the direction toned down Morlan Higgins' performance of Huguenet and built up William Hurley's Playwright – namely, Fugard himself when he was young. Voice, in Higgin's case, was moderated, Hurley's given more fire. Hurley's was at first too submissive, so he was told to be more defiant.

Fugard refers to his being a director as wearing the third hat; the first was a playwright's – and he would never give that up – the second an actor's. In 1997, he decided to give up acting (he was finding it more and more difficult to remember lines), and in 2001 he gave up directing, though in 2014 he took up both again, but only in a special circumstance, what Charles Isherwood called a 'very slight new play' (*The Shadow of the Humming Bird*),[15] in which a grandfather reads from notebooks and other texts while conducting brief conversations with a Californian grandson.[16] His main intent is to tell a story well and he works in particular with monologues, trying to give life to the delivery. He hates directorial conceits that interfere with Aristotelian catharsis, the emotive experience filled with pity and fear that renews an audience, enabling them to view the serpents of Medusa and emerge eager to live their lives fully rather than being turned to stone.

Every time he directs, the experience fills him with terror, he says, as well as self-doubt, as he begins the arduous task of eliciting the best performances for the play he is directing. The terror only increases with his assessment of the calibre of the actor or actress. He says he depends on several days of table-reading at the beginning, and during this time the cast members all get to know the text as well as each other, and experiment with interpretations. At first, he tells his actors to read the script like a telephone directory, and not to act. Since they are not required to 'perform' immediately, they are free to become intimately acquainted with the text. Questions are encouraged. I've noticed that other directors I've worked with find this table-time essential to a good end product.

A month of rehearsals is Fugard's preference, followed by several previews, during which he continues to make suggestions, sometimes even rewriting, a procedure I find that I've instinctively followed with my own classical translations and adaptations. (In America, though, I have had to spend a lot of time pointing out the correct pronunciation of classical words and names, which is not the case to the same degree as directing in Britain or Europe.) In Fugard's discussion with Trevor Nunn and Jonathan Miller on the optimum period for rehearsals, Miller said that, although he usually took a month, he felt he had given his actors what they needed after two weeks. Nunn wanted at least six weeks, then a break, followed by more rehearsals – the longest time possible with the actors – and was forced by the theatre schedule to stop rehearsing. Fugard believes in a muse that overlooks his directing as well as his writing.

Fugard especially looks for an actor that trusts him and that takes risks. He recollects the example of Laurence Olivier, as the dare-devil father in O'Neill's *Long Day's Journey into Night*, getting up to change a light bulb, doing a backflip to get down, then continuing his performance. The risks that Fugard himself takes demand a lot from both his actors and his audience. For instance, *The Island* begins in silence, which lasts for about ten minutes, with mimed activity. The prisoners perform useless, brutal tasks like digging a hole on a beach and emptying the sand into a bucket, which is immediately filled in by another prisoner. Both are forced to repeat the same backbreaking action, back and forth, illustrating not only the brutality of the regime but the patience needed to bring about change.

Fugard's *Orestes* and an actor's commitment

For an *Orestes*, Fugard also devised a sequence of mainly silent action. First, Clytemnestra gives birth to Iphigenia; then a brilliant scene is staged to illustrate her loss – there is a call to her, as if she were in the next room, then silence, then another call, a little louder, as if she were playing outside, then silence, then still louder, as if she were far away, then silence. Then Clytemnestra screams out her name, shouting it, and finally whimpers it through her tears. Silence. Lastly, she stutters out the name Iphigenia, breaking it into each syllable: 'If ... ee ... gain ... ya.' Her tears are translated into syllables. Fugard encouraged Yvonne Bryceland (as Clytemnestra) to weep with her whole body; she said he could make her feel her own personal pain, the loss of a beloved, whose only response was silence.

Since Fugard thought Bryceland was not throwing herself adequately into the assassination of Agamemnon, he re-arranged chairs and tables in the rehearsal room into Agamemnon's boat. He took off all his clothes and strutted back and forth on the tables, banging on his chest, saying: 'I am Agamemnon the King! I am returning from Troy with Cassandra, the princess, as my personal prize!' He noticed the evil glint in his actress's eyes. No more problems with her hatred and subsequent anger.

Each performance, 'Clytemnestra' finds a new wooden chair onstage that she designates as Agamemnon, carefully hitting it on the floor or table, finding its weakness, then smashing it to bits, venting her anger in each performance. In the second part of the play, Orestes shows up as a terrorist, in the guise of John Harris, who blew up an elderly woman in a railroad station, a true story. He is spurred on by Electra, who has him kill their mother to avenge their father, now in a new, modern context.

Antigone: Actors and ends

Sometimes the choice of actors has been based on serendipity ('What was the actor pool?'). For instance, my translation of

Antigone, performed in Ireland in 1999, which Fugard directed, featured a cast of graduate students and professionals honing their basic skills in a summer acting programme run by American directors from the Yale School of Drama.[17] Fugard had six weeks for rehearsal in a charming barrel of a building, hence the name the Firkin Crane theatre, built in Cork in the nineteenth century. After the opening and several performances, it moved on to St John's Theatre in Listowel, County Kerry, a Protestant (Church of Ireland) church converted into a theatre in 1990. J. B. Keane, the playwright and novelist, attended a performance in which some nuns sat in the front row, laughing at even the suggestive jokes.

In casting, Fugard was also influenced by who was eager for which role. Patricia Logue of Belfast, who suffered as a Catholic at the hands of Protestants, was a natural for the role of Antigone. Creon was played by an African American, Damen Scranton, who ran a school in one of New York's ghetto areas, which demanded an iron hand to earn the respect of the students. At times, this Creon treated Antigone as an unruly student. But ultimately, Antigone was to teach him more of a lesson than the one he taught her. One wonders if Antigone learns anything. One knows that Creon did.

Fugard thought the way to lose the audience was to demonize Creon and make Antigone into a flawless heroine. He retained the dichotomy articulated by Hegel, who considered '*Antigone* ... one of the most sublime, and in every respect most consummate work of art human effort ever produced. Not a detail in this tragedy but is of consequence. The public law of the State and the instinctive family-love and duty towards a brother are here set in conflict.'[18] Antigone and Creon are rather like immovable forces in their refusal to compromise, which leads to their mutual destruction.

Instead of a male chorus announcing victory, an English actress delivered the choric lines alone. This is the first time the stage is fully lit, as then the chorus begins, 'First ray of sun, fairer than any seen before!' Having lines delivered in Cork by a single person avoided the abominable slurring that so often occurs when actors no longer have a living choral technique. Many directors (like Peter Stein in his *Oresteia*, Michael Cacoyannis in his *Iphigenia* and Ariane Mnouchkine in *Les Atrides*) succeed by having one actor deliver lines for the most part, perhaps alternating with others in the chorus.

The chorus concludes this first ode with 'May Bacchus be the lord of a dance/ That will shake the land of Thebes.'[19] After this, Creon (Scranton, the American) enters to cries of 'King Creon' and is cheered. He charms the audience, goes around shaking hands and speaking directly to them. They seem to agree with him. He is modest and tries to win the audience over. He is totally charming until he must confront Antigone over breaking his law. Fugard directed him to stand behind the audience then, to seem as if the audience itself is interrogating her.

Fugard let the actors and actresses at first make their own mistakes, then used a firm hand to lead them back to his vision. He always did this in a way that tricked them into thinking that they had made those decisions. For example, 'As you were saying the other day, perhaps you cut down on waving your hands and arms at this point.' He had all the actors and actresses seated on stage in a circle, emerging only to play their part. Sometimes they were distracted, and Fugard lost his temper ... once. He's like a volcano erupting, and the cast didn't want that happening again. It showed them how loss of focus would destroy a scene for the audience. They should never be static, nor lose concentration on what was going on before them.

Antigone: The music of voice, the accents of contemporaneity

Fugard used only the music of the human voice. His overture was also verbal: at first, the theatre is in darkness, and four actors choose the Greek names they like to repeat, like 'Acheron, Dirce, Thebes, Dionysus, Salmydessus', with many sibilants, beginning softly in fugal entries, now growing louder, then fading; the audience hears Antigone calling the name 'Ismene' softly, then louder, and then Ismene answers on the fourth call, 'Antigone', and the lights go up slightly. The sisters embrace and the play has begun.

When Antigone curses Creon, Fugard had her do it like an Irish witch:

I honoured what should be honoured, and yet stand convicted of dishonour. If the gods think that my punishment is deserved, then I forgive my executioner. But if instead he is guilty, I curse him and I demand that the gods make him suffer the same pain he unjustly inflicts on me. (*Antigone*, 37)

During one rehearsal, there was a rainstorm raging outside, and as Antigone said these words church bells rang and lightning struck the bell tower. Only in Ireland. In both Ireland and Greece words and curses have particular power because the gods listen. Tiresias was played by a tall, pale-blond Serbo-Croatian who struck the right notes of sexual ambiguity, coupled with a fey quality.[20] Just before his entrance, when Tiresias delivers his warning to Creon, the ensemble makes sounds like a wind blowing, intensifying the supernatural spiritual quality and the inevitability of what the prophet will say. The actors observing his entrance were directed to look nervous as Tiresias approached, tapping his way, guided by a youth from Listowel. At the end of the play, the dead bodies are symbolically represented by articles of clothing. Haemon hurls his cloak at his father, and Eurydice, who has hanged herself, lays her cape at Creon's feet. Antigone puts the flower crown that she wore on her way to death next to the two 'bodies'.

The four actors begin reciting the names again as they did at the beginning, rising then fading away, and finally we hear Ismene call for Antigone three times. Silence. The soul-wrenching performance at the end of the play when Creon sees he has lost everyone he loved establishes this as mainly Creon's tragedy. Damen Scranton as Creon had the audience in tears as he mourned over the bodies of both his son Haemon and his wife Eurydice. Fugard had led Scranton's Creon into his personal hell, and they took the audience on this nightmarish journey. Antigone gained immortal fame, whereas Creon earned immortal infamy. The punishments fitted both: one defied the government and was executed; the other defied the family's needs and was punished by loss of family. Then, as now, cooperation sometimes seems an impossible dream.

Both Ismene and Haemon were English and their accents contrasted with Antigone's Irish accent. There were other Irish Catholics and British Protestants in the cast, which enhanced the cultural and political resonances in their interchanges, namely the discrimination of the British Protestants against the Irish Catholics in both Northern Ireland and the Republic. There is sometimes a desire for revenge that exacerbates the craving for Justice.

Both Ismene and Haemon represent the voice of reason and compromise in the original play, but theirs is a truth Antigone will never accept, given her unyielding sense of justice (and the stubborn nature of Oedipus that she, his daughter, inherited). Finally, both are pushed too far: Ismene then sides with Antigone and Haemon takes his own life after discovering Antigone has hanged herself. Creon's American accent adds even more political commentary – here is someone with power that goes too far.

Just before opening night, Fugard wanted to infuse some humour to relax the actors, so he asked them each to give an abbreviated performance. Patricia Logue, in true Belfast fashion, gave the shortest performance of all: she walked past Creon glaring at him with her middle finger raised in the universal vulgar gesture of 'up yours'. Fugard is usually a wreck before opening night, as are most of the actors. If in his opinion mistakes are still being made, he will rage in silence. At other times, he shouts at the actors and rages out of the rehearsal room. By the end, he usually gets what he wants, as everyone tries to win him back. His approach generally pays off. Soon the performance 'finds its legs', as he says.

What Fugard learned early on is that there is no one approach to directing. What will work with one actor fails completely with another. Most good directors discover gradually that theirs is an art, not a science – a craft by which director shapes actor. He adds verbal music, rhythms, fast and slow, and alternates humour with seriousness, like movements in a sonata. He also feels actors and actresses should stop intellectualizing their performances, but deliver more emotional truth. As he told one actress, 'If you follow the heart, you will produce good theatre; if you follow the head, you won't.' He also told her that what she needed in her performance was 'more cunt, dear, what you need is more cunt'. He wanted more female passion and guts. He wanted her to find her innermost Medea. Three things, Fugard maintains, are necessary for any good performance: a text of quality, good actors and an attentive audience. This allows a flower to grow between the first two ingredients and the audience, the *hana* that the Noh master Zeami considered essential.[21]

Other *Antigones*, Irish and American

Antigone appeals to Americans particularly because the heroine is construed as the first civil disobedient. As a tragedy of the defender of the individual against an abusive political system, *Antigone* has also been popular in Ireland: in 1984, there were four versions, by Tom Paulin (*The Riot Act*), Brendan Kennelly and Aidan Carl Mathews, and Pat Murphy's film. Seamus Heaney added his *Burial at Thebes* in 2004.[22]

Translations now are to be found in accessible English, not the archaic English of versions meant to lend the play a 'classical' quality. In May 2005, there was a specifically American version directed by an African American, Delicia Turner Sonnenberg, at 6th At Penn Theatre in San Diego that expressed the war-weariness with the Iraq invasion – a war enlisting many African Americans and Hispanics who went to escape economic hardship and were possibly duped by the propaganda. The cast was fittingly multi-cultural and the chorus praising God (Dionysus) became a black spiritual.

There were many telltale signs that this was an American and specifically Californian production. For instance, when the chorus prayed to Dionysus at the beginning to bless their play, they used Buddhist gongs and a quartz crystal for the invocation. The modern costumes also made political statements. Antigone was dressed in a sweatshirt, fatigues and hiking boots. She reminded the audiences of a strident Cindy Sheehan, who protested against the war after her son was killed. Many who had initially been won over by President Bush's rhetoric were now changing their minds.

Ismene, by contrast, was dressed like a wealthy Republican, with hair up, heels and a fashionable suit. Eurydice, Creon's wife, also came on in even more elaborate formal dress to celebrate the recent victory. Both wore expensive jewellery, suggesting now not only wealth but the conservative politics that amassed it. A large sign at the back of the stage spelled out 'Mission Accomplished' in letters that suggested the Greek alphabet. One recalled the banner that Bush had displayed in 2003 on the aircraft carrier USS *Abraham Lincoln*, when he addressed the nation. He suggested the war was over. It wasn't. One could say it is still continuing.

At the end of the play, that backdrop took on an intensified meaning as Creon mourned over the corpses of his wife and son. In the final lyric, the concluding lines of the play, the chorus chanted:

If a person is to be happy,
He needs good sense.
Never show disrespect to the gods.
Loud words from those with high pretensions
Lead to heavy blows of punishment;
Good sense is hammered out on the anvil of age. (*Antigone*, 53)

The gods' mission to send punishment was accomplished. Sonnenberg directed Dale Morris's Creon as a southern gentleman with an accent reminiscent of Bush's. She had him try to win over the audience as he politely invited his wife to join him in a waltz to celebrate this victory.

Two reviewers called Jennifer Eve Kraus, who played the feisty Antigone, 'a hothead with a heart'.[23] As the play opens, before Ismene enters, we see Antigone kissing Haemon, African American actor Mark Broadnax, who is very winsome and gentle, until he confronts his father. Tiresias was played by Sylvia M'Lafi Thompson, another African American actress, whom few would recognize onstage as a woman. As she entered, the stage darkened, enhancing her terrifying presence – an apparition that startled both this Creon and the audience.

Sonnenberg called for a southern spiritual quality in some of the choruses, as if one were at a gospel revival, the place where southern slaves could find freedom every Sunday. Her direction was also strong in political commentary, explicitly manifesting the concerns she shared with this Antigone for the rights of the individual against the state, and for avoiding the abuse of minorities, for which America can still be indicted. Behind these productions lurked the realities of Iraq and the Patriot Act, though current surveillance operations make the Patriot Act pale into insignificance: 'Creon's eyes and ears are everywhere.'

Productions like this can sometimes lose the power of the Greek original, as I've noted, in that Creon becomes a villain, and Antigone a heroine who will reappear again and again throughout the world whenever she is needed. Greek tragedy, on the other hand, was a mastery of ambiguity; there is rarely one right, and good and bad are mixtures in everyone. This translation of *Antigone* took on new life in Salt Lake City in 2012, under the direction of L. L. West at the Classical Greek Theatre Festival. The backdrop of the Arab Spring influenced him to set the play in present-day Syria, with an Assad-like Creon, who is driven to prevent the civil unrest and loss of his power that might follow should this woman show him to be weak.

West's Antigone is gentler than many, but still brave. The chorus was brought to life as members of the press, clearly a modern but apposite note. Headscarves, as well as Arabic music, suggested the Middle East. The artistic director and dramaturg James T. Svendsen – another splendid American director who sees how relevant Greek tragedy is today – ably educated the audience before the performance.

Trojan Women: An American political version

Seret Scott's direction of my *Trojan Women*, a version, conveyed other political messages. Jack O'Brien, then director of The Old Globe theatre in San Diego, asked me to write this because he wanted a play by a woman that celebrated peace, and one directed by a woman to usher in the millennium (2000). Obviously, Euripides was there at every step, and his *Trojan Women* has rightly been called the greatest anti-war play ever written. Because Scott's mother had seen the war in Vietnam, Seret set this *Trojan Women* there, to show America's imperialist thrust, including abuse of the indigenous peoples (one thinks of the My Lai Massacre in 1968 or Oliver Stone's 1989 *Born on the Fourth of July*).

Scott also featured a prologue, which showed Paris's abduction of Helen as the cause of the war. However, this Helen was willingly seduced rather than kidnapped. Poseidon, following this scene, ends the prologue with the appropriate observation: 'People are mad to fight wars. Everyone thinks he'll never die; it's always the other person. But the winner today is the loser tomorrow, and everyone loses eventually. Death comes soon enough.'

This was a dream director. One never felt her bullying or using emotional blackmail as Fugard sometimes would, though of course both methods can achieve good results. Since this was a woman's play showing women as the victims of every war, I wrote Helen as an excuse for war, not as the cause. (Even Herodotus questioned the cause of the Persian Wars: 'Who would ever go to war for a woman?') Look for the economic reasons. So this Helen was a feisty seductress who finally wins sympathy thanks to Scott for her deft direction.

Where Sonnenberg brought in gospel, Scott brought voodoo and curses. Cassandra was played by African American actress Rayme Cornell who was dressed in rags suggesting a voodoo priestess. At one point, the lights low, Cassandra cursed Talthybius and all those abusing her – and she was frightening in her power. She predicted for him the post-traumatic stress that ruined the lives of so many soldiers, few of whom could avoid witnessing the atrocities of bloody war. A monologue of his own showed Talthybius' confusion about fighting in a foreign war and what was happening to his capacity to be human.

Cornell subsequently directed this *Trojan Women* herself, staged by the Nevada Conservatory Theatre at the University of Nevada, in Las Vegas, in 2011. She said in an interview that it was written about a year before 9/11 ('which was foreshadowing and a little eerie'). With rap choruses added to her production, this was hip-hop softened by a woman's voice.

Americratic themes: Justice and freedom and music

American versions of the ancient plays often convey a sense of, a need for, justice, and this is reinforced by the interpretation and choices of the director. To revert once again to Sellars, his *Ajax* (1986), set in front of the Pentagon, protested against America's gratuitous wars (a contemporary issue as alive now as it was then). He featured a deaf-mute actor (Howie Seago),[24] sloshing around in a large plastic container filled with blood and gore, with lines delivered by his obedient chorus and other soldiers as shell-shocked as he was. Sellars seemed to be suggesting that all warriors have to be rather sense-deprived to commit the atrocities they do. Again, Sellars' *Persians* showed the bias against, the unfairness to, one people as against another: the Persians misjudged the Greeks, misunderstanding how they were in the service of their entire city rather than being simply units of a force headed by one sole ruler (Greek democracy versus Persian tyranny). His later *Children of Heracles* (2005) dealt with Hispanic immigration and with refugees from recent wars.

Americans also bring their own specifically national and historical concerns to the stage, for example, in replicating a historical phase like Lee Breuer and Bob Telson's *Gospel at Colonus* (1983, based on the work of Ben Halley, Jr and Fourteen Karat Soul) and featuring the African American spiritual that shaped jazz and led to the one space where slaves could experience freedom.[25] By merging Greek tragedy with Christianity, this production became as problematic as Rodosthenous' 2012 production of Euripides' *Orestes*, set in Northern Ireland.

Freedom, then, is another American concern, since the republic's founding fathers demanded release from the dictatorship of a British king and from excessive taxation. But the quest for freedom, or the escaping from oppression, also fuelled the Irish exodus in the 1850s during the Great Famine. Starving people risked the infamous coffin ships, and many did not survive the crossing to America. The horror of such an experience also marked the slaves exported from Africa. Both became the new Americans.

Whereas English versions of the classics rarely incorporate music, most American versions consider it essential. Music was essential in the ancient Greek productions, as was dance. Martha Graham (1894–1991) conveyed the mixed passions of the heart in her danced productions of Greek tragedy. Many of her staged dances used particularly American features, combining elements of the Old West with the classical tradition. Along with Eva Palmer and Ruth St Denis, Graham shaped dance in America, with many works based on the classics. In so doing, this great trio showed how women in America could head up companies and be creative directors.

Conclusions

As Athol Fugard has seen, perhaps most clearly, there is no one path to success. As I mentioned at the start of this chapter, theatre is a collaborative effort, so that any success is a negotiation of best outcomes from limiting conditions, and the limitations are as varied as the people both on the stage and off.

Further, though, what we have seen in American directing is a sensitivity to issues that are in a sense timeless – justice and freedom – but with modern or even contemporary facets: racial and sexual harmony, the latter powered by a feminism that recognizes the enhanced role women can play in the modern world. This in itself makes for the new, but to make a topic of reason or sensibility work on the stage requires dramatic and theatrical imagination. This incarnation of the new will, as it should, surprise the audience, certainly, but often the actors and their directors too. Fugard's agonies on opening night are only one response to the newness, the freshness, he is struggling for; Yvonne Bryceland's discovery in herself of Clytemnestra's anger and hatred is another. And one could go on enumerating for each of the successes that we have seen above.

That is not to deny that there is a sort of continuity of effort informing the modern translation and staging of ancient theatre, just as there has been a kind of continuity of scholarly interest in these developments, from the 1980s and 1990s through to today. Just as Huguenet's example influenced Fugard, Fugard's work, like Breuer and Telson's, can be seen as giving suggestive example not just to younger playwrights but also to directors like Sellars, Sonnenberg and Scott, however much their styles might differ.

One generality, though, may well stand. American directorial directions have much in common with modern Irish and African American creativity; this speaks to our shared impulse towards personal dignity, even nobility, something the ancient Greek tragedians represent so excellently – and which, then, we also share with them. Further, in accord with Greek tragedy's multi-dimensional reach – voice in its many tones and modes, music, dance, even spectacle – modern American stagings (especially) reach out to other media to capture and to enhance the living fullness of such impulses and aspirations. As well, modern translations and versions provide a similar service and are another key ingredient in helping directors work towards the best possible performance. For underlying these aspects of innovation is the recognition that the re-presentation of ancient tragedy on our stages is a matter of representing *our* lives *today*, in ways that speak to us in our natural idiom.

Bibliography

Foley, H. P. (2012) *Reimagining Greek Tragedy on the American Stage*, Sather Classical Lectures 70. Los Angeles: University of California Press.

Fugard, A. (2005) *Exits and Entrances*. Claremont, South Africa: David Philip.

Fugard, A. (2007) 'Jason – The End'. *Arion* 15.1 (Spring/Summer): 138–46. Online at http://www.bu.edu/arion/files/2010/03/Fugard-Jason.pdf (accessed 1 August 2016).

George, N. (ed.) (2015) *The Oxford Handbook of Dance and Theatre*. Oxford: Oxford University Press.

Hall, E. and Macintosh, F. (2005) *Greek Tragedy and the British Theatre 1660–1914*. Oxford: Oxford University Press.

Hardwick, L. and Stray, C. (eds) (2008) *A Companion to Classical Reception*. Oxford: Blackwell.

Heaney, S. (trans.) (2004) *The Burial at Thebes: Sophocles' Antigone*. London: Faber & Faber.

Hegel, G. W. F. (1962) *Hegel on Tragedy*, A. and H. Paolucci (eds and intro.). Garden City NY: Anchor.

Jones, S. (1995) *American Medea*, unpublished play.

McDonald, M. (1983) *Euripides in Cinema: The Heart Made Visible*. Philadelphia: Centrum.

McDonald, M. (1992) *Ancient Sun, Modern Light: Greek Drama on the Modern Stage*. New York: Columbia University Press.

McDonald, M. (trans. and intro.) (2000) *Antigone by Sophocles*. London: Nick Hern.

McDonald, M. (2001) *Sing Sorrow: Classics History and Heroines in Opera* (Westport CT; London: Greenwood Press, 2001).

McDonald, M. (2003) *The Living Art of Greek Tragedy*. Bloomington IN: Indiana University Press.

McDonald, M. (2007) 'Medea: The Beginning'. *Arion* 15.1 (Spring–Summer): 127–56. Online at https://www.bu.edu/arion/files/2010/03/McDonald-Medea.pdf (accessed 1 August 2016).

McDonald, M. (2012) *The Craft of Athol Fugard: Space, Time and Silence*. Los Angeles: Murasaki Press.

McDonald, M. and Walton, J. M. (eds) (2007) *The Cambridge Companion to Greek and Roman Theatre*. Cambridge: Cambridge University Press.

Walton, J. M. (1987) *Living Greek Theatre: A Handbook of Classical Performance and Modern Production*. Westport CT; London: Greenwood Press.

Walton, J. M. (2006) *Found in Translation: Greek Drama in English*. Cambridge: Cambridge University Press.

Wetmore, K. J., Jr. (2002) *The Athenian Sun in an African Sky*. Jefferson NC; London: McFarland.

Wetmore, K. J., Jr. (2003) *Black Dionysus: Greek Tragedy and African American Theatre*. Jefferson NC; London: McFarland.

Wetmore, K. J., Jr. (2005) *The Empire Triumphant: Race Religion and Rebellion in the Star Wars Films*. Jefferson NC; London: McFarland.

Wetmore, K. J., Jr. (2013) *Black Medea: Adaptations in Modern Plays*. Amherst NY: Cambria Press.

Zeami, M. (1984) *On the Art of the Noh Drama: The Major Treatises of Zeami*, J. Thomas Rimer and Yamazaki Masakazu (trans). Princeton: Princeton University Press.

2

Greek contemporary approaches to tragedy: Terzopoulos' revisions of Aeschylus

Avra Sidiropoulou

Researching the (post-)tragic body

Greek auteur Theodoros Terzopoulos' elegant, violently elemental work has gained him broad international recognition increasingly since the mid 1980s. He has had numerous performances staged all over the world, his formalist style and radical reinterpretations of Greek tragedy establishing him as a permanent fixture in major theatre festivals across the globe. After studying at the Berliner Ensemble (1972–6)[1] and becoming well versed in Brechtian techniques and in the sparse, geometric aesthetic of the Bauhaus, Terzopoulos returned to his native country, where he directed at the National Theatre of Northern Greece for a number of years.[2] Soon to realize the need to experiment more thoroughly with an ensemble of actors committed to carrying out extensive research and a unique type of training, he formed

Athens-based Attis Theatre in 1985.[3] A year later, the ground-breaking production of Euripides' *Bacchae* ushered in a new era for an alternative approach to Greek tragedy, placing Terzopoulos among the most reputable international *avant-garde* directors of his generation, among the likes of Robert Wilson, Tadashi Suzuki and Vallery Fokin. Terzopoulos' artistic acumen duly afforded him administrative acclaim as well: from 1985 to 1987, he served as the artistic director of the European Cultural Centre of Delphi, a position that encouraged him further to introduce to the Greek public leading-edge theatre practices – namely, an emphasis on minimalist staging, textual deconstruction, abstract design and intense physical forms – from both East and West. Moreover, he became a founding member of the International Institute of the Mediterranean Theatre in 1990 and was also appointed Chairman of the International Committee of the Theatre Olympics. In 1999, he actually chaired the second Theatre Olympics held in Shizuoka, Japan, while in 2001 he acted as chairman of the Theatre Olympics in Moscow.

This chapter discusses Terzopoulos' work on Aeschylus, and, more specifically, his readings of the tragedies *Persians* and *Prometheus Bound*. Terzopoulos' return to these plays over a span of years, from 1992 to 2010, with different and increasingly mature versions of the plays, testifies not only to his investment in the genre of Greek tragedy, but also to his determination to put his own directorial philosophy and method to continual test, inventing new forms as well as redefining existing theatrical codes. Suspicious of the temptations that lurk behind adapting classics (such as re-contextualizing action and setting through and through), Terzopoulos is adverse to restoring tragedy by means of straightforward metaphors and paltry directorial quirks, convinced that restorations give birth to 'stillborn babies.' More than anything, he is concerned to highlight those elements and currents in the ancient tradition that would still be pertinent today. Fundamentally, in his revision of Aeschylus' texts, he creates an energy of collective integrity and a balanced, yet fierce play of actors, which takes him away from small detail and particular-case aesthetics (Sidiropoulou 2011: 170).

Ways of working: Interculturalism, corporeality and visceral energy

Over several years of working meticulously on Greek tragedy, returning to earlier versions of the same plays and re-working them anew, Terzopoulos has perfected a style that mixes formalist movement and abstract staging with a frenetic – alternately chaotic and contained – energy, originating in the performer's bodily organs.[4] Indeed, in Terzopoulos' theatre, the body is heavily textualized, inscribed with signs that transcend discursive meaning, and, as a result, in its extraordinary transformability, becomes a vessel for *logos* to unravel its mysteries as pure sound. The Artaudian notion of speech as incantation informs the director's aesthetic through and through; body and voice are treated as one big channel of biodynamic energy: physically exhausted, the actors struggle to speak, until eventually, physical pain (*ponos*) turns into speech (*logos*). The body in ecstasy documents both a transgression and an expansion – the body has well crossed the borders of all human capacity, becoming an instrument of primal energy and liminal expression. Terzopoulos borrows from Artaud and Grotowski the purist's trust that rigorous training will eventually render the actor both physically and emotionally cleansed. Essentialist in his approach, he treats the body as a hieroglyph, an opportunity for archetypes to be communicated, a medium that can house our collective unconscious, since 'all knowledge of the world resides inside our bodies' (Terzopoulos, quoted in McDonald 2000: 206). Influenced by the Jungian notion that our bodies bear memories, the director links body to myth, further stipulating that it is necessary for the latter 'not to make a story but to remake a memory' (Terzopoulos 2010a: 5), making clear that his exploration of tragedy is more than an affair of highlighting its West-revered classical paradigms.

Denouncing tragedy's long-held role as a repository of the ideals of Enlightenment, Terzopoulos nevertheless is ruled by an altogether humanist perspective, part of the trust that people carry within them the same emotional matter – a conviction that allows him to move comfortably from one culture to the next, incorporating languages and traditions, and having them stand in dialogue with each other. This type of intercultural exchange is ultimately more than just a wistful, utopian proposition; as the international reception of his productions testifies, the emphasis on corporeality as medium for generating universal meaning procures an idiom both vital and flexible enough to survive across national borders, encouraging global communication, while simultaneously inculcating the culture-specific elements of the tragic plays with a distinctly universal scope.[5] Suspicious of the monomaniac euro-centric 'regulation by culture,' a 'repression of individual, instinctive spontaneity and an expression of human creativity' (Pavis 1991: 11), Terzopoulos explores the visceral element that exists in any act of creation: a product generated through the synthesis of different cultures and/or a focus on the essentialist supra-cultural cell, a constitutional element of all humans.

It is not difficult to fathom Terzopoulos' attraction to Aeschylus, a poet celebrated for the grandeur of his verse, the sheer stature of his characters and the archaic solemnity of his world. Terzopoulos sees theatre as a means of existing at the 'threshold of death' and is ready to acknowledge the religious nature of his own work in terms of a feeling that 'God is always around our heads'[6] (Terzopoulos, quoted in Lalas 2000). The affinity to the Aeschylean ceremonial aspect seems well compatible with his ubiquitous religious concern and the belief that the Greek plays evoke within the spectator a sense of (divine) consternation: 'Without awe there is no tragedy' (Terzopoulos, quoted in Paridis 2010).

Terzopoulos and *The Persians*: Themocentricity, lament and ecstasy

Of all three great tragedians, Terzopoulos has claimed closer affinity to Aeschylus, in so far as the liturgical nature of his tragedies informs an aesthetic based on an emphasis on the ritualistic and a reliance on non-verbal ciphers. In *The Persians* he used the play's static loftiness to devise an extreme rite of mourning. Revisiting *The Persians* three times (1990, 2003, 2006), he was keen on exploring not so much the main dramatic characters as such, but, more notably, the chorus of the Persian elderlies.

Aeschylus' play, the only surviving Greek tragedy of purely historical subject matter, was originally presented as the second part of the trilogy at the dramatic competition of the City Dionysia festival of Athens (472 BCE), winning the first prize. Set in the aftermath of the Persian army's defeat by the Greeks in the battle of Salamis (480 BCE), it relates the native responses to King Xerxes' excessive pride (hubris), but the point of view is surprisingly sympathetic towards the fallen Persians.[7] The action takes place in front of the royal palace in the city of Sousa, one of the main governing centres of the Persian Empire. The agony of the Persians' wait gives way to the horrible recounting – name after name – of the lost Persian warriors by the Messenger, thereafter solemnly contextualized in the Ghost of Darius's speech, and reaching an excruciating climax in Xerxes' own sonorous wailing, when he returns from the battlefield. The accumulated emotional affliction of the text becomes for Terzopoulos an opportunity to explore the concept and expression of woe, which duly builds the performance into a jarring universal ritual of mourning. Thus, the tragedy's *themo-centricity* becomes a strong point of attraction, given that Terzopoulos is much more interested in examining the concept and physical expression of lament, instead of psychologizing the suffering dramatis personae involved in it.[8] Characteristically, he contends that he does not see the background of a myth in the play; rather, it is as if 'the centre of ecstasis has been exploded and everything gets covered in the material that has formed out of it' (quoted in Kyriaki 2009).

Recognizing the patriotic and political dimension as a marked aspect of Aeschylus' plays (Collard 2008: xx) makes it even easier to see how Terzopoulos' increasing politicization has brought him even closer to the world of this text, traditionally acknowledged to be a timeless commentary on the evils of war. Ambitious to unearth and fortify the communal and universal core of the tragic plays, Terzopoulos also brings up the process of both deconstructing and reconstructing the material that has resulted from the abrupt explosion of the tragedy's centre,[9] from a kind of blast that causes a series of extreme actions, manifest in the performer's external and inner expression. Yet, while it is certainly tempting to attribute to Terzopoulos' work the unrelenting revisionist aesthetics of postmodernism, whereby the focus is on formal pattern and emphatic visuality, it may be more useful to pay attention to his constant return to the idea of an essentialist centre as the source of all artistic creation, which may actually, if anything, suggest a fundamentally modernist outlook.

The Persians: First version (1990–92)

Terzopoulos' first attempt at *The Persians* (1990)[10] features a cast of five actors (three women and two men) and just a couple of props, set in motion by the principles of abstract, minimalist staging. Within a simple circle of white canvas with just one red splotch of red, the actors stand on low platforms, dressed in black robes and approximating received notions of the representational style of Greek tragedy. In what feels like a contained and intimate space, the movement is markedly ceremonial, with highly rhythmic rocking – front to back – and wavelike physical patterns. Featuring an array of Asian dance forms[11] that typically accentuate the tragedy's sacred element,[12] Aeschylus' play is viewed as a protracted scene of suffering, the sense of imminent doom that the Messenger eventually communicates, slowly building into a crescendo of physical and vocal anguish:[13] the actors weep and shudder, forcefully beating their chests, clasping their heads and tearing their hair in an expression of profound grief.

Intense bodily exertion predominates; for example, the Messenger narrates the names of those killed in the battle, while lying on his back on the floor, in obvious physical strain, until the obsessive wailing that ensues brings about the Ghost of Darius in majestic golden robe, a light-drenched presence interrupting the densest point of mourning. While everyone else has literally collapsed well underneath him, Darius dominates the stage through his sheer stature, introducing clarity and vision into a cosmos enmeshed in darkness and confusion. When the Ghost departs, the Persians' lament resumes and reaches a paroxysmic climax with the arrival of Xerxes. Rendering both performers and spectators witnesses to a condition of irreparable liminality has been for Terzopoulos a constant and worthwhile endeavour.

On the whole, the production's physical action is slow, in tune with the play's notable stillness.[14] The starkness of the staging, featuring just a handful of symbolic overtones (such as the black and white photographs of children, presumably depicting victims from the Bosnian war), coupled with the semi-nudity of the actors – so appropriate within a rite of mourning – remains an overriding aesthetic principle that lets the emotional content of the play culminate naturally and economically. Behind the production's early monotony of grieving, there also lurks a sense of intimacy, as if we are witnessing a family drama, as opposed to a historic national tragedy.

The Persians: Second version (Meyerhold Centre, Moscow, 2003)

In this second version of *The Persians*, Terzopoulos worked with Russian actors, incorporating traditional forms of lamentation from the Soviet regions. With this production, the director returns to the practice of structuring performance geometrically: the acting area consists of a circle pierced with a red thread, in and out of which revolves the play's action. Terzopoulos' popular staging patterns and recurring gestural motifs intensify dramaturgical intent. The performers move in and out of the circle semi-naked; in fact, the circle operates as an off-limits zone, an area of concentrated energy. Lit gradually, the Ghost of Darius separates the two worlds – the inside of the circle (a blazing locus of suffering and mourning, the actual site of Salamis) and its outside, a place of distant reflection. Transformation becomes a key feature of the abstract *mise-en-scène*, visually eloquent stage props – such as the photographic portraits of war victims, the white stiletto shoes and the metal stands, which turn into buckets revealing a 'bloody' red inside – being subjected to endless symbolic transmutations.[15] Typically, the painterly perspective predominates, the exacting composition of the stage sharpening directorial focus through and through. Similarly, the performing body assumes symbolically meaningful postures, which, in combination with the other bodies on stage, strikingly replaces verbal exposition.

As in the earlier production of the play, here too, Terzopoulos communicates the extremity of human suffering somatically: repeatedly, the bodies of the Persians quiver violently, possessed, as it often seems, by supra-human anarchic forces. Notably, the primordial properties of myth are present in both the heightened speech and the movement, which intermittently contradict each other, generating extra layers of perceptual tension for the audience. There is surely something shamanistic in this mixture of anxiety and pain, a frenzied, altogether disquieting effect, much though the director contends that rhythm has a 'logical kernel' (Terzopoulos in Terzopoulos 2000b: 55).

After extensive exposure to the production's peculiar cadences, the audience becomes more and more drawn into a state of emotional transcendence, experiencing the manner in which physical exhaustion stimulates and multiplies the performer's energy; in this light, speech becomes an expression of the body's need to release tension, as it alternately tightens and relaxes, surpassing its natural boundaries to enter a condition of liminality.

The Persians: Third version (Aghia Irini, Istanbul and Ancient Theatre of Epidaurus, 2006)

With his last take on *The Persians* – co-produced by the International Istanbul Festival and the Epidaurus Festival in 2006 – Terzopoulos unlocks a broader political statement on the common fate of humankind. While Aeschylus' play merges the lamentations of the Persian chorus with the pained experiences of the ancient Greek spectators, who had incurred similar losses in the war, Terzopoulos formalizes the tragedy's anti-war statement further, by uniting two conflicting nations' (Greece's and Turkey's) sensibilities on stage.

The production features a mixed cast of seven Greek and seven Turkish actors, who jointly, and in their native tongue, narrate the defeat of the Persian army in Salamis, simultaneously foreshadowing the Persian Empire's decline. Queen Atossa is performed by a Greek, Darius by a Turk, whereas the part of Xerxes is shared by one Greek and one Turkish actor. Terzopoulos now departs from Aeschylus' tragic tale of hubris; he also downplays the sombre tone, investigating, instead, common manifestations of mourning in both Greek and Turkish cultures. Against the sparse, monumental space of the Aghia Irini in Istanbul first, and later in the ancient theatre of Epidaurus, a number of men of different national origins, dressed in modern costume, stand next to each other along a horizontal line that splinters into chaotic configurations, once the reality of loss takes over. East meets West, as distinctly Eastern music fuses with Byzantine melodies that make the performance resonate with suggestive religious overtones. Once again, as with the previous version of the tragedy, the production's visual layering with photographs of war victims is pronounced: portraits of Greek, Cypriot, Turkish and Kurdish casualties parade on stage in black and white, haunting reminders of how commonly fatal wars are. In addition, the director conjures up as another strategy of contemporizing the play, having the actors display pieces of paper that feature names of the dead Persian soldiers. Significantly, the emphasis is on highlighting the political dimensions of a remote historic fact, such as the battle of Salamis.

Terzopoulos' intercultural approach raised controversy in Epidaurus; some critics and spectators resisted the production's trans-national scope, arguing that this reading of the play did not do justice to Aeschylus' intention of condemning Xerxes' ill-fated audacity.[16] Yet, while the tragedy is certainly not about the reconciliation of two enemy states, its strong anti-war sentiment can certainly vouch for Terzopoulos' use of joined lamentation as a cross-cultural bridge, albeit imaginary. The shift in emphasis from the formal rigidity of the previous versions to the ubiquity of grief no doubt suggests a changed approach to the play; Terzopoulos is no longer interested in simply telling the story of the palace dignitaries that bemoan the Persians' defeat, but rather, in researching the role of the mourners, the dirge-singers of various ethnic backgrounds, and in investigating how the latter respond to the 'explosive frenzy' of the mourning, the 'extreme state of stimulation, the annihilation of the body' (Terzopoulos, quoted in Angelikopoulos 2006).

On the whole, one might certainly speak of an evolution in political awareness, in the light of the two earlier versions of the play; Terzopoulos' formalism is predictably still there, yet it is also transfused with moments of collective suffering – especially when the large bilingual cast speaks of the human plight – which clearly transcend the specifics of time and space. To this end, the meeting of cultures is also conspicuous in the desperate embrace of the Greek and Turkish actors, who also share a variety of similar gestures. Terzopoulos' stage is turbulent, vibrating both visually and aurally with bodies that shake and roar, disturbing any tentative symmetry in explosive movement. Repeatedly, the performers lose their composure utterly: they alternately struggle, embrace, undress in an unruly fashion and whirl like dervishes, singing dirges in both Turkish and Greek.[17] Oftentimes, the violence of the battlefield is conjured up physically: on the floor, the chorus members fight and shake, all the while becoming more and more physically involved with each other. They toss their red 'bloody' kerchiefs on the floor fiercely, throw coins to one another and set up a scene of anarchy, until they slowly emerge cleansed, their soldiers' boots in hand.

Eventually, the chorus is nothing but a series of red dots, blurring into history. Reflecting an encounter as well as a confrontation between two nations torn in universal conflict, this version of *The Persians* brilliantly encapsulates Terzopoulos' conception of intercultural approach:

> When we meet the other, the stranger, and we look at him in the eyes, in that terrifying moment, there are two options for us: either we reach eros in its ontological meaning, or war, in its literal meaning. Perhaps, in the end, the deeply political can be identified with the deeply erotic. (Quoted in Dimadi 2006)

Terzopoulos and *Prometheus Bound*: The aesthetics of (anti-) heroism

The humanistic perspective is addressed even more forcefully in Terzopoulos' work on Aeschylus' *Prometheus Bound*, staged successively in 1995, 2008 and 2010. The play, composed circa 456 BCE,[18] has always been identified with such venerated values as resistance, intelligence and generosity, defiance against tyranny and civic responsibility.[19] An archetype of rebellion and of faith in human progress, the universal figure of Prometheus has been a fascinating subject for several auteur revisions of the exemplary myth of heroism (see Richard Schechner's *The Prometheus Project: Four Movements and a Coda* in 1985, Heiner Goebbels' *The Liberation of Prometheus* in 1993; Robert Wilson's *Prometheus* in 2001, Rimini Protokoll's *Prometheus in Athens*[20] in 2010 and Jan Fabre's *Prometheus – Landscape II* in 2011, among others).

Terzopoulos uses a classical character at the centre of a myth that 'easily transcends cultural boundaries', someone who is 'at the dawn of several Enlightenments with all their philosophical, ethical and political problems' (Decreus 2012: 182). Positing axiomatic questions as to the value and viability of the Prometheus paradigm in today's ostensibly dehumanized world, Terzopoulos' emphasis on the necessity of heroism displays a deep anxiety for the personal and existential to become political. Transcending the distinctly ontological focus of the first Prometheus version, Terzopoulos gradually deconstructs the tragedy's heroic stature, offering a fresh interpretation of Prometheus as an anti-hero who bears little relation to the universally idealized conception of the Titan's tortured son. Prometheus' fall now becomes a multilayered icon, charged with echoes of Western civilization's decline and the collapse of all faith in the values and promulgations of the Enlightenment. By having his modern Prometheus display characteristically non-tragic responses towards the imperious torture to which he is subjected, Terzopoulos actually tries to reconsider 'the absolute metaphors we still use today' (Decreus 2012: 191). For him, as Decreus argues, 'tragedy is not a soteriological construction (unlike the three Western book-religions), it is man-made, diverse in its historical periodization, and today questioned in its post-tragic characteristics' (Decreus 2012: 193).

Prometheus Bound: First version (Tuscany, 1995)

Aeschylus sets his play in a rocky mountain of Caucasus, where Prometheus, son of Zeus, is being chained by Hephaistos, on the orders of Kratos (Power) and Bia (Violence); he is eternally punished for defying the Gods by daring to provide the mortals with the gift of fire. Given the actual immobility of the Aeschylean protagonist, Terzopoulos' stage kinetization of Prometheus is truly remarkable. The 1995 production of the play – which premiered in the Church of St Francesco, in Montalcino, Tuscany – reflects how, paradoxically, the constriction of space and blocking can free up the actor's biodynamic movement of the lower part of the body. Thus, in an acting area that feels firmly defined – communicating both intimacy and imprisonment – Prometheus is anything but static. Interestingly, the tension between the hero's perpetual cognitive and moral restlessness and his prohibitive physical circumstances is made manifest visually.[21] At the same time, in contradistinction with Terzopoulos' overall solemn staging, the colour symbolism of the first 'take' on the myth seems uncharacteristically saturated. For instance, the stage, which is initially infused with cobalt-blue lighting and dramatically dominated by the red ribbon that holds the protagonist prisoner, gradually also absorbs cool greys, until in the end the captive Prometheus emerges in fiery orange lighting focus. While some traces of literalness can also be detected in the production's geometric blocking, these are actually followed through consistently and are therefore effective in their function. The triangle that places Prometheus pinned down in the middle, hanging from some imaginary roof by thin red ribbons, is quite characteristic of Terzopoulos' emphasis on clear shapes not simply anaesthetizing space, but also decoding dramaturgy.

In the end, the performance's expressionist undertones surreptitiously immerse us into a landscape loosely referencing Hades. One can easily recall the director's habitual stylization, the shuddering semi-naked bodies in all their rhythmic convulsion, but this being an earlier work, one also notices a level of descriptiveness in the staging, as well. Yet, while the red ribbons by which Prometheus dangles from the imaginary rock are semiotically weak, the white ghostly figure of the single-person chorus that materializes at the end of the performance, wrapped up in a semi-transparent cloth, is quite striking, as is indeed the final vertical configuration, where all the performers are positioned single file, in anticipation of Zeus's destructive force.

Prometheus Bound: Second version (Central Drama Academy of Beijing, 2008)

Being commissioned to stage *Prometheus Bound* in China, Terzopoulos blended in elements of the local culture, turning the production into an overtly political statement against totalitarianism. Within a distinctly Brechtian perceptual framework, one recognizes the director's desire to manipulate the aesthetic mandates of social realism. For example, the cheerful song in the opening parade of Kratos's representatives – a chirpy group of young women dressed in white suits, accompanied by their male commander – is repeated throughout, echoing popular propaganda practices common in communist regimes globally. Characteristically, upon entering the stage, the agents of Kratos sit among the audience, avid observers of all that is happening on stage, who make sure that they intervene when things get out of hand, as when the rebellious spirit of Prometheus threatens to spread chaos all over. More than anything, we are being caught in a game of surveillance, control and resistance, as we observe the chorus engage in a carefully orchestrated alternation of lament (in Chinese as well as in Greek[22]), rapprochement and violent repeal. One cannot help but admire Terzopoulos' 'chorusization' of the protagonists: the characters of Kratos and Bia, the Oceanids and Prometheus do not so much function as independent entities, but rather as leaders of three separate groups, which tag along with them. These consist of three sets of men and women, of female and of male performers, respectively, while the members of each group are dressed identically in uniform-like costumes, which are also symbolically conceived.[23] This choice is crucial in lifting the characters up to the level of archetypes and heightening the tragedy's communal aspect. While it is difficult to distinguish Prometheus at first, it is this challenge precisely that affords a different angle, namely, of the play being less a personal drama of a heroic personality and more a debate on issues of democracy, personal responsibility and civic duty.

It is perhaps no accident that the only visible coryphaeus in the production spreads terror and violence to his own set of subordinates when things become troubled: when the male performers inside the circle become increasingly mutinous, red placards of numbers in hand, he irritably slashes his whip or rips pages off a book, referencing habitual methods of totalitarianism.

In general, the conspicuous shift of focus in Terzopoulos' treatment of Aeschylus over the years is worth noting: while identifying a process of maturation might perhaps suggest an attitude of condescension, evidently there is an inner movement from the existential (and thus, personal) to the political (and thus, communal) dimension. This turn is obvious in the director's work on both *The Persians* and *Prometheus Bound*. The small cast/ intimate space/private mood elements of the early versions have given rise to pluri-vocal, politically conscious productions of a much more global scope. This 'opening up' is also manifest in the very fact that some of the later works also feature culturally mixed casts, having actors speak in their native language (as was the case with the 2006 Greek–Turkish *Persians* or the 2010 *Prometheus Bound*, in which the actors communicate in Greek, German and Turkish). Inevitably, over the years, Terzopoulos' travels have rendered him progressively sensitive to how language can be more of an empowering, rather than limiting, mechanism for encouraging universal perspectives, all the while illuminating anew potent aspects of Greek tragedy. The reality of having different idioms exist in dialogue with each other on stage could be a sign that notwithstanding its inherent 'locality' language can still address the desire to connect and transcend. The anxiety to simul-taneously preserve one's own cultural identity and still contribute its unique features to a more generous quest towards understanding our primal and essential humanity becomes especially pronounced in Terzopoulos' later work.

Prometheus Bound: Third version (Elefsina, Old Oil Mill Factory, 2010)

The natural setting of the Elefsina Oil Mill factory, sparsely refashioned by the arte povera visual artist Yannis Kounellis, was one of the three locations accommodating Terzopoulos' most recent take on *Prometheus*. In fact, the production belonged to a larger, tri-partite project (*Promethiade*) relating to the myth of Prometheus, also staged in Istanbul, Turkey and Essen, Germany.[24] The old oil mill factory in the industrial area of Elefsina, near Athens, now defunct, becomes a haunting landscape of reflection on current socio-ideological anxieties.

At the onset of the performance, the actors enter the stage separately and at a different pace; attuned to the sensuous tango music, they position themselves slowly on the ground, stomach down, as if waiting for the earth itself to comfort them. However, the fragile equanimity of the beginning is short-lived, abruptly interrupted by a siren that officially kicks off the play with a looming sense of urgency. Notwithstanding the production's stillness, at least for its biggest part, the 'real-timeness' of the rhythm is truly engaging. Against the amber colours of the surrounding mill, lit in warm hues, the drama of Prometheus is being played as a piercing political parable.

It is language that is the protagonist here: Greek, German and Turkish mix at all times, repeated in key phrases, splitting fiercely or fusing harmoniously. Paradoxically, the performance's surface unintelligibility forces us to pay attention to the non-discursive elements of language and allow ourselves the pleasure of immersion in its purely incantatory aspect. In this respect, Terzopoulos seems to reference Artaud's urge to 'let words be heard in their sonority rather than be exclusively taken for what they mean grammatically, let them be perceived as movements' (1958: 120). The ambition to 'resurrect the word' from [a movement of] 'energy and ecstasis' is part of the understanding that 'elevation of the word means exaltation of speech, not speech as a proper expression – academic speech, explanatory speech – but speech of pain, speech which comes from the soul' (Terzopoulos, quoted in McDonald 1992: 165). Significantly, nationality – foregrounded linguistically – is rendered inconsequential. Linguistic dissonance ultimately stimulates feelings of empathy, corroborating a valid mechanism of establishing a truly global perspective of reception.

Terzopoulos suggested that the 2010 production was far from a predictable portrayal of the perennially idealized liberator of humanity, but more of a self-derisive mirroring of the extremes of self-sarcasm and disparagement that an individual can reach in the attempt to reclaim one's own. Accordingly, Aeschylus' tragedy is viewed in a much less solemn light than the one in which it is ordinarily perceived, and the conflict between Prometheus and Zeus proposes a series of metaphors regarding resistance against any form of tyranny. The director manufactures an extreme world, where, in Brechtian manner, the very victims introduce to the public their victimizers, who come 'from within' (Terzopoulos, quoted in Paridis 2010). A tragedy of a 'dehumanized man,' who exists at the threshold of ridicule, the 2010 version of *Prometheus Bound* is an aggressive, almost anarchistic portrayal of contemporary social, political and ideological turbulence, and certainly a far cry from Terzopoulos' first handling of the Prometheus myth.

Such emphasis on communal plight is richly supported by current-day references interpolated in different moments of the performance. Emotionally loaded phrases drawn from Greece's long history of strife and dissent altogether universalize the scope of the play. Spoken in unison, lines such as 'the army is coming,' 'take him away!,' 'no, I will not sign' are only some of the hypnotic mottos that add to the generally impassioned effect. The prophetic undertones of 'there will come a day' [«θα έρθει μια μέρα», 'bir gün gelecek', 'der Tag will kommen'], taken up in three different languages, are chilling statements of hope and courage, which are, however, instantly annihilated by the negative 'it will not come' [«δεν θα έρθει»]. After a choral recounting of characteristic modern predicaments ('everything burns – forests, factories, books, universities, children'), bearing a number of haunting associations, the triple-facet Prometheus, performed by a Greek, a Turk and a German, delivers an unequivocal political message: 'after I am dead, the world will change' [«όταν θα έχω πεθάνει, ο κόσμος θα αλλάξει»].

Repetition builds obsession, as languages, bodies and ethnic histories clash and then mesh, until, in the end, the intentionally cacophonous 'klausigelos,' a prolonged sequence where laughter and crying interchange, is cut short by the unnerving siren, which takes us straight back to the beginning, as the cycle of coercion and defiance repeats itself ad infinitum. It is no wonder that this production, too, being a variant of other Terzopoulos' productions, demonstrates noted occasions of 'klausigelos'; much like in this version of *Prometheus Bound* (as well as in the 2006 production of *The Persians*), the spectator becomes enmeshed in an extended scene of suffering, which is, nonetheless, anti-Aristotelian in that it renounces the dignity of psychological pain. Characteristically, the director sees sarcasm and laughter as the only possible remains of human decency, after all dramatic or tragic dimensions have been left (un)resolved:[25]

> 'We are in a post-tragic space. This means we constantly make mistakes. We are a machine full of errors. Of the promises of progress, nothing has been left. This is a post-tragic vision. It's not like it used to be in the myth where the God says: You are my marionette and I'm blinding you to make you commit a mistake' ... Therefore, he says, '(T)his is the absolute end, this darkness must be shown by art [...] We must accept the evil and make people aware of it instead of speaking on behalf of a utopia.' (Quoted in Raddatz 2010: 96, 98)[26]

Exploiting the emotive dimensions of intercultural collaboration, Terzopoulos turned his production into an obsessive, if loving, study in communal pain, a utopian, if necessary, depiction of cultural and most notably, of political solidarity. Aeschylus' heightened poetry yields a commanding weapon against oppression, as Prometheus' predicament unfolds its ecumenical dimensions.

It may be true that in the earlier Terzopoulos productions the tight geometric design has on occasion undermined the director's much discussed endeavour to make his performers manifest a (Dionysian) loss of control, having approximated states of ecstasy through extreme bodily exertion. The form, in other words, was often too clean and too sleek to accommodate the liminal perspectives of tragedy, and as a result the accumulated pain that we were expecting to see explode in the staged lamentation of Xerxes or the suffering of Prometheus actually felt overly staged, stylized well beyond the 'mess' in which real anguish is normally experienced. However, notwithstanding the unapologetic formalist aesthetic, the principle of 'verticalization' that Terzopoulos speaks of, namely the 'omission of the literary framework', the 'extra-literary perspective' (in Sampatakakis 2008: 177), helps shape and form dictate dramaturgy in compelling ways. At the same time, the notion of abstracting the text is for Terzopoulos a necessary step in capturing 'the meaning without the meaning,' in discovering the 'profound meaning' that lies underneath the obvious meaning (177). The ambition to perfect a style of composition based on lines and shapes within a general discourse of abstraction that eliminates whatever the director considers tangential, in favour of a kernel of 'dramatic essence' carefully extracted through research and bodily exertion, has certainly been present in most of Terzopoulos' work on Aeschylus.

Final thoughts

The gradual shift from the existential to the political has expanded the breadth of Terzopoulos' work to fierce expressions of the essentialist *us*. The subject is now deconstructed and the heroic stature of tragedy interrogated further in a clearly communitarian perspective. The director assumes complete authorship of the original text, rejecting a straight 'loyal' reading – what Pavis aptly describes in terms of a 'faithful philanthropic philology' (2008: 125) – instead stretching its physical, rhythmic and sonar boundaries through the actor's body and placing the original play in a context that is simultaneously timeless and contemporary. This is surely clear in how Terzopoulos treats both Aeschylus' tragedies herein examined. In many respects, the rigid formalism of his early productions is cracked open in the later ones, becoming more aggressive and yet, curiously, also more humane. The manifesto-like vitality of the 2010 version of *Prometheus Bound* is a by no means facile reconciliation between the tragic play's stature and the final cry-revolt against the utter disenchantment of our un-heroic, indeed, 'post-tragic' era. In effect, the death of heroism is a continual and poignant reference in contemporary directorial revisions of Greek myths.

As McDonald points out, while modernists were able to 'make collages out of the fragments of the past' (1992: 6), today's artists can only point to how fragmentary everything is. Terzopoulos is perhaps unique in staging this damaged, disjointed, post-tragic universe, all the while anxious to expose through a deconstructed form his own religious search for a centre, for meaning, for a sense of human connection. The plunge into the depths of communal conflict, lament and (non-)heroism is his own way of bringing time and space together into the heart of meaningful art. After all, what makes a work of art truly global is, in the director's view, analogous to the degree in which 'the creator has managed to touch on the centre that concerns us all.' The encounter of a truly deconstructionist post-modern form with a modernist search for centre and meaning renders Terzopoulos' contribution to directing practice quite compelling and unique. In his work, the absolute content of a work can be released through the form wherein 'cause and effect are identified as one, they co-exist' (Terzopoulos quoted in Lalas 2000).

Bibliography

Artaud, A. (1958) *The Theatre and its Double*, M. C. Richards (trans.). New York: Grove Press.

Burian, P. and Schapiro, A. (2009) *The Complete Aeschylus Vol. II. Persians and Other Plays*. Oxford: Oxford University Press.

Collard, C. (2008) *Aeschylus, Persians and Other Plays*. Oxford: Oxford University Press.

Decreus, F. (2010) 'Theodoros Terzopoulos' *Promethiade*, or the revolutionary power of contemporary theatre'. *Classical Papers* XI: *The Proceedings of the International Symposium Drama and Democracy from Ancient Times till the Present Day*, Festschrift in Honour of Prof. Ahmed Etman. A. El-Nahas (ed.). Cairo: University of Cairo, Faculty of Art: 3–5 March 2012: 181–96.

Decreus, F. Bodies (2014), 'Back from Exile'. *Gramma Journal of Theory and Criticism* 22:1 63–74.

Dimadi, I. (2006) «Είδαμε τους Πέρσες στην Κωνσταντινούπολη» ['We saw the Persians in Istanbul'], 27 June. Online at http://www.athinorama. gr/theatre/article.aspx?id=2784 (accessed 11 August 2014).

Hatzidimitriou, P. (2007) 'The "Bacchanalian Body in Theodoros Terzopoulos" Theatre'. In *The Flesh Made Text: Cultural and Theoretical Returns to the Body*. New York: Peter Lang.

McDonald, M. (1992) *Ancient Sun, Modern Light*. New York: Columbia University Press.

Marinou, E. (2010) 'Next-Door Prometheus'. *Epta*, 4 July.

Pavis, P. (1991) *Theatre at the Crossroads of Culture*. London and New York: Routledge.

Pavis, P. (2008) 'On Faithfulness: The Difficulties Experienced by the Text/Performance Couple'. *Theatre Research International* 33: 117–26.

Raddatz, F. M. (ed.) (2011) *Promethiade. Athens, Istanbul, Essen 2010*. Essen: Klartext.

Ruffell, I. (2012) *Aeschylus: Prometheus Bound*. Bristol: Bristol Classical Press.

Sampatakakis, G. (2007) *Geometrontas to Chaos: Morphe kai Metaphysike sto Theatro tou Theodorou Terzopoulou*. Athens: Metaichmio.

Sidiropoulou, A. (2011) *Authoring Performance: The Director in Contemporary Theatre*. New York: Palgrave Macmillan.

Sidiropoulou, A. (2015) 'Adaptation, Recontextualization and Metaphor. Auteur Directors and the Staging of Greek Tragedy'. *Adaptation* 8: 31–49.

Stone Peters, J. (1995) 'Intercultural Performance, Theatre Anthropology, and the Imperialist Critique: Identities, Inheritances, and Neo-Orthodoxies'. *Imperialism and Theatre: Essays on World Theatre, Drama and Performance*, J. Ellen Gainor (ed.). London; New York: Routledge: 199–213.

Terzopoulos, T. (2000a) 'Interviewed by Thanassis Lalas'. *To Vima*, 20 August.

Terzopoulos, T. (2000b) *Theodoros Terzopoulos and The Attis Theatre: History, Methodology and Comments*. Athens: Agra.

Terzopoulos, T. (2006a) 'Interviewed by Vassilis Angelikopoulos, Fired-up Persians Examines Violence in the World Today'. *Kathimerini*, 11 June.

Terzopoulos, T. (2006b) «Πέρσες από το Θέατρο Άττις» ['Review of Persians from Attis Theatre'], 14 July. Online at http://www.nooz.gr/ page.ashx?pid=9&aid=103353 (accessed 15 July 2014).

Terzopoulos, T. (2010a) 'Director's Note'. *Theatre Olympics: Crossing Millenia 5*.

Terzopoulos, T. (2010b) 'Interviewed by Christos Paridis', «Αντι-Προμηθέας» ['Anti-Prometheus'], 19 May. Online at http://www.lifo.gr/mag/features/2123 (accessed 4 September 2014).

Terzopoulos, T. (2012) 'Interviewed by Maria Kyriaki', «Αφιέρωμα Τερζόπουλος-Εμμονή και Μνήμη» ['Terzopoulos: Obsession and Memory'], 20 December. Online at http://www.episkinis.gr/2009-05-31-09-20-01/2009-06-04-11-06-13/964-2012-12-20-15-58-21 (accessed 14 December 2014).

Tsatsoulis, D. (2008) Seimiologikes Prosegiseis tou Theatrikou Phenomenou. Athens: Ellinika Grammata.

3

British auteurship and the Greeks: Katie Mitchell

Andrew Haydon

This chapter looks at the professional productions of classical Greek texts directed by Katie Mitchell – seven productions of four plays (*Trojan Women, Phoenician Women, The Oresteia* and *Iphigenia at Aulis*) spanning a cycle of twenty-three years. I intend to situate these productions in the wider context of English theatre during the period, demonstrating the trajectory in which the most progressive theatre was moving, the relationship of the critical establishment to that work, and how it fits within the wider artistic development of Britain's most accomplished director. In doing so, I hope to illuminate the trends and fashions in modern British stage practice in relation to Greek Tragedy, focus on her feminist approaches to Greek Tragedy,[1] and to examine the overarching questions about directors' licence and the concept of authorship.

It is interesting to note that while the style of the productions evolves over the course of the years covered by this study – from the 'anthropological' phase (Rebellato 2010), heavily influenced by Eastern European theatre, especially the Polish company Gardzienice, to what can be described as Mitchell's distinct, trademark style, bearing traces of her myriad previous productions – throughout her entire career, the super-narrative of her work has continually been about trying to discover an ever more pure, rigorous form for naturalistic acting. It is also worth acknowledging at the outset of this piece that, while taken across the totality of her work – her celebrated productions of Chekhov, her world premières of Martin Crimp and Simon Stephens pieces, her 'camera shows'[2] – naturalism isn't an especially controversial choice of predominant form, there is a school of thought within classical scholarship, and perhaps some theatre criticism, which argues that because the plays pre-date naturalistic theatre, such a mode has no place being used in productions of them (see Cole 2015). However, banning such practices on the basis of anachronism seems wilfully literal-minded, and this is not really a theatrical argument. Directors are free to use whatever means they wish to realize their artistic vision. Indeed, it is often argued elsewhere that 'the/a text' is merely an initial impulse for the director. Mitchell is in fact more modest. Her work should be undertood as the combination of her abiding, ongoing fascination with naturalism, a clear love of stage aesthetics, and a desire to make the theatre experience as clear, vivid and moving as possible for an audience.

Trojan Women at The Gate: Poor theatre in Notting Hill

The story begins in 1991 at London's Gate Theatre in Notting Hill, then a tiny room above a pub run by subsequent Royal Court artistic director and Oscar nominee-to-be Stephen Daldry. Mitchell has just returned from several months in mainland Europe studying directing in Georgia, Russia, Lithuania and Poland. The Berlin Wall has fallen, and across Eastern Europe and the former Soviet Union seismic social and political changes are taking place. In the Middle East British and American planes have bombed Baghdad, while in Northern Europe Russia has carried out covert military actions against Lithuania.

Against this backdrop, informed by both the spirit of these uncertain times and her recent training, particularly with Gardzienice, Mitchell created her first version of Euripides' *Trojan Women* with her newly formed company Classics on a Shoestring. It starred Paola Dionisotti, Kathryn Hunter and Barbara Flynn, with future Kneehigh and Shakespeare's Globe artistic director (and Classics on a Shoestring co-founder and production choreographer) Emma Rice as the chorus leader. The piece was presented on a bare stage, save for the covering of red earth on the floor. The chorus performed Bulgarian-style music, recently popularized by the release of *Le Mystère des Voix Bulgares* on the 4AD record label (also home of Pixies and Cocteau Twins). At the same time as this 'ethnographic' slant, Mitchell had already begun her deep exploration of Stanislavski's Method, so while the choric scenes had a ritual wildness and abandon to them, the ferocity of the scenes between named characters was also rigorously psychological and meticulous. Mitchell characterizes the production as 'bare, visceral, physical and vocal' and also recalls that, thanks to the then configuration of the seating in The Gate, 'the audience were pinned in. No one could get out. And no one dared exit across the stage.'

Trojan Women received near universal rapturous reviews, often brimming with critical insight. Writing in the *London Evening Standard* Michael Arditti opened by suggesting: 'Imagine Howard Brenton writing a play in response to the recent bombing of Baghdad, equating it with the Nazi raids on London and you will have some idea of the background to Euripides' *Trojan Women*' (Arditti 1991); Jane Langdon-Davies in *What's On* vividly saw:

> These women are not wailing drabs or archaeological fictions, but real people with a vibrant religion and culture. Even as they're being shipped off to Greece as slaves, and while they watch their city burn, they bravely uphold their traditions of singing and dancing: a tragic last gasp of Trojan civilisation. (Langdon Davies, 1991)

It was only Nicolas de Jongh, then writing for the *Guardian*, who, alongside hailing a 'daring, inventive and imaginative' production, claimed: 'It is also enraging and misguided from start to finish' (de Jongh 1991).

This fusion of British text-work, Russian psychology and Eastern European physicality and viscera must have seemed like a revelation at the time, as Mitchell was bringing the fruits of original research undertaken in countries that had until recently been 'behind the Iron Curtain' straight into her rehearsal rooms.

Yes, a new theatrical *avant-garde* – Théâtre de Complicité, Forced Entertainment and the like – were already tapping this rich mainland European seam for inspiration. The mainstream, however, was still counting the cost of a decade of arts funding cuts by the Thatcher government. Nevertheless, it is significant that Mitchell's first move prior to embarking on her directing career was to look to mainland Europe, and particularly Eastern Europe, for influences and possible new directions. That this search – for what we might think of as a kind of 'purity' in her work – took place against the most vast, unexpected shifts in European history since 1945 cannot have failed to have made an impression on her, and doubtless also informed the wider perspective of the productions.

Phoenician Women at the RSC: Stanislavski in Bosnia

The next Greek text undertaken by Mitchell, five years later, was again by Euripides, this time *Phoenician Women* at the Royal Shakespeare Company's Other Place theatre in Stratford-upon-Avon. The production itself, when described by Mitchell, sounds like a direct continuation of the elements that she brought to *Trojan Women*. There was once more a simple bare stage, with various natural elements. This time, she had sprigs of thyme handed out to the audience as they entered the space, so that the heavy, ritual smell of the herb suffused the atmosphere, while the space was lit partially by numerous candles. Once again, the setting was an 'a-historical zone', with the performers wearing simple tunics that carried 'very little data'. Mitchell recalls that prior to this production, she had recently attended a workshop series with Peter Brook, so that his ideas about theatre also permeated the rehearsal process. However, the twin spirits of *poor theatre* company Gardzienice and the psychological truth of Stanislavski continued to be the dominant influences on the work.

The greatest influence on the thinking behind this comparatively rare outing for a Greek play in 'Shakespeareland' was not theatrical at all, however. In June 1991, Slovenia declared its independence from the former Yugoslavia, triggering a complex series of events that led to a series of wars, civil wars, massacres and ethnic cleansing on a scale not seen in Europe since the end of World War Two. That the conflict had suddenly blown up inside what had seemed, to outside eyes, like an entirely peaceful country made it all the more horrific. The wars were also to inspire arguably the most famous original drama of 1990s Britain: Sarah Kane's debut, *Blasted*. Mitchell describes the era as 'a very difficult time to be young', remembering how every night the television news would relentlessly bring reports of fresh horrors being perpetrated or discovered. During the conflict, Mitchell travelled to the former Yugoslavia, driving through Serbia to Montenegro (her father knew a cultural attaché who managed to get her the necessary paperwork):

> We drove round the border with Bosnia and you would see these troops cutting down a hillside or crossing the road. Or you'd stop at a roadside café and there'd be all these men who'd just come from the fighting popping over to the non-fighting-country to have their breakfast and were then going to go back to fight. So it was very close, I think, that ... violence. (Mitchell 2015)

Unlike Kane, however, rather than writing a play which contained an analogous situation (albeit part-transplanted to an expensive hotel room in Leeds), Mitchell discovered in *Phoenician Women* a perfect text to explore the particular barbarism of the civil war. Here, instead of the Trojan War, the audience is confronted with the conflict between Oedipus and Jocasta's two sons, Eteocles and Polyneices, sparked by the latter reneging on a power-sharing deal between the two.

It is fascinating to note that, in spite of the 'Eastern European' influences on her work (none of them ex-Yugoslavian), and again the use of Bulgarian singing, there was nothing in the production to explicitly tie this production to the conflict in the Balkans. Instead, Mitchell plainly trusted the power and precision of the Euripides itself to imprint on the minds of the audience, and for the similarities between these mythical, ancient horrors, and the ones taking place only a short flight away from the theatre, to be readily appreciable.

At its first performance at the RSC's Other Place, the reviews largely bear witness to a revelation. Nick Curtis in the *Standard* argued: 'The Greeks and Katie Mitchell were made for each other.

This director's uniquely solemn, ensemble approach to theatre finds its stripped-down apotheosis in the universal, formal, choric tales of Greek tragedy' (Curtis, 1995). *The Times*'s Benedict Nightingale suggested that 'to say that everything Katie Mitchell touches turns to gold might annoy Katie Mitchell. Like Shakespeare's Bassanio, she knows the value of plain lead' (Nightingale 1995). It is interesting to note the over-familiarity creeping into some press assessments of Mitchell's work: 'Her setting is in her favourite colour – black ...' (Kingston 1996); 'You get a fair idea of the high-mindedness with which Katie Mitchell approaches Euripides' tragedy when you are told you can't buy a programme until the performance is over ...' (Stratton 1996), but: 'Such touches testify to the completeness of Mitchell's fiercely focused vision' (Curtis 1996) and 'Mitchell's productions have always been characterised by their clarity, austerity, and a dramatic intensity' (Smith 1996). For all the chummy familiarity of the reviews, *Phoenician Women* remains one of Mitchell's most fêted British productions to date, winning her the *The Evening Standard* Best Director award after the 1996 London run.

Oresteia at the National: Between two styles

Of all the Greek plays that Mitchell has directed, her *Oresteia* is the production with which she was least satisfied by quite some margin. Indeed, in her book *The Director's Craft* she holds up her National Theatre production of *The Oresteia* as a perfect example of 'an accurate reflection of my first over-excited and uneven reading of the text' (Mitchell 2009). 'It's impossible to do and you want to rub it out of your memory,' she said. Mitchell also suggests that on reflection she much prefers the plays of Euripides, which she characterizes as 'more discursive' than Aeschylus' oeuvre.

The production also marked a very specific, deliberate new phase in her directing career and aesthetic, although in this instance it is a change of direction that Mitchell herself counts as a misfire. In his chapter on Mitchell in *Contemporary European Directors*, Dan Rebellato suggests that her work has three phases or modes: an 'anthropological phase, an actor-centred phase, and the technological phase' (Rebellato 2008: xx). *The Oresteia* marked an abortive early attempt to usher in the technological phase a full six years before it sprang into more fully realized life in her adaptation of Virginia Woolf – *Waves* – for the National. Nonetheless, *The Oresteia* was her first attempt (in Britain) to incorporate video work into the fabric of a production. Indeed, this 'failure' perhaps partly informed the shape of the 'actor-centred phase' that followed. Part of Mitchell's dissatisfaction with the video elements in the production came from her irritation with the whole:

> The main thing to say about [*The Oresteia*] is that anyone can have a go at the first play. You need to be *very good* to have a go at the second play. And you need to be at the top of your game or a genius to do the third. You shouldn't embark on the whole unless you've got an idea for the third. So [this/mine] was a production with diminishing returns: it got worse and worse. We did a fantastic Agamemnon, and we did a really awful Eumenedies: cheesy, embarrassing, clutching at the worst, cheap Complicité and Peter Brook [rip-offs]. But it did have a different type of edge and colour to it ... (Mitchell 2015)

It is worth noting that Mitchell's *Oresteia* was the first at the National Theatre of Great Britain since Sir Peter Hall's almost – in places – 'original practices' production in 1981, with Jocelyn Herbert's Greek robes and masks and Sir Harrison Birtwhistle's score, a focus on rhythm and ritual, and an all-male cast. The aesthetic of Mitchell's *Oresteia*, by contrast, still carried traces of the Eastern European work that had so far informed her productions of the Greeks, but this time it was mixed in with that more recent 'European' aesthetic popularized by, for example, Complicité's *Street of Crocodiles*. At the same time, the translation used had been written by Ted Hughes, who completed it only shortly before his death. This posthumous production was its première performance. It was published in 1998, the same year that Hughes also released *The Birthday Letters*, the collection of poems regarded as the poet's most explicit response to the suicide of his wife, Sylvia Plath, thirty-five years earlier. As a result of this dual proximity – both culturally and for Hughes as a writer working on this translation – Mitchell suggests 'all of the horror of that seeped into the soil of the play, and the production as well'.

This was an *Oresteia* founded on the idea of the middle-class family and the potential for horrific abuses to take place within such structures: 'the family looked middle-class. It wasn't heroic, it wasn't royal: [this *Oresteia* was about] bourgeois violence and abused children, basically.' In a way, this was a bigger departure for the political terms of Mitchell's aesthetic than the video work. If the previous two Greek productions were plainly looking outward to national and international conflicts for their resonances, here the production looked inwards, into the middle-class family – a much smaller scale – for its foundations. If her *Phoenician Women*, spurred by the Bosnian war, was one aspect to 'Mitchell's *Blasted*' depicting the overt violence of a civil war, then this *Oresteia* could be suggested as its other half – the part where we see that the horrors of war are symbolically echoed in abusive relationships.

Despite mixed reviews – Oliver Jones in *What's On* hailed it as 'one hell of a production' (Jones 1999); Michael Coveney, praised 'Katie Mitchell's hypnotic production ... A really superb occasion' – the majority of the critics concurred with Mitchell's own analysis: 'The production mingles flashes of inspiration with moments of elephantine clumsiness' (Edwardes 1999).

It is in the reviews of the *Oresteia* that Charles Spencer first gives voice to the problematic 'Euro-sceptic' notion that was to grow over the next decade: 'Mitchell has such a distinctive and overbearing style as a director ... that you sometimes feel you are watching Katie Mitchell's, rather than Aeschylus', *Oresteia*' (Spencer 1999). It is a problematic assertion, and sadly not the last time we shall see it in this chapter.

Iphigenia at Aulis: The birth of a new aesthetic

Following on from the *Oresteia*, the next Greek play Mitchell chose to direct was Euripides' *Iphigenia at Aulis*. The play depicts the event from which – arguably – all the action of the *Oresteia* flows: the sacrifice at Aulis of Agamemnon and Clytemnestra's daughter, Iphigenia, merely in order that the Greek fleet might reach Troy.

Interestingly, Mitchell's production had two related lives, opening first at the Abbey Theatre in Dublin in 2001, and then transferring, with much of the same cast, to the National Theatre in London some three years later in 2004. It is also a crucial production in terms of the growth of Mitchell's aesthetic. Following on from the transitional *Oresteia*, in close collaboration with her regular designers, *Aulis* moved from the bare stages and natural elements of the Gardzienice/poor theatre-inspired early productions to a new conception for staging Greek tragedy. The natural elements, physical theatre and Bulgarian *a cappella* singing were cleared out, and in their place now stood large, cinematically detailed interiors and sudden bursts of the great German dance–theatre choreographer Pina Bausch-inspired ballroom dancing. The emphasis on psychological exactitude and actors'/characters' intentions remained intact, and was indeed further explored and expanded in this new overall vision.

The set for *Aulis* was an abandoned hotel, which Agamemnon has commandeered as his HQ ('because it overlooked the bay, so [he] really liked it', Mitchell explained to me in an interview 14 years later, demonstrating the longevity of her productions' psychologizing of these 2,000-year-old characters, giving a glimpse of just how closely she and the actors spent time under their skins). Mitchell describes the journey of the women, the chorus of the piece, as that of 'ladies on a day trip who stumble into Hitler's bunker' – into hell, essentially. It is worth noting that following on from the Dublin *Aulis*, and sandwiching the National Theatre version, Mitchell had directed a series of high-quality Chekhov productions and that this new direction/aesthetic for her stagings of Greek plays moved them – at least visually – far closer together. The 'Katie Mitchell Production' had been born.[3]

For the London version, Mitchell also introduced aspects from the work of the neuroscientist and writer Antonio Damasio, whose work on the biology of emotion she read together with her actors. Connecting to Stanislavski's probable reading of William James's famous essay *What is an Emotion?*, Mitchell was immersed in work looking at what actual physical responses the human animal has, particularly to intense emotional moments. Primarily, she argues, these physical responses are much bigger in real life than are ever portrayed in theatre, giving as an example the actor Justin Salinger's reaction to seeing a rat: where in real life he jumped back some distance, in theatre this is something that would typically be toned down physically. Alongside these large-as-actual-life gestures, Mitchell's other key physical invention for *Aulis* was to have the full cast performing the physicality of extreme anxiety – essentially continual movement for the entire duration of the piece. This, she argues, bled through to the audience's experience of the piece. Because of this relentless shifting on stage, the audience were also made so tense that they were far more alert to the ideas and meaning in the text. For Kim Solga,

> This kind of performance – call it a feminist performance of violence – does not ask how it might make the experience of violence's loss seem real on stage. Rather, it asks Taylor's question: how stage a blinding? When a woman's body in violence, suffering, panic and fear promises to go so spectacularly missing – as does Iphigenia's here – this rebel transformation returns not just that body but the chilling echo of its absence to the scene of representation, and asks us to engage with the sounds, the sensations, of loss. (Solga 2008: 160)

It is significant that *Aulis* was the first Mitchell Greek production on a larger, traditional proscenium arch stage. This shift necessitated a different dynamic for talking to the audience, something which, within the scheme of Mitchell's work with 'radical naturalism' (Solga 2008: 150), needed a good deal more thinking about than it might for directors happy to 'chop and change' between registers. Mitchell is revealing on this point:

> [If the naturalism is not retained, the actors] just physically relax and you lose tension. Choruses are really hard because they let steam out, and what you want to do is tighten [the situation, the tension], not make it go soggy ... If the character inside naturalism believes in a life-threatening situation and you then say to the character: '[Now] you're just an actor talking to the theatre audience now' they just go [*she relaxes into a slouch*]: 'Oh, well, y'know, the thing is there's this great story ...' The literal tension goes out of the actor's body, and you have to start the tension again in the situation. I remember Mark Lithgoe and I watched *Iphigenia*, and he said 'The problem for the brain receiving this kind of work, is this switch between the naturalism and the more stylised work. It lurches. That's the problem with it. So, if you can remove that lurch ...'

If the *Oresteia* had failed in Mitchell's eyes and disappointed the critics, the reception of *Iphigenia* offered the exact reverse. The production also benefited hugely from the immediacy of Britain being at war. Where in previous reviews only a handful of critics spotted possible parallels between *Phoenician Women* and the war in Bosnia, here, Britain's illegal invasion of Iraq with America ensured everyone sat up and took notice. Only Sheridan Morley in the *Express* believed the costumes to be modern dress and 'clearly inspired' by 'certain Iraqi parallels'. Elsewhere, however, it is intelligently discerned that 'As an attack on the moral hypocrisy of warfare ... [it] drops some pretty serious ordnance. But it doesn't target its subject directly' (Marminon 2004). 'Was Katie Mitchell thinking of a current conflict when she staged her *Iphigenia*?' asks Benedict Nightingale in the *Times*. 'Perhaps. But Don Taylor's punchy, colloquial translation predates the Iraq war and Mitchell's revival transcends it ... This is one of the finest productions the National has ever mounted' (Nightingale 2004). However, even with praise like this, and with even previous Mitchell-sceptic Nicholas de Jongh, here clearly moved, describing the piece as 'Astonishing', Spencer's niggling doubts begin to be seen in other reviews. Despite the piece being 'fresh, daring and stylish' in Spencer's eyes, it is also apparently 'a little too pleased with its own virtuosity'. Michael Billington offers the indecipherable objection that he 'wish[es] she had edited out some of the naturalistic detail' and John Gross, largely positive, still finds time to grumble about a 'weary succession of gimmicks and tricks'.

Nevertheless, *Iphigenia at Aulis* was an enormous success, but much more importantly it established what appears to be a complete, wholesale, successful transformation of Mitchell's aesthetic vision for the presentation of Greek plays. From the bare stages, ritual and red earth of her first *Trojan Women*, audiences now found themselves confronted with concrete, recognizable, Chekhovian rooms immersed in a nightmare of endless war.

Women of Troy: Chekhov and Bausch in hell

Mitchell's next Greek project was her second production of *Women of Troy*, this time for the National Theatre, in 2007. It was, however, more in dialogue with her (relatively) recent *Iphigenia* than her first version – *Trojan Women* – now seventeen years earlier. It was a continuation of Mitchell's new exploration of an almost dream-like (or nightmarish) naturalism, fused with intense psychological acuity and incredible levels of tension. The genesis for this National Theatre production was apparently largely down to the fact that Euripides' *Women of Troy* was on the British A level Theatre Studies syllabus (such is artistic decision-making/dramaturgy in the National Theatre of Great Britain). As a result, Mitchell's primary impulse, beyond the ongoing development of her own director's craft, was to create a version of the play that was exciting and visually stunning, to really bring home the idea that Greek drama need not be considered stuffy or old-fashioned. To 'put some fire in the belly' of the classics. To breed in young audience members a real appreciation of just how good Greek drama was.

Mitchell describes the version as 'very filmic' and there's certainly something in that. Bunny Christie's ultra-naturalistic, two-storey warehouse set would easily have stood up as a film set, including close-ups. It is interesting that, because of the increased level of naturalism, one of Mitchell's strongest memories is that the murder of the baby – Andromache's son Astyanax – was almost unbearable to either direct or perform, more so than in her first production, where the ritual nature of the production perhaps made the baby's death feel more symbolic than 'actual'.

Again, like *Aulis*, the play centres around a group of women who suddenly find themselves in this brutal, male, military environment, and again, as with *Iphigenia*, there were sequences of ballroom dancing, reminiscent of the work of Pina Bausch. In *Women of Troy* these sections became more complex and evolved, often adding in sequences where the dancing appeared to be slowed down or moving backwards. Mitchell has written before of her artistic debt to Bausch. In an article for *The Observer* she suggested that *Café Müller* 'has probably inspired me for about 10 years;

even now, I'm probably derivative without knowing that I am. Nothing's come close to it. I'm maybe cursed by having seen it in some ways! I'm certainly haunted by it' (Mitchell 2010).

It is perhaps this further evolution of style that tipped the mainstream media critics over the edge. Between *Iphigenia* and *Women of Troy* it felt as if a very British consensus had amassed against Mitchell's work in the mainstream media. Observe the opening of the *Telegraph* review:

> [Mitchell's] particular speciality, however, is smashing up the classics. Faced with works of genius ... Mitchell's primary aim isn't to serve the dead author. It is to come up with her own personal response to the piece, using what she needs, discarding what doesn't suit her, and leaving her grubby fingerprints all over whatever survives of the original masterpiece. Common practice among the directorial auteurs of Europe, this overweening arrogance is mercifully less often seen in Britain and seems to be the speciality of a group of mostly female directors such as Mitchell, Deborah Warner and Emma Rice, who all attract a devoted coterie of admirers while outraging reactionary white males such as myself. (Spencer 2007)

It's an almost-comic bit of bluster, and when located in Britain's most right-wing broadsheet its chauvinist Euro-scepticism might pass without comment had the *Guardian* not also used the same word with the same disapproving tone: 'Once she was content to realise an author's text, now she has become an auteur whose signature is on every moment of a production' (Billington 2007).

There is not space in this chapter to address the contested view that a director should be 'content to realise an author's text'.[4] In fact, the production achieved both a viciously lucid telling of the story, sublime comment on human capacity for inflicting suffering and a horrifying vision of what the effects of that suffering actually look like up close. Without directly suggesting contemporary parallels – fewer than Euripides himself intended when writing the play during the Peloponnesian War – its bleak picture managed to suggest the all too real victims of any war you cared to name. In my review, I argued that '[the production] does so without once preaching, seeking to score points, or sacrificing any artistic integrity. Its use of metaphor – the way it engages the audience, requiring them to interrogate as well as be "shown" – is perfectly judged. The whole is moving beyond words, visually ravishing, and utterly harrowing' (Haydon 2007).

By sheer coincidence, *Women of Troy* was also critic Matt Trueman's first ever review posted online. His conclusion – 'There are few more delicate images of hopelessness to be found' (Trueman 2007) – could almost have been conceived as a perfect rebuttal to the 'Dead White Males'⁵ who had stopped watching and started reciting dogma. It is significant that as Mitchell developed more as an artist, experimenting less with aspects of others' practices, as she had done in the first *Trojan Women* and in *Phoenician Women*, and into a fully realized aesthetic of her own – an aesthetic powerfully informed in particular by her feminism, most noticeable in its critique of the uninterrogated misogyny in the original texts, but also in the emphasis on strengthening women's roles – that elderly male critics began to rail against her having stopped 'serving' the texts.

By this point, however, the opinions of a few parochial old men were as good as irrelevant to the wider picture of Mitchell's work. The clarity and rigour of her productions inspired a new generation of directors, and her influence can already be seen running through the veins of new productions of the Greeks produced in Britain since. From Carrie Cracknell's *Medea* (National Theatre, 2014) through to Rob Icke's *Oresteia* (Almeida and West End, 2015), the spectacle of Greek tragedies played in modern dress within recognizable interiors and interspersed with contemporary dance have already crossed from experiment to near-default.

Phoenician Women in Deutschland: An artistic landmark

Thanks to Mitchell's reputation as a director abroad, her most recent production of a piece of Greek theatre had its world première at the Deutsches Schauspielhaus, Hamburg, in November 2013 (where it is still in repertoire, three years later, at time of writing). *Alles weitere kennen sie aus dem kino* (*The Rest Will Be Familiar to You from The Cinema*) is British playwright Martin Crimp's radical reworking of Euripides' *Phoenician Women*, bringing the so-far cycle of Mitchell's Greek stagings to a neat, near-circular conclusion.

Crimp's *Alles weitere* works like this: he has effectively removed the original chorus – the Phoenician women of the title – and replaced them with 'sphinxes' (although they are never referred to as such in the script) performing a complex ritual or procedure. In Alex Eales's brilliant crumbling mansion set, the Sphinxes hold the principal characters of *Phoenician Women* captive, dragged out of their graves just after death, reanimated, and made to re-enact their stories over and over again. As such, we are given both the action of the original play, and an entirely new conception of why we are watching it, integral to the staging.

In place of the original Phoenician women's plaintive woes we are instead challenged by a series of contemporary riddles. The questions are sometimes nonsensical ('If a stone that weighs 75 grams / and is flying through the air at 200 km per hour / can it shatter a human pelvis / why are we all so beautiful?'), sometimes oblique ('If two boys, both pierced by a sword of copper and tin need / 3 hours until they bleed to death at an ambient temperature of 30 degrees Celsius / then who is this woman? Is she / (1) mother of Oedipus? / (2) wife of Oedipus? / (3) Mother of 2 boys or / (4) all of the above? And / how can the dead live?') and sometimes chilling ('Or if Steffi has taken a tiny child – / ... / yes, takes a tiny child / and paints its face like a cat / and blindfolds it and leaves it one metre from the edge of the cliff / then what is the meaning of justice?').

An additional effect of this rewrite, beyond the new contemporary understandings and resonances to which it gives voice, is the complete shift in power from masculine to feminine. Granted, the men in the original are prey to the whims of the Gods, some of whom are women. But ultimately, all the Gods are under the power of the male god Zeus. In this new version we find ourselves in a godless world where some mixture of science and necromancy holds sway, and where women are very much in control. In this, *Alles weitere* forms perhaps the most complete vision yet of Mitchell's constant evaluation of gender in her work. It is notable that, with the arguable exception of the *Oresteia*, all the Greek plays she has directed are concerned primarily with women. Following on from her radical remake of Strindberg's *Miss Julie* (2010) at the Berlin Schaubühne, which told the story of the play from the perspective of the maid, in *Alles weitere* we see female power at its most fully realized in her work.

It is also interesting to note that, when placed in a German context, it is the ultra-naturalism of her work that makes it most alien. Where in Britain critics cavilled at the slow-motion dancing and 'rewinding of scenes', in Germany, the only note Deutsches Schauspielhaus artistic director Karin Beier gave Mitchell on seeing an early dress rehearsal was that the naturalistic costumes of tattered tunics worn by the named characters of the original text could maybe be substituted for modern dress as a German audience 'wouldn't get' why they were wearing bronze age costumes (Mitchell 2013) – an ironic reverse of British critics' concern at the 'overweening arrogance' of 'not serving a dead author'.

Indeed, seeing *Alles weitere* in Hamburg, you get a sense of a director set free from having to deal with a deadening set of conventions and critics, and instead given the proper time, resources and respect necessary to explore further than ever before the full possible extent of her artistic vision. It is a vision that, while characterized as 'European' and 'auteur'-ial back in Britain, when placed in a German context is suddenly seen as 'very English'. The British attraction to renewing repeatedly the relevance of a particular text remains very much in evidence, but the deep commitment to the Russian Stanislavski's Method, the early awakening to the possibilities of the physical within theatre by both Poland's Gardzienice and Germany's Pina Bausch, and the more 'European' conception of a piece of theatre as a contract of signs between director and audience all play their part in a journey toward a vision that is both unique and inspiring.

Conclusions

In this, *Alles weitere kennen sie aus dem kino* is not only the conclusion of this chapter, but also the apex of artistic achievement in this twenty-three-year-long (so far) journey of constant research, effort, experimentation, trial and error, and ever-increasing artistic vision. On the face of it, Mitchell's vision for the stage has always been a singular one, characterized by a commitment to the affects of naturalism, perhaps traceable to both their use in a systematic rehearsal room and the effect on audience. In applying the psychology of Stanislavski to the ritual and verse of these ancient texts, Mitchell's productions effectively repurpose these pre-dramatic texts for the post-dramatic age. By also bringing modern, politically left, feminist thinking to bear on these ancient, plutocratic, male documents, her productions also serve as live critiques of the original structures – living, breathing interrogations of form and purpose. And, within the context of the British/English theatre establishment, we also see this corpus as a successful challenge to the old, problematic assumption that a director can 'serve' a text. These are theatre productions that have succeeded as experiments, as milestones, as influences across generations and as great art in their own right.

Bibliography

Arditti, M. (1991) 'Review of *Women of Troy*', *Evening Standard*. *Theatre Record*, 921.

Billington, M. (2004) 'Review of *Iphigenia at Aulis*', *Guardian*. *Theatre Record*, 821.

Billington, M. (2007) 'Review of *Women of Troy*', *Guardian*. Online at www.theguardian.com/stage/2007/nov/29/theatre.euripides (accessed 15 November 2015).

Billington, M. (2009) *State of the Nation*. London: Faber.

Clapp, S. (1999) 'Review of *Oresteia*', *Observer*. *Theatre Record*, 1592.

Cole, Emma (2015) 'The Method behind the madness: Katie Mitchell, Stanislavski, and the classics' *Classical Receptions Journal* 7 (3): 400–21.

Coveney, M. (1999) 'Review of *Oresteia*', *Daily Mail*. *Theatre Record*, 1591.

Curtis, N. (1995) 'Review of *Phoenician Women*', *Evening Standard*. *Theatre Record*, 1514.

Delgado, M. M. and Rebellato, D. (eds) (2010) *Contemporary European Theatre Directors*. London: Routledge.

Edwardes, J. (1999) 'Review of *Oresteia*' in *Time Out*. *Theatre Record*, 1591.

Enwright, L. (2016) 'Katie Mitchell: The Feminist Visionary Making Theatre about the Female Experience'. Online at www.the-pool.com/people/women-we-love/2016/7/katie-mitchell-the-feminist-visionary-making-theatre-abut-the-female-experience (accessed 1 August 2016).

Gross, J. (2004) 'Review of *Iphigenia at Aulis*', *Sunday Telegraph*. Theatre Record, 823.

Haydon, A. (2007) 'Review of *Women of Troy*'. Online at http:// postcardsgods.blogspot.de/2007/12/women-of-troy.html (accessed 27 July 2016).

Haydon, A. (2013a) 'Review of *Alles weitere kennen sie aus dem kino*'. Online at http://postcardsgods.blogspot.de/2013/11/alles-weitere-kennen-sie-aus-dem-kino.html (accessed 15 November 2015).

Haydon, A. (2013b) 'Waves and Traces: An Interview with Katie Mitchell'. Online at http://exeuntmagazine.com/features/waves-and-traces/ (accessed 15 November 2015).

Hughes, T. (1999) *The Oresteia: A Translation of Aeschylus' Trilogy of Plays*. London: Faber & Faber.

Jones, O. (1999) 'Review of *Oresteia* in *What's On*'. *Theatre Record*, 1593.

Jongh, N. de (1991) 'Review of *Women of Troy*', *Guardian*. *Theatre Record*, 923.

Jongh, N. de (2004) 'Review of *Iphigenia at Aulis*', *Evening Standard*. *Theatre Record*, 822.

Kingston, J. (1996) 'Review of *Phoenician Women* in the *Times*'. *Theatre Record*, 820.

Langdon-Davies, J. (1991) 'Review of *Women of Troy*', *What's On*. *Theatre Record*, 922.

Marminon, P. (2004) 'Review of *Iphigenia at Aulis*', *Daily Mail*. *Theatre Record*, 821.

Mitchell, K. (2009) *The Director's Craft*. London: Routledge.

Mitchell, K. (2015) Unpublished interview with the author.

Morley, S. (2004) 'Review of *Iphigenia at Aulis* in the *Express*'. *Theatre Record*, 823.

Nightingale, B. (1995) 'Review of *Phoenician Women*', *Times*. *Theatre Record*, 1516.

Nightingale, B. (2004) 'Review of *Iphigenia at Aulis*', *Times*. *Theatre Record*, 824.

Pavis, P. and Kruger, L. (1991) *Theatre at the Crossroads of Culture*. London: Routledge.

Pavis, P. and Anderson, J. (2012) *Contemporary Mise en Scène: Staging Theatre Today*. London: Taylor & Francis.

Radosavljević, D. (2013) *Theatre-Making: Interplay Between Text and Performance in the 21st Century*. Basingstoke: Palgrave Macmillan.

Solga, K. (2008) 'Body Doubles, Babel's Voices: Katie Mitchell's *Iphigenia at Aulis* and the Theatre of Sacrifice'. *Contemporary Theatre Review* 18:2: 146–60.

Spencer, C. (1999) 'Review of *Oresteia*', *Daily Telegraph*. *Theatre Record*, 1594.

Spencer, C. (2004) 'Review of *Iphigenia at Aulis*', *Daily Telegraph*. *Theatre Record*, 825.

Spencer, C. (2007) '"Euripides All Roughed Up". Review of *Women of Troy*', *Daily Telegraph*. Online at www.telegraph.co.uk/culture/theatre/drama/3669609/Women-of-Troy-Euripides-all-roughed-up.html (accessed 15 November 2015).

Stratton, K. (1996) 'Review of *Phoenician Women*', *Time Out*. *Theatre Record*, 822.

Trueman, M. (2008) '"Carousel of Fantasies", review of *Women of Troy*'. Online at http://matttrueman.co.uk/2008/02/review-women-of-troy-national-theatre.html (accessed 15 November 2015).

4

Tadashi Suzuki and Yukio Ninagawa: Reinventing the Greek classics; reinventing Japanese identity after Hiroshima

Penelope Chatzidimitriou

Even if Artaud's polemical call 'for no more masterpieces' is not heard by the Japanese directors Tadashi Suzuki and Yukio Ninagawa, still their *tour de force* partly lies in their strong clash with the classical tragic texts. 'Only strength is memorable; only the capacity to wound gives a healing capacity the chance to endure, and so to be heard,' writes Harold Bloom in accordance with Artaud's vision of theatre as a purgatorial epidemic (in Rabkin 1983: 60).[1] Thus, Suzuki's provocative readings of the classics result from his focus on tension and struggle in human existence. There is a fissure between the upper and the lower parts of the body, Suzuki supports, that is, between '*the conceptual and the physical, the conscious and the unconscious, dream and reality, script and body language*' (Saitoh in Mitter and Shevtsova 2007: 170, my emphasis). Classics are collaged and replayed through the distorted consciousness of a marginalized or insane central character. Such a kind of dramaturgical collage of play materials creates a new textual vortex that escapes psychological interpretation (Suzuki in ibid., 2007: 171) – an issue we will come back to later.

On the other hand, Ninagawa's revisioning of tragedies like *Medea* (1978) remains more faithful to the original text: 'I do all that is written in the script, stage directions and all. But I allow myself to add what is not written' (Ninagawa in Mitter and Shevtsova 2007: 135). In his theatre, it is the non-verbal additions, the Japanese or Asian aura, which permeates the visual context of his productions and reveals what words cannot. Rejecting long reading sessions around a rehearsal table, he asks that his actors read the play with their body. 'That is to say, his approach is from the visible (the ocular) to the invisible; from the outer factors (movements, position, pose, stance, direction, facial expression and costumes) to the inner workings of the characters' (Mitter and Shevtsova 2007: 136). Simultaneously, he makes his Japanese spectators feel at ease while watching a performance of ancient Greek tragedy, for they recognize the *mise-en-scène* as culturally their own.

Bodies in contaminated contexts

When Antonin Artaud composed his 'poetics of contagion' in Theatre and the Plague, he could not have foreseen the atomic bombing of Hiroshima in August 1945 in the aftermath of World War II, not to mention the tuna fish boat *Lucky Dragon 5* incident in Bikini Atoll in 1954. The high levels of radiation found in the tuna that was fished and distributed to the Japanese local markets, finally, though belatedly, made a whole nation feel that nuclear power was a threatening insider, an enemy that had invaded their bodies.[2] Thus, be it the case of food pollution or the Artaudian plague, both theatre and medicine prove to be 'technologies of the body' that share a common interest in 'the interaction of the human organism with its environment, the relationship of inside and outside, the nature of visibility and somatic disclosure, and the definition of individual and social pathology' (Garner 2006: 2).

To return to our discussion of the *Lucky Dragon 5* incident in 1954, anti-nuclear movements swept the whole country, transforming 'Hiroshima' into the absolute symbol of Japan's atomic victimhood. To put it differently, 'the A-bomb survivor was elevated to the status of a "totem"' (Durkheim in Saito 2006: 369), and all 'Japanese identified with A-bomb survivors and saw themselves as nuclear victims' (Saito 2006: 369). Alongside, the perpetrator was no longer the faceless atomic bomb, a 'natural disaster rather than a human wrong', 'an "actor" in its own right' (ibid. 2006: 362), but acquired a face, an American one in specific, ensuing for the first time discussions of responsibility and culpability. That is, as many as nine years after the nuclear bombing in Hiroshima, politics entered the national master narrative, tarnishing the post-war image of the United States as the 'benevolent liberator' in Japan (ibid. 2006: 364). Similarly, Japan tried to erase its military past and belligerence, building on the argument that it was the only country worldwide that had fallen prey to atomic bombing. This was not only a period of hectic reconstruction of the country's economy and infrastructure; what was equally feverishly reconstructed was the Japanese national identity on the world stage.

In such turbulent times, the traumatized Japanese national body emerged as a site of resistance against politics, for the body is always culturally and linguistically inscribed and cannot escape 'the pitfalls of politics or logocentric thinking' (Marshall 1992: 5).[3] Thus, the aesthetics of *butoh* or Tadashi Suzuki, for example, are rooted in the cultural specificity of post-war Japan. If at the turn of the twentieth century the Japanese *Shingeki* (new theatre) totally surrendered itself and embraced Western modern drama and theatre – a possible form of Japanese self-hatred and self-depreciation, in the Japanese director Kawamura Takeshi's view (Martin 2000: 83) – the *angura* theatre practitioners of the 1960s decided to overcome Western realism, built-up noses and blonde wigs, and transform the Westernized Japanese body into a body of resistance. The exotic Japanese national body, beautified according to the Western cultural standards – thus mutilated and muted – gives way to 'Japanese models of the body' that self-consciously mirror Western society and 'the violence it has inflicted on nations with different cultural backgrounds' (Marshall 1992: 6).

'Burn the Louvre': Escaping classical beauty, escaping history

When the Greeks stripped their sculptural mortal and divine bodies of drapery to reveal their nakedness and beauty (*kalos*), they instantly conceptualized the human form, setting the ideal through centuries of Western art. Nakedness was no more a sign of humiliation and defeat of the foe or the victim as seen in Assyrian and Middle East art. Nor was it shameful, as the Christian Edenic vision would later want it to be. Even today, the classical Greek standards of naked beauty exhibited in museums around the world persistently negate the modern sexually burdened perception of pornographic nudity, restricted to the private sphere.[4] Created to please and delight the senses in public, the classical naked body holds a kind of (inner) beauty perceivable both to the eye and the mind's eye. Physical qualities and qualities of the soul and personality are combined to inextricably associate Beauty and Goodness, the *Kalokagathia* (Eco 2004: 45).

Nonetheless, the impossibility of universal standards of beauty is widely accepted nowadays as well as the assumption that the aesthetic gap becomes even wider when it involves such distant and different cultures as Western Europe and East Asia. In fact, any comparative aesthetic judgement of different races or ethnicities involves not so much good looks but power relations between cultures. Not surprisingly, when the first Europeans came to Japan in 1542, they described Japan and the Japanese as a world that is the opposite of Europe:

> Europeans were tall, the Japanese were short. Churches were high, temples low. European women whitened their teeth, Japanese women blackened theirs. Japan was an antipodean universe, ever yielding, ever prostrate. (Smith 1998: 2)

Once again a wide range of criteria, from socio-economic and cultural to religious and moral ones, affect physical beauty judgement. Beauty is attributed to insiders, the noble, the affluent, the holy and the good. By contrast, ugliness is assigned to the outsiders, the humble, the secular, the evil (Kyo 2012: 5).

Throwing off the 'mantle of Westernism' (Sanders 1988: 148), the newly emerged Japanese performance aesthetics 'explore[s] the dark truths that hid beneath the Japanese social mask' (Stein in Sanders 1988: 148), foregrounding complexity and heterogeneity. Governed by anger at the historical control exercised on the Japanese body, a fundamental aesthetic conflict emerges with anything that is imported from the West – from urban alienation and the cult of technology and novelty to Western styles of dance, ballet and theatre. As Vicki Sanders concludes, *butoh* could only have emerged in Japan. Its 'squat-bodied movement', its 'post-Hiroshima rebelliousness', its 'crudeness', 'vulgarity', 'commonness', its 'spirituality', are exclusively Japanese, anti-Western forms (1998: 161–2). What Hijicata Tatsumi, for example, does with performances like *Forbidden Colours* (1959) is to scrub off their Oriental [*sic*] classical beauty from Japanese bodies and launch instead an Artaudian grotesque, freakish anthropomorphism that could have very well been a chapter of its own in Umberto Eco's treatise *On Ugliness*.[5] In his exploration of the monstrous and the repellant in the arts, Eco cites, among others, Adorno's belief, as expressed in his *Aesthetic Theory*, that through the depiction of ugliness, art engages itself in social criticism, protesting against and denouncing a beautiful life in an ugly world. Ultimately, '[t]he transformation of the ugly into form results in the cruel' (Hohendahl 2005: 184). All in all, Eco's perspective helps us see *butoh* as a rejection of any rules of a beautiful life, thus beauty itself, in an ugly society. Interestingly enough, this is a captivating, even seductive kind of ugliness, a sort of 'terrible' nocturnal beauty.

What about texts of the Western canon, particularly the Greek classics and Shakespeare? Why did they escape the menace of the post-Hiroshima Japanese artists? Tadashi Suzuki's answer proves illuminating at this point. As opposed to the performance-oriented Japanese texts that seem to him 'boring [*sic*]', for they lack intellectual sophistication and profundity, Greek drama is 'an archetype of the fundamentals of what it means to be alive as a human being' (Suzuki to Toni Sant 1988: 151). If Shakespeare attracts him for his probing investigation of interpersonal relations among individuals who flee the 'collective centre' only to create an innerscape in which (their) loneliness is the protagonist, the ancient Greeks give him a larger ontological scale of the human experience in its confrontation with the divine or mortal other. Individuality is, thus, simultaneously transcended and yet paradoxically grounded within a plagued collective and social sphere (Varopoulou 2002: 475–6).

As for Yukio Ninagawa, the fact that Greek tragedies and Shakespeare form the core of his repertoire may be the result of the challenge posed in bridging 'the spatio-temporal gap between present-day Japan and his audiences (usually Japanese) and the classical dramatic world' while overcoming 'the embarrassment [...] he feels when Japanese actors play the parts of European characters in Shakespeare or Greek tragedies' (Mitter and Shevtsova 2007: 134–5). More importantly, Ninagawa's fusion of heterogeneous elements of the East and the West manifests how Western classical artifacts can be appropriated and explored instead of being blindly respected as imported masterpieces of a superior culture. Ultimately, with the Japanification of the classics what is subverted is the Japanese inferiority complex toward Western culture (Brokering 2007: 371).

From the above it becomes clear that in its post-Hiroshima era the Japanese theatre can no longer be received as 'the art of a "nation of children"' (Lequeux in Brandon 1989: 38) and this can also be partly attributed to the changes in international politics. The latter definitely opened the way to cultural changes in the second half of the twentieth century and onwards. As an economic superpower, Japan today receives the West's attention and respect, no longer being treated as culturally inferior. Likewise, the Japanese directors' attraction to the Greek classics and Shakespeare grants them a valid passport to the West, making their work appealing to both Japanese and non-Japanese audiences (Marshall 1992: 14). After all, Western theatre has long revealed its urgent need of the East to escape its aesthetic logocentric impasse, a need that the emerging global culture could satisfy. Japanese directors like Suzuki and Ninagawa could now become an essential part of an international theatre *avant-garde*.

Trojan Women: Tragic female bodies in resistance

Interestingly enough, the Japanese body of resistance in both Suzuki and Ninagawa's first productions of Greek tragedies – *The Trojan Women* (1974) and *Medea* (1978) respectively – is gender specific. It is on the female body that masculine aggression and violence is inscribed, especially at times of war. 'I intended to express the disastrous fate of women caused by war, which was initiated by men [...]', Suzuki writes in the programme (Suzuki in Allain 2002: 154). Warfare, with the aid of technology, turns women into commodities to be used, abused and discarded. Suzuki's *The Trojan Women*, for example, is set amongst the ruins of a bombarded cemetery immediately after World War II. Japan is a twentieth-century Troy, a victim of the American military and cultural imperialism. Thus, Suzuki's (Trojan) women, though surviving a war, have a life and destiny far worse than that of the ghosts.[6]

The Euripidean communal tragedy is, consequently, transformed into the tragedy of women against the backdrop of a scorched wasteland. This should not come as a surprise as, in the historical process of the nationalization of the collective memory of 'Hiroshima', young female survivors were assigned a leading role. The photographs of the so-called 'A-bomb maidens' with their keloid (overgrown scar tissue), their deformed faces and bodies, became the ultimate emblem of the tragedy caused by the American 'Little Boy' – as the nuclear bomb that devastated Hiroshima was named – hitherto the tragedy of a whole nation. As Susan Sontag observes, 'photography has kept company with death; ever since its invention "as a memento of the vanished past and the dear departed"' (2002). The moment, however, cameras became portable, they could 'seize death in the making' and 'picture taking acquired an immediacy and authority greater than any verbal account in conveying the horror of mass-produced death'. For Sontag, the year that the camera proved its supremacy in defining horrible realities was 1945, specifically in the first days after World War II concentration camps had been liberated and the days of August 1945 after the incineration of the populations of Hiroshima and Nagasaki. To return to our discussion of the physically deformed 'A-bomb maidens', what was alongside destroyed was any hope of their marriage and birth giving. To put it differently, in the Japanese collective imagination, the Japanese maidens' ugliness triggered fears of infertility, thus suspension of a hopeful national future. Their deformed face was turned into a death mask that urgently demanded plastic surgery intervention to at least erase the externally visible marks.[7]

It is true, however, that in Tadashi Suzuki's *The Trojan Women* the female victims succumb to their ill fate. Suzuki seems to deprive his Japanese women of any cathartic tragic glory and his spectators of any hope for the coming of a harmonious future for humankind. 'The fundamental drama of our time is anxiety in the face of impending disaster,' Suzuki comments in his director's note, expressing his view that peace is only a temporary interval between long, destructive periods of war. Suzuki sees in tragedy the depiction of a world in which catharsis or reconstitution cannot be achieved as the laws of the evil finally triumph (Sampatakakis 2015: 491).

Yet, unlike the vanity of human passions against an eternal backdrop – as is the case with Noh theatre – the ancient Greek tragic heroes' dignity lies in the fact that despite their failure and their defeat they are driven by their desire to fully meet and grasp their misfortune. This is their admirable power and grandeur, a valuable moral lesson for the (post-)modern human condition (Suzuki in ibid.: 495–6).

What, after all, Suzuki's female bodies successfully resist is their representation as the silent commodities that the dominant Western and Japanese cultural discourses wished for, a fate that the silenced 'A-bomb maidens' could not escape. The success of such representational resistance largely lies in what Paul Allain identifies as the creative symbiosis of directorial technique and vision with the notorious Suzuki actor training method. The result, though, is not a harmonious but a clashing relationship of those two with the text. The Greek tragedies offer Suzuki the theme of mania – be it ecstatic, erotic or vengeful – to justify and foreground the high levels of energy that his trained performing bodies unleash on stage. Kayoko Shiraishi's – Suzuki's muse and protagonist from 1967 to 1990 – madness is not anymore a construct but an essential element of the classical texts to be unearthed and offered to the audience (Allain 2002: 153). Suzuki employs the 'metaphorics of disease' as theatre has done from classical times and the ravaged-by-plague city of Thebes in *Oedipus Rex* to 'the epidemic drama of Tony Kushner and other AIDS dramatists'.[8] Particularly in modern theatre, disease provided 'a discursive ground for addressing questions of individual, social, and political (dis)equilibrium and for locating the body within a field of pathological and other influences. It also provided this theatre with a network of metaphors for its own modes of corporeal interaction' (Garner 2006: 2–3).

Likewise, Suzuki's recurrent framing device of the world as a mental hospital in his productions of Greek classics, Shakespeare and even Chekhov can be partly attributed to 'Japan's instability and social conflicts and the sensibilities these created' (Allain 2002: 140). This is a man's world, Suzuki implies – that is, a mad world in which texts and bodies lose their 'sane integrity', ending up butchered and irrational. In our modern times, *teatrum mundi* has become a mental hospital. This is a sort of Artaudian plagued theatre, which directs itself at those physical sites where human will, thought and consciousness reside, a 'contagious delirium' in which the Suzukian actor is the central figure.

A gender-ambiguous *Medea*

Similarly, Yukio Ninagawa's most celebrated Japanese body of resistance is female. In the character of Medea he sees the Japanese female body revolting against a repressing patriarchy that considers weakness and modesty to be the ultimate female virtues. The challenge for him is to make such a revengeful, ruthless heroine pitiful and sympathetic, especially to his Japanese audience. Such a challenge may not be that big if one takes into account how dear other Western female characters like Hedda Gabler and Nora have been amongst the Japanese, at least when Ibsen's plays were first introduced to the island at the end of the nineteenth and the beginning of the twentieth centuries. Still, the latter fact does not eliminate the threat that classical Medea poses. Under this light, Ninagawa's major success is that his Medea proved to be irresistible to the Japanese.

Mae Smethurst goes to great lengths to analyse the aesthetic means employed by the Japanese director to achieve his set goal. According to her, his liberal and subversive use of the traditional Japanese conventions of Kabuki and Bunraku are the key to his achievement. Interestingly enough, an all-male cast is used, a convention typical of ancient Greek theatre and *avant-garde* Kabuki theatre. In the Tokyo performance of 1993, Medea was played by Tokusaburo Arashi, a Kabuki actor trained as an *onnagata* – a male actor, that is, who plays female roles – creating, thus, a strong Kabuki presence (2002: 8–9). There is a contrast between the male body that performs Medea and the assumed female voice, gestures and costume of an *onnagata*, a sort of representational rupture that allowed for the revolting female character to smoothly emerge and capture the Japanese's sympathy.

As a rule, femininity in men was recognized and accepted as early as pre-modern Japan although there is a long history of disregard for women in the Japanese patriarchal culture with the warriors rejecting their weakness, Buddhism depriving them of the possibility of Enlightenment, and Confucianism limiting women to the role of obedient wives and wise mothers. Thus, the mighty Japanese warriors could be poets as well, 'shedding unashamed tears over the beauty of cherry blossoms and the dew on the morning glory flower' (Hoffman 2013). Even Buddhism allowed women their reincarnation as men in their next life. It seems that there is more of a female to a male and vice versa in the Japanese culture than in the Western one, argues the American anthropologist Ruth Benedict in her 1946 classic treatise on Japan *The Chrysanthemum and the Sword*, and this is reflected in Kabuki theatre as well. The *onnagata* male impersonators of female roles starred on the stage, with Yoshizawa Ayame (1647–1709), for instance, being a big star. Married and father of four sons, Ayame believed that a skilful *onnagata* should dress, make up and live in exquisite female coquetry. All in all, sex tolerance and diversity have long been accepted in Japan, although this was not the case for Japanese women, who could only see heaven in their husbands' eyes.

Still, the cases of unyielding Japanese women who escaped the social norm are not that rare. The peasant poet and local political activist Matsuo Taseko (1811–94), for example, left behind her family to go to the chaotic then capital of Kyoto and join the Imperial cause against the Tokugawa Shogun and the Western intruders.[9] The masculine within the feminine, the blending of the chrysanthemum with the sword, seems to be found, though not often, in the tradition of Japan, too. In that sense, Ninagawa's sympathetic depiction of the rebellious Medea by a male actor, an *onnagata*, seems to make use of the accepted aesthetic conventions of traditional Japanese theatre only to serve other social purposes, prevent any possible objections, finally enriching the gallery of emancipated females on the Japanese stage. In this regard, Ninagawa's Medea as a female body of resistance is an example of a neo-*onnagata* – a term coined by William Hamilton

Armstrong to embrace those recent *onnagata* performers who challenge and expand the gender performance and customs of their traditional art on the contemporary Japanese stage. In his view, not only does a neo-*onnagata* expand the Kabuki definition of *onnagata*, but liberates conventional cross-dressing practices and models possible new sex role behaviours for men and women: 'They challenge the fixed sexism and staid conventions of Kabuki, the fossilized images of Woman, and, by extension, the images of Man' (Armstrong 2002: 2, 6). Broadly speaking, contemporary Japanese theatre does not any more see manhood or masculinity as sex-specific, but as 'an existential mode of being, or, more precisely, [...] the courage to be at all', to do 'what one has to do or what one feels is right' (Goodman 1971: 164). Placing masculinity within this wider and more flexible frame sheds new light on Ninagawa's Medea performed by a neo-*onnagata*.

Whether our discussion revolves around Tadashi Suzuki or Yukio Ninagawa's restagings of Greek tragedy, it becomes clear that both articulate 'some fundamental injury, [...], a narrative about a horrible destructive social process and a demand for emotional, institutional, and symbolic reparation and reconstitution' (Alexander 2004: 11). Rejecting the psychoanalytic theory of collective trauma and what he names 'the naturalistic fallacy', Jeffrey C. Alexander supports the view that collective trauma is constructed by society: 'For traumas to emerge at the level of collectivity, social crises ["events"] must become cultural crises,' he says (ibid. 2004: 10). In between the experienced event and its representation, there is an empty space that should be filled by the trauma process, a sort of 'spiral of signification'. Only through this process can a new master narrative of social suffering be constructed. The latter is affected by the 'institutional arena', be it the religious, scientific, legal, state bureaucracy, and the aesthetic carrier groups. Thus, the disrupted-by-suffering-and-pain collective identity is revised and reconstructed after experiencing, imagining and representing the trauma (ibid. 2004: 22).

Conclusions: Utopian visions vs dystopian realities

Nevertheless, Suzuki and Ninagawa do not only assume the role of aesthetic agents in the construction of a new Japanese master narrative. Rather, to do so, they also renegotiate and redefine the Japanese theatre aesthetics and its ideology in an attempt to bridge personal memory and national memory, the past with the present, the old with the new, the East and the West. This is why David Goodman proves right when he says that the Japanese modern theatre has been political from its birth but the 1960s generation of theatre practitioners was forced to reformulate both politics and theatre after the renewal of the US–Japan Mutual Security Treaty (ANPO) in 1960. In Mobile Theatre: Prospectus 1970, Tadashi Saito and Nakamura Masaki, for example, write: 'We have been atomic bombed and nothing changed. We have been occupied by a foreign army and nothing changed. We have organized demonstrations of our citizens and nothing changed' (Goodman 1971: 165).

Against the background of such a collective traumatic memory, the *angura* theatre practitioners in the 1960s moved away from blind reproduction of Western theatre toward 'a nostalgia for a pre-modern Japanese world', as Takeshi Kawamura describes it, and traditional Japanese theatre codes. This is particularly true of Tadashi Suzuki, who 'looked to noh, the "art of walking," to provide "feet" for the modern theatre' (Armstrong 2002: 242). Likewise, he was inspired by Noh's non-realism, its '"do-or-die" battle mentality', in performing and the fixed, eclectic security of the *mise-en-scène*. These, combined with the dramaturgical collage of play materials, reveal a mistrust for the modern global age and linearity for they are blamed as 'responsible for the atrocities of our age, since they justify inhuman expedience' (Goodman 1971: 165). In effect, the dramaturgy of tragedy is rejected, for the tragic vision it offers enunciates 'the logic of lethal expedience in theatrical terms' (ibid. 1971: 165). *The Trojan Women* offers a telling example as Suzuki does not endorse the Euripidean praise of those courageous enough to survive a war and start their life anew when he portrays a dead Hecuba. As Marianne McDonald notes, the major difference between Euripides and Suzuki concerns the themes of death and tragedy (1993: 60). Summed up, Suzuki's effort is binary – to overcome, on the one hand, what he saw as the main problem of pre-modern Japan, its static nature, and, on the other hand, to protest against an apocalyptic future.

The essentialized notions of the *angura* performing body as a pseudo-mystical narrative and the international career of Japanese directors like Suzuki and Ninagawa have monopolized scholarly attention in the West. Still, we should keep in mind that the *angura* theatre practice and ideology has been severely criticized by a younger generation of Japanese theatre practitioners who emerged in the 1980s and chose to interact 'not with Japan's fractured history, but with the dystopic atmosphere of today's society and culture' (Eckersall 2000: 97). Such is the case of the director Takeshi Kawamura and his group Daisan Erotica. The appropriated-by-capitalism-and-the-West nostalgic and escapist *angura* theatre with its optimism of the 1960s 'self'-liberationist politics is superseded by a kind of theatre that wants to criticize the 'bubble economy', the 'fake culture and surface euphoria' that covers up the serious problems of Japanese society at the end of the twentieth century. Daisan Erotica, negating any revolutionary agenda, represents the 'urban trash' as it is unquestionably consumed by the average Japanese, revealing a 'dystopic rather than utopian' Japan, 'fractured rather than cohesive', 'violent and coercive rather than safe and free' (ibid.: 100).

As mentioned above, modern Japanese theatre has always been political. Be it *Shingeki*, *butoh* or *angura*, twentieth-century Japanese theatre goes hand in hand with the milieu in which it is born and lives, reflecting or resisting the dominant ideology. Thus, *Shingeki* imitated Western theatre practices whilst *angura*, led by charismatic directors–auteurs like Tadashi Suzuki, Terayama Shûji, Satô Makoto and others, revolutionized Japanese theatre practice by criticizing 'the limitations of modernist art in Japan' (Eckersall 2006: 41). Surprisingly, though, their enthusiastic reception and influential presence on the international theatre stage coincided with the weakening of their resistance to the indigenous and international capitalistic ethos. At the same time, the globalization of the economy came about in the bubble space of 1980s Japan, in a decade of rapid but unsustainable growth.[10] Resisting the above, a wave of third-generation *angura* artists emerged, among them Takeshi Kawamura. As he says:

In 1989, the emperor died and it was the end of the Shôwa era. The Berlin Wall also came down. In other words, there seemed to be many important historical events unfolding during that time. As a result, my work began to reflect a need to face these big moments in history [...]. Another kind of theatre making was becoming necessary. (Kawamura Takeshi in Eckersall 2006: 41)

Whatever the future of the new-millennium Japanese theatre may hold,[11] it is certain that the traumatic twentieth-century historical course of the country has stimulated a protean course in Japanese theatre practice. From the nuclear-polluted tuna fished in the Japanese waters in 1954 to McDonald's international fast food chain and the accompanied cultural homogeneity of globalization in the late twentieth century, Japanese practitioners have been alert to the social, cultural and aesthetic challenges posed each time. This can be seen as a crucial aspect of the significant, multifold contribution that Tadashi Suzuki and Yukio Ninagawa have made to the indigenous and international theatre practice in the post-war twentieth century era. In that sense, their traumatized and redefined Japanese bodies break through national borders to travel on the world stage, giving the tragic *logos* modern validity. Likewise, the directors' undercurrent post-Hiroshima political and social considerations find in the classical texts their perfect match. They blend to address the suffering but also the beauty of the traumatized modern human condition, playing with the verbal and the non-verbal, with dark ontological depths and shimmering visual surfaces.

Bibliography

Alexander, J. C., Eyerman, R., Giesen, B., Smelser, N. J. and Sztompka, P. (2004) *Cultural Trauma and Collective Identity*. Berkeley: University of California Press.

Allain, Paul (2002) *The Art of Stillness: The Theatre Practice of Tadashi Suzuki*. London: Methuen.

Armstrong, W. H. (2002) *Neo-Onnagata: Professional Cross-Dressed Actors and their Roles on the Contemporary Japanese Stage*. PhD Dissertation, Graduate Faculty of the Louisiana State University and Agricultural and Mechanical College.

Βαροπούλου, Ελένη [Varopoulou, E.] (2002) Το Ζωντανό Θέατρο: Δοκίμιο για τη Σύγχρονη Σκηνή. Αθήνα: Άγρα.

Benedict, R. (2005) *The Chrysanthemum and the Sword: Patterns of Japanese Culture*. Boston; New York: Houghton Mifflin.

Brokering, J. M. (2007) 'Ninagawa Yukio's Intercultural *Hamlet*: Parsing Japanese Iconography'. *Asian Theatre Journal* 24.2 (Fall): 370–96.

Eckersall, P. (2000) 'Japan as Utopia: Kawamura Takeshi's Daisan Erotica'. *The Drama Review* 44.1 (Spring): 97–108.

Eckersall, P. (2006) 'After Angura? Recent Works by Kawamura Takeshi'. In *The Ends of the 60s: Performance Media and Contemporary Culture*, Peter Eckersall and Edward Scheer (eds). Sydney: UNSW and Performance Paradigm, 41–51.

Eco, U. (2004) *On Beauty: A History of a Western Idea*, Alastair McEwen (trans.). London: Secker & Warburg.

Eco, U. (2007) *On Ugliness*, Alastair McEwen (trans.). London: Harvill Secker.

Garner, S. B., Jr. (2006) 'Artaud, Germ Theory and the Theatre of Contagion'. *Theatre Journal* 58.1 (March): 1–14.

Goodman, D. (1971) 'New Japanese Theatre. Theatre in Asia'. *The Drama Review* 15.2 (Spring): 154–68.

Hoffman, M. (2013) 'Gender Bending in Japan'. *Japan Times*, 13 July. Online at www.japantimes.co.jp/life/2013/07/13/general/gender-bending-in-japan/#.VYuD9hvtlHx (accessed 25 June 2015).

Hohendahl, P. U. (2005). 'Aesthetic Violence: The Concept of the Ugly in Adorno's "Aesthetic Theory"'. *Cultural Critique* 60 (Spring): 170–96.

James, B. R. (1989) 'A New World: Asian Theatre in the West Today'. *The Drama Review* 33.2 (Summer): 25–50.

Jenkins, I. (2015) 'Defining Beauty: The Body in Ancient Greek Art exhibition'. The British Museum, London, 26 March–5 July. Online at www.britishmuseum.org/about_us/news_and_press/press_releases/2015/defining_beauty.aspx (accessed 28 June 2015).

Kyo, C. (2012) 'The Search for Beautiful Women in China and Japan: Aesthetics and Power'. *The Asian-Pacific Journal: Japan Focus* 10.49.1, 3 December: 1–9.

Marshall, J. (1992) 'Bodies Across the Pacific: The Japanese National Body in the Performance Technique of Suzuki and Butoh'. Revised edition of a seminar in MUSU Theatre Department Workshop series, 9 September: 1–23.

Martin, C. (2000) 'Japanese Theatre: 1960s–Present'. *The Drama Review* 44.1 (Spring): 82–4.

McDonald, M. (1993) Αρχαίος Ήλιος, Νέο Φως: Το Αρχαίο Ελληνικό Δράμα στη Σύγχρονη Σκηνή. Μτφ. Παύλος Μάτεσις. Αθήνα: Βιβλιοπωλείον της «Εστίας».

Mitter, S. and Shevtsova, M. (2007) *Fifty Key Theatre Directors*. London and New York: Routledge.

Rabkin, G. (1983) 'The Play of Misreading: Text/ Theatre/ Reconstruction'. *Performing Arts Journal* 7.19: 44–60.

Saito, H. (2006) 'Reiterated Commemoration: Hiroshima as National Trauma'. *Sociological Theory* 24.4 (December): 353–76.

Σαμπατακάκης, Γιώργος [Sampatakakis, G.] (2015) 'Η Τραγωδία ως Ανάπτυγμα του Κακού. Η Μήδεια του Miyagi Satoshi και η Ιαπωνική Παράδοση'. *Το Αρχαίο Ελληνικό Θέατρο και η Πρόσληψή του*. Κωνσταντίνος Κυριακός (επιμ.). Πρακτικά του Πανελλήνιου Θεατρολογικού Συνεδρίου. Πάτρα: Τμήμα Θεατρικών Σπουδών, Πανεπιστήμιο Πατρών.

Sanders, V. (1988) 'Dancing and the Dark Soul of Japan: An Aesthetic Analysis of "Butō"'. *Asian Theatre Journal* 5.2 (Autumn): 148–63.

Smethurst, M. (2002) 'Ninagawa's Production of Euripides' Medea'. *American Journal of Philology* 123.1.489 (Spring): 1–34.

Smith, P. (1998) *Japan: A Reinterpretation*. New York: Vintage.

Sontag, S. (2002) 'Looking at War: Photography's View of Devastation and Death'. *New Yorker*, 9 December. Online at www.newyorker.com/magazine/2002/12/09/looking-at-war (accessed 25 June 2015).

Sontag, S. (2003) Παρατηρώντας τον Πόνο των Άλλων. Μτφ. Σεραφείμ Βελέντζας. Αθήνα: Scripta.

Suzuki, T. (2003) 'Suzuki Tadashi and the Shizuoka Theatre Company in NY. Interview with Toni Sant'. *The Drama Review* 47.3 (Autumn): 147–58.

Walthall, A. (1998) *The Weak Body of a Useless Woman: Matsuo Taseko and the Meiji Restoration*. Chicago: University of Chicago Press.

PART TWO

Directing as Dialogue with the Community

5

Directing Greek tragedy as a ritual: Mystagogy, religion and ecstasy

Magdalena Zira

The original context of the performances of Greek drama in the fifth century BCE in the festival in honour of Dionysus was marked by various rituals that were known and shared by the entire community, and thus carried their own emotional or ideological weight. There were religious events that preceded and surrounded the plays[1] and a variety of ritual actions performed by the chorus in the plays themselves, with which the audience was deeply familiar and which could stir the collective cultural memory, emotions and subconscious. The religious role of the non-dramatic chorus outside the theatre[2] was also part of the original audience's cultural context: it was manipulated by the playwrights, through the characterization of the dramatic chorus. The religious content of the odes, especially the abundant references to myth, gave the chorus's utterance authority and weight: myth was the moral map, the way of interpreting the cosmos.[3] The connection between mystical religions and the origins and structure of drama,[4] although a contested issue, may have been an important part of the cultural context in which these plays were experienced in performance.

In this chapter the predominant case study will be one significant production from the 1970s: Euripides' *Suppliants* by the Cyprus Theatre Organization, directed by Nikos Charalambous, which achieved the successful convergence of the ritual and the political. This production exemplifies the many aspects of the use of ritual in contemporary staging of Greek tragedy, such as: the innovation of the tragic form through the use of contemporary ritual and the 'borrowing' from living traditions and cultural frameworks; the realization of the play's political potential for the contemporary audience through the use of ritual; the role of Christian dogma and ritual in contemporary interpretation of tragedy; the seamless and vital integration of singing and dance in the dramatic identity of the chorus and the aesthetic of the production as a whole; and, finally, the audience–chorus interaction through the spiritual participation of the audience – a *methexis* achieved through the characterization of the chorus and through the fruitful exploration of contemporary ritual.

Directors who choose to stage a Greek tragedy in a contem-porary setting, in what theorists call *retopicalizations*, are generally driven by a political interpretation of the text and by the need to respond to contemporary historical parallels.[5] Even though contemporary re-imaginings of tragedy in Western theatre often tend to do away with large singing and dancing choruses who pray and perform ritual,[6] there are cases when a contemporary setting can provide fruitful contextualization of the play's ritual content and the chorus's religious role. In such retopicalizations that use the framework of a traditional culture to interpret Greek tragedy, we very often find a vital integration of choral music and dance in the dramatic role of the chorus and the action of the play, through the use of ritual. Thus, the complete integration of the ritual and dramatic role of the chorus, staying within the emotional reality of the plot, is one contemporary solution to the 'problem' of choral singing and dancing. In these cases singing and dancing are interpreted as behaviours that are codified, ceremonial, of high significance to the entire community and marking an important community event, such as a religious occasion or a rite of transition.

The discussion of ritual touches on *avant-garde* experiments, intercultural theatre, and also theatre that explores the 'roots' of a particular culture, and often becomes theatre of protest.[7] This is theatre that explores cultural identity, often a *suppressed* cultural identity, through traditional religious and ritual patterns. Through reference to living religious traditions, such productions bring Greek tragedy to the heart of a contemporary community faced with crisis. The theatrical experience and the theatrical ritual allow the community to see this crisis enacted before them, creating an emotional and historical context not unlike the original context of Attic drama that dramatized the internal conflicts of the *polis*.

Christianity and tragedy: Laments and female ritual expressions

In a discussion of productions in the West, Christianity is a crucial part of the contemporary religious context. On the one hand, drawing parallels between Christian theology and the theology of tragedy is rife with problems. At the same time, a religious context that makes sense to a contemporary audience may offer great solutions to the problem of the chorus's integration and role. The *Gospel at Colonus* is perhaps the most well-known Christian adaptation of tragedy, both in the USA and internationally (see Chapter 1). *Gospel* is remarkable also for finding a successful contemporary parallel, in form and content, for the Greek chorus. By setting the play in a Pentecostal church, the chorus becomes integrated, engaged, integral to the play, while its singing and dancing makes complete contemporary sense.[8]

On the other hand, the discrepancies between the theology of Sophocles and those of *Gospel* have also been widely discussed. The main differences with the Sophoclean theology and tone of the play show that a great amount of modifications and adjustments to the text was needed to fit the story of Oedipus's final days into a Christian setting: the Christian elements of redemption and making peace with death, twin cornerstones of the belief systems of all Christian denominations, receives great focus in Breuer's production, but does not have an ancient Greek parallel. Oedipus does not curse his sons in *Gospel*. Rather, paternal curses and disastrous family feuds, so important in the Theban saga, become deserved divine rage of the deified Oedipus. The identification of Oedipus with a Christ figure, who goes down to the underworld and comes back, to rise to the heavens, is also very different from the original, in which there is no apotheosis of Oedipus. The best he can do is to become a spirit of Colonus. Furthermore, there is nothing in the original to match the jubilation and elation at the end of Breuer's production.

It is easy to understand why Christianity, and monotheism in general, offer a limited prism through which to view religious behaviour in Attic drama, especially with reference to the afterlife, the relationship between humans and god, and most of all with the moral landscape that governs human relationships. The conflict between religious and state issues, for example, is expressed in various ways in tragedy, involving the transgression of secular rulers, the power of divination, the corruption of the clergy and, also, what humans can learn from myth. But this issue takes a completely different tone in the history of the Christian European West, where issues of dogma, proselytism, religious freedom, church power, persecution of 'heretics', witch-hunting, Christian martyrdom and so on have historically marked the relationship between organized religion and civic life. In Greek tragedy the gods do demand respect, and their priests do warn rulers against transgression, but the sheer number of gods, their multiple, complex, often unfathomable motives, create a different landscape. The one certain 'sin' is *hubris*, but that can be as much an issue of secular morality (one person behaves hubristically towards another) as a religious issue (one person behaves hubristically towards a god). In their relations with humans, gods seem often cruel, or self-serving, or vengeful. Sometimes they are in direct conflict amongst themselves, as in the *Eumenides*. Furthermore, although there is no such clear-cut theory about the underworld, or the afterlife, analogous to the Christian heaven–hell duality, life after death is generally described in Greek literature as a dark, sad place, a far cry from the Kingdom of Heaven to which all good Christians aspire.[9]

It is hard to imagine a Greek play being transported to a Christian setting without making significant alterations to the text and its meaning. On the other hand, we have seen what a tempting parallel it can be for solving 'the problem of the chorus'. What this means though, is that a contemporary religious parallel can create more intimacy between the chorus and the audience, can make up for hidden/lost layers of interpretation, can give meaning to the collective voice and can do away with the awkwardness surrounding the lyrical parts.

In our contemporary world, expressions of Christian faith are not limited to churches; they may be connected to a variety of social issues and perhaps there are cases when the chorus as a congregation or as religious followers would be a fruitful direction to take in the right context. Each nationality, each country and each denomination has distinguishing characteristics, touching on social, historical and cultural issues that have dramatic potential. Also, in each play each tragedian's concerns with religion, and especially the chorus's role with regard to it, are greatly differentiated. I feel that this realization can liberate our own way of thinking.[10]

Perhaps it would be valuable to consider another possible direction, as an example, connecting the ritual and the political, and Christianity with tragedy: the instances where religious practice is connected to the social issue of gender. This may be a very interesting area to explore, especially in relation to the female chorus. I would like here to offer some parallels between the tension dramatized in tragedy between women as agents of ritual and the male authority and attitudes still prevalent in Christian dogma today in some areas of the world.

Margaret Alexiou,[11] Helene Foley[12] and Casey Dué[13] have written about patriarchal society's fear of 'subversive' female lament. The implied attitude today behind the suppression of female ritual expressions or actions, is always that it is uncivilized, primitive, unruly, inappropriate, whereas male authority wishes to impose order and the central authority of an institution on all important rites of passage in life. Thus, the suppression of female lament still exists in the context of the Christian Orthodox church services, which are at once male-dominated, and also, as Alexiou has shown, have an ancient web of connections, primarily through the Virgin Mary, to ancient female-dominated cults, such as the mourning for the death of Adonis and community funeral rites.

This is a powerful tension that can be used in our exploration of staging the chorus, and it is an issue of male and female spheres of authority, frequently explored in tragedy. The ingrained idea that 'women must be silent in church'[14] is a part of the Christian doctrine analogous to the tensions of the fifth century BCE caused from the suppression of public female manifestations of mourning.[15] Lament played an important part in Nikos Charalambous' production of *Suppliants*.

Euripides' *Suppliants*, the Cyprus Theatre Organization: Creation of a strong contemporary historical/political parallel[16]

I believe that the most important factor contributing to the valid claim of our *Suppliants* as a positive proposal for the revival of Greek drama, was the social and political atmosphere of the time and its significant impact on the psyche of everyone involved in this adventure of producing Euripides' play. [...] The performance worked aesthetically and politically, but it worked mostly because of its effect on our collective consciousness, as an enactment of tragic catharsis or even as 'return of the unjustly lost dead who demanded restitution and justice'.[17] (Author's own translation)

Euripides' *Suppliants* was produced by THOC (the Cyprus Theatre Organization, the State Theatre of Cyprus) in Cyprus in 1978, translated by Kostis Kolotas, directed by Nikos Charalambous, with set and costume design by Yiorgos Ziakas and music by Michalis Christodoulidis. It was presented in Greece (Athens Festival – Lycabettus Theatre, 1979 and Epidaurus, 1980), marking a new era for the participation of the State Theatre of Cyprus in the Epidaurus festival.

The theatre theorist Andri H. Constantinou writes about this production of *Suppliants* that '[t]he Greek audience was to experience a Cypriot production on the evils of war, only six years after the events of 1974. The play generated a great deal of emotional reaction. Here the concept of the director linked the play to Cyprus history and folklore' (2011).[18] This production achieves innovation in an effective way, in its historical and aesthetic context, especially with regard to the chorus, by drawing from local folk and Christian Orthodox tradition. I would like to concentrate on the use of ritual and how effective it becomes, due to the said cultural context. This marriage between *laiki paradosi* (folk tradition) and a ritual staging was an innovation at the time and a key to the power of the production.

First reviews (when it was first performed in Cyprus) show to what extent this iconoclastic approach to Greek drama broke the norms, often causing hostile reactions. These suspicious reactions revolve mostly around the all-time favourite of conservative critics, the question of what is 'appropriate' for Greek drama. At times, the comments are similar to the general outcry Karolos Koun received in his homeland for his staging of Aristophanes' *The Birds*,[19] which went on to become an international sensation. Karolos Koun, the influential Greek director and founder of Theatro Technis, revolutionized the staging of Greek tragedy and comedy through his seminal productions of *The Birds* (1959) and Aeschylus' *Persians* (1965) and contributed to a new direction in the staging of the chorus.[20]

The most striking objection of the critical community was the inability or refusal to acknowledge the political and ritual reading in Charalambous' *mise-en-scène*. Allusions to the recent history of Cyprus, which, in the international and Greek tours were one of the main ingredients for the success of the production, were dismissed by most Cypriot critics as an unnecessary intervention to the original, with the notable exception of Christos Zanos, who accepts this as a valid directorial intention but at the same time finds it unsuccessful in its execution.[21]

I shall argue that both the parallels with Cypriot history and the anti-war message behind the ironic reading of the characters of Theseus and Athena were essential to the meaning of this production and the interpretation of its stage metaphors, its use of the design and music as well as its treatment of the spoken word. Thus a new 'meaning' that overrides the original story provides the throughline for the interpretation of every choice in spectacle, lyrics parts and text. Most notably, theatre critic Eleni Varopoulou praises the innovative directorial approach, as an effort to restore a living communication between the ancient text and the contemporary Greek.[22] Costas Georgousopoulos is even more enthusiastic, characterizing Charalambous' *mise-en-scène* as 'the only solution to staging Greek tragedy today', meaning the creation of a strong contemporary historical/political parallel. 'Myth becomes a symbol through which history is not explained, but verified.'[23] The critic Thymele praises the bold and innovative directorial choices, and appreciates the fact that the established codes of performance of Greek drama were subverted through the use of expressionism, symbolism, realism and simplicity in the acting, as well as through the use of ritual and folk tradition.

The historical and political contexts were crucial in the realization and success of the production. In this context, the ritual acts of supplication and the burial of the dead have very strong parallels in the audience's reality. This context was the emotionally charged atmosphere of the post-invasion Cyprus, with the collective trauma of the refugees and the missing vividly present in everyone's consciousness. We have, here, another case in which the religious and ritual atmosphere is inextricably linked with the political goals of the production. The 1974 invasion of Cyprus by Turkey was very recent, and the human tragedy it caused was still very much an open wound in 1979–80: a great number of refugees were displaced and living in temporary camps, and thousands of soldiers and civilians were missing, from both sides of the conflict. The humanitarian tragedy of the missing in particular was the direct historical connection to the subject matter of the *Suppliants*.[24]

In the years following the Turkish invasion of Cyprus, the female relatives of the Greek Cypriot missing persons – mothers, wives, daughters, dressed in black and clasping black and white photos of their relatives – would march to the line of separation in the divided city of Nicosia, by the famous Ledra Palace Hotel roadblock, and protest to the UN, to the world, to anyone who would listen.[25] The imagery surrounding the missing is not dissimilar to the imagery surrounding the mothers of the disappeared during the Dirty War in Argentina. In fact, the artistic team of this production mentions the strong parallels between the Cypriot relatives of the missing and Argentinian demonstrations at Plaza de Mayo in the production's programme note. These women had, by 1978, become iconic, their daily marches to the border a ritual, the photographs symbols of the entire war. Only very recently has the discovery of the bodies and their identification through DNA testing begun, after mass graves on either side of the border were revealed. But when the play was performed, the demonstrations for the missing were at their peak.[26]

It is also important to bear in mind the living religious context of the production: a great percentage of the Greek and Cypriot population are churchgoers, or are at least very familiar with some of the Greek Orthodox rites whose echoes were used in the staging. These rituals have an emotional resonance regardless of the viewer's personal religious faith. This familiarity, together with the recent experience of the war, created the environment in which audience participation/experience of the event made the ritual 'work'. Aithra's totem-like figure during the chorus's supplication becomes then in the collective imagination of the audience almost like a *Panagia*, a Byzantine image of the Virgin Mary. Jenny Gaitanopoulou (Aithra) describes the whole experience as:

> a ritual scene. One minute you are one of the crowd, and then gradually you get into a state, you become something else, you become a totem, through ritual, you become a god, you become a king [...] This dressing scene, was such an important part of the ritual and of the actor's performance. You start off almost like a normal person, and every time they put [a piece of the costume] on you, you enter deeper into a different state. It is gradual [...] Don't priests do the same during the liturgy? They wear a special costume, in order to be able to perform a ritual.[27]

My impression of the production was of watching one continuous ritual throughout the entire performance, a liturgy, a process of purification or invocation of the recent dead. The production was marked by a visual clarity; it drew from local folk and religious traditions but at the same time supported its concept with inventiveness and the use of symbolism. The treatment of the chorus was essential to this: the characters emerged out of the collective of the chorus, then returned to it; on-stage characters and chorus were often intermingled; the choral odes spilled into the action. The prominence of the collective of the ensemble that was, at times, inseparable from the collective of the chorus was significant.

As such, this production is an example of group ritual used towards theatrical innovation, and specifically towards making the ancient play contemporary, in terms of both political meaning and aesthetic. This was clearly Charalambous' goal: 'Euripides is contemporary and that's how we approached the text.' The director, in an interview quoted in an article in the Greek newspaper *Ta Nea*, describes the process by which the prologue came about based on the actors' personal experience of the 1974 war:

> We created a work group, which you don't normally see in National theatres, and from the darkness of the first rehearsal

we arrived at the fateful phrase 'we have come here to demand
our dead to be returned to us for burial, which the enemy has
denied us'.[28] (Author's own translation)

If the whole play was a re-enactment of the recent 'tragedy' in
Cypriot history by the ensemble, with emphasis on the missing dead
who remain unburied, then the religious theme inevitably becomes
particularly strong. Thus, theatrical renditions of recognizable
church rituals are one way in which the ritual atmosphere is
achieved.

But there are other elements of the *mise-en-scène*, formal or
symbolic, belonging to the sphere of the imagination that enhance
the ritual atmosphere. One of them is the use of the half-mask: the
effect is not quite that of estrangement, but of sacredness. It gives
the characters and the chorus a quality that transcends time and
place, and also connects the human with the divine plane. Jenny
Gaitanopoulou describes working with the mask:

> You leave your identity behind, it takes away your person-
> ality as a normal everyday person and gives you the enlarged
> characteristics of the role you are playing. There is no personal
> commentary on the work by you: an actor. It is gone, lost, you
> become one with the ensemble.[29]

Another crucial element is the use of rhythm: there is a constant
interchange between fast and slow, but at the same time a
sense that the whole thing is connected like a musical score.
Everything is interconnected through imagery and sound, there are
no gaps, no jarring changes of direction.[30] The composer Michalis
Christodoulidis in his programme note emphasizes the importance
of the lament, as a universal expression of grief. In his opinion, the
lament is a traditional ritual that is recognizable and emotionally
resonant in any country and in any era. Many of the choral
odes were structured or sounded like laments. Christodoulidis'
inspiration came not only from Cypriot folk music, but also from
Byzantine church music, traditional music from northern Greece, as
well as African music. A notable characteristic of the soundscape,
which later on became almost a trademark for Charlambous'
productions, was the use of Ancient Greek together with or instead
of Modern Greek in the choral odes. The ancient language was

used as part of the score, for its musicality and its mystical quality. The actual meaning of the words was of secondary importance.

Above all, the chorus-ensemble is the connecting presence and force that gives the ritual elements vitality and resonance. They perform the main rites, such as the supplication and burial, but also 'give birth' to the main characters, connect the scenes with the odes seamlessly, stage atmospheric tableaux and sounds and, perhaps most importantly, create a communion with the audience. The whole play then becomes a ritual enactment of events by the ensemble, aimed at awakening collective memory. Through this ritual the events of the play have a double meaning, as reflections of the recent events that the people of Cyprus had experienced.

In 1979, these were innovative elements in the staging of Greek tragedy. Many of them became staples of Charalambous' directorial style in the years that followed, but their successful use in the *Suppliants* was never repeated with such force.[31] They, in turn, became 'old fashioned' aesthetically, but, most importantly, subsequent productions lacked the urgency of the *Suppliants'* political message and the corresponding historical context that had made Euripides' plot and its ritual context extremely 'real' and relevant.

Conclusions

The way this production of *The Suppliants* affected the participants – its extensive touring and frequent revivals that marked a generation of Cypriot artists who took part in the chorus of the several re-stagings – is also a testament to its power. Is there a heightened sense of the production's goals among the cast because of the direct experience of enacting known rituals, combined with the historical context?

It seems to me that the merging of the performers' and the characters' experience as well as the strengthening of the play's impact on the audience through the enactment of ritual during a theatrical performance are common goals of many productions of Greek drama that incorporate recognizable, contemporary ritual and religious elements in the world of the play. Charalambous' *Suppliants* was driven by a recent traumatic event within a community and by using living folk traditions in the staging enhanced the political message of the play. This production managed to evoke a specific contemporary culture and historical moment while remaining faithful to the text.[32]

In ritual, the *here* and *now* is particularly important: the audience is not merely watching a mimesis, re-enactment of a story that happened *sometime somewhere*. Instead, ritual happens in the present moment, in the moment of communion between the performers and onlookers within *this* space *here*, a ritually charged space, a space that becomes sacred. The sacredness of the space can be created or evoked by the enactment of ritual, as in the case of environmental stagings, a technique used for example by Richard Schechner in his famous adaptation of the *Bacchae*, *Dionysus in 69*.[33] Alternatively, the location of the performance can be an already sacred place, where rituals have been performed in the past, such as in Peter Brook's *Orghast*,[34] an adaptation of Aeschylus' *Persians* performed in Persepolis and at Naqsh-e-Rustam, the mountain cliff where Darius I and Xerxes I are actually buried.[35] The necessary component in each instance is the communion between the performers and the audience, an aspect of ritual theatre that was the focus of the work of another influential twentieth-century director, Jerzy Grotowski, whose theatrical manifesto stresses the communion between actor and spectator, as a means to rediscover the dynamic of ancient theatre when it was still part of religion.[36] Charalambous' *Suppliants* is then a part of the theatrical *avant-garde*'s experimentation with ritual that reached its apogee in the 1960s and 1970s. A central aspect of this ritual theatre was its emphasis on the here and now, on the place and the audience as participants in the ritual event. In Charalambous' *Suppliants* the lines added in the prologue of the performance, 'we have come *here* to demand our dead to be returned to us ...', signify the beginning of a ritual *here*, in the audience's presence, who have experienced a recent war, in a space that will become sacred through ritual acts, one of which is supplication.

Μυσταγωγία (mystagogy) is a word used often in Modern Greek to describe extremely successful theatrical or musical performances in which the audience is completely engrossed, participating spiritually in the events on stage and transported to another plane. This word expresses the similarities between the power of theatre and the power of ritual, their ability to bring the participants, spectators and performers alike to the point of ecstasy. The experience of ecstasy and mystagogia in theatre, through ritual that either draws from contemporary religion, is created by the company and the directorial vision with the active participation of the audience and uses elements from the community life of living traditional cultures. The ecstasy and mystagogia experienced by the collective of the performers and the collective of the audience at the same time in a shared space happens frequently in the context of a politically charged theatrical production. Shared ritual, in the process of mystagogia, is a way to create bonds within a community while at the same time enhancing the impact of the socio-political message of the play. This ecstasy is not a way to escape this world, but to see it for what it really is. Music and movement, diachronically and universally important elements of most kinds of ritual, become especially significant and integrated in these productions. The role of the chorus is naturally crucial here, as the main agent of ritual in the original text, but also the embodiment of a collective on stage: the collective without which ritual cannot exist.

Bibliography

Alexiou, M., Yatromanolakis, D. and Roilos, P. (2002) *The Ritual Lament in Greek Tradition*. Lanham MD: Rowman & Littlefield.

Bridges, E., Hall, E. and Rhodes, P. J. (2007) *Cultural Responses to the Persian Wars: Antiquity to the Third Millennium*. Oxford: Oxford University Press.

Burkert, W. (1966) 'Greek Tragedy and Sacrificial Ritual'. *Greek, Roman and Byzantine Studies* 7:2 (Summer): 87–121.

Burkert, W. (1983) *Homo necans: The Anthropology of Ancient Greek Sacrificial Ritual and Myth*. Berkeley: University of California Press.

Burkert, W. (2001) *Savage Energies: Lessons of Myth and Ritual in Ancient Greece*. Chicago: University of Chicago Press, 2001.

Chang, D. (2011) 'Democracy at War: *Antigone: Insurgency* in Toronto'. In E. Mee and Helene P. Foley (eds), *Antigone on the Contemporary World Stage*. Oxford: Oxford University Press, pp. 267–85.

Charalambous, N. (2005) *Kathimerini* Athens, 19 June.

Constantinou, A. H. (2011) 'Four Hundred Productions: A Review of the Plays Staged by the Cyprus Theatre Organization'. Downloadable from https://www.thoc.org.cy/About-four-hundred-productions-a-review-of-the-plays-staged-by-the-cyprus-theatre-organisation,EN-ABOUT-01-02-02,EN (accessed 1 August 2016).

Dué, C. (2006) *The Captive Woman's Lament in Greek Tragedy*. Austin: University of Texas Press.

Foley, H. (1993) 'The Politics of Tragic Lamentation'. In Alan H. Sommerstein (ed.) et al., *Tragedy, Comedy and the Polis: Papers from the Greek Drama Conference, Nottingham, 18–20 July 1990*. Bari: Levante.

Foley, H. (2003) 'Choral Identity in Greek Tragedy'. *Classical Philology* 98.1: 1–30.

Foley, H. (2009) *Female Acts in Greek Tragedy*. Princeton: Princeton University Press.

Gamel, M. K. (2010) 'Revising "Authenticity" in Staging Ancient Mediterranean Drama'. In E. Hall and S. Harrop (eds), *Theorizing Performance: Greek drama, cultural history and critical practice*. Bristol: Bristol Classical Press.

Georgousopoulos, K. (1979) 'Review of Euripides' *Suppliants* by the Cyprus Theatre Organisation', *Vima*, 19 September.

Georgousopoulos, K. and Gogos, S. (2002) *Epidauros: To archaio theatro, oi parastaseis*. Miletos.

Goff, B. and Simpson, M. (2007) *Crossroads in the Black Aegean: Oedipus, Antigone, and Dramas of the African Diaspora*. Oxford: Oxford University Press.

Goldhill, S. (1996) 'Collectivity and Otherness: The Authority of the Tragic Chorus'. In M. S. Silk (ed.), *Tragedy and the Tragic: Greek Theatre and Beyond*. Oxford: Oxford University Press, 244–56.

Grotowski, J. (1991) *Towards a Poor Theatre*. New York: Routledge [1968].

Hadjikosti, I. (2013) Σχετικά με τον ΘΟΚ 'αναμνήσαντα οικήια κακά': Το 1974 μέσα από τις παραστάσεις αρχαίου δράματος. *Ancient Theatre and Cyprus Conference Papers*, Nicosia: The Bank of Cyprus Cultural Foundation.

Hall, E. (2007) 'Aeschylus' Persians via the Ottoman Empire to Saddam Hussein'. In E. Bridges, E. Hall and P. J. Rhodes (eds), *Cultural Responses to the Persian Wars: Antiquity to the Third Millennium: Antiquity to the Third Millennium*. Oxford: Oxford University Press, 167–200.

Hall, E. (2010) *Greek Tragedy: Suffering Under the Sun*. Oxford: Oxford University Press.

Hall, E., Macintosh, F. and Wrigley, A. (2004) *Dionysus Since 69: Greek Tragedy at the Dawn of the Third Millennium*. Oxford: Oxford University Press.

Herington, J. (1985) *Poetry into Drama: Early Tragedy and the Greek Poetic Tradition*. Berkeley: University of California Press.

Lianis, G. (1979) Kyprioi Kallitechnes sta Nea, *Ta Nea*, 21 August.

McConnell, J. (2014) 'Lee Breuer's New American Classicism: The Gospel at Colonus's "Integration Statement"'. In Kathryn Bosher, Fiona Macintosh, Justine McConnell and Patrice Rankine (eds), *Oxford Handbook of Greek Drama in the Americas*. Oxford: Oxford University Press, 474–94.

Mee, E. and Foley, H. P. (2011) *Antigone on the Contemporary World Stage*. Oxford: Oxford University Press.

Schechner, R. (1994) *Environmental Theater*. Milwaukee: Hal Leonard.

Seaford, R. (1994) 'Sophokles and the Mysteries'. *Hermes*: 275–88.

Smith, A. C. H. (1972) *Orghast at Persepolis: An Account of the Experiment in Theatre Directed by Peter Brook and Written by Ted Hughes*. London: Methuen.

Thymeli (2012) 'Oidipodes (Tyrannos kai epi Kolono) sto Ethniko Theatro', *Rizospastis*, 12 March.

Van Steen, G. (2007) 'From Scandal to Success Story: Aristophanes' *Birds* as Staged by Karolos Koun'. In Edith Hall and Amanda Wrigley (eds), *Aristophanes in Performance, 421 BC–AD 2007: Peace, Birds and Frogs*. London: Legenda.

Varopoulou, E. (1979) 'Euripidi Iketides apo ton Thoc sto Lykavito'. *Proini Eleutherotypia*, 23 August.

Zanos, C. (1978) 'Iketides apo to Thoc', *Nea Epochi*, 131–2 (July–September).

Zeitlin, F. (2004) 'Dionysus in 69'. In E. Hall, F. Macintosh and A. Wrigley (eds), *Dionysus Since 69: Greek Tragedy at the Dawn of the Third Millenium*. Oxford: Oxford University Press.

6

La MaMa's *Trojan Women*: Forty-two years of suffering rhythms from New York to Guatemala

In Memoriam Elizabeth Swados, 1951–2016

Adam Strickson

This chapter is concerned with a production that is both historical and contemporary, *The Trojan Women*, part of *Fragments of a Greek Trilogy* (versions of Euripides' *Medea*, *Electra* and *The Trojan Women*), originally directed for The Great Jones Repertory Company by the Romanian director Andrei Serban and composed by Elizabeth Swados in 1974, who will be considered as co-directors. It is an auteur–director(s)-led piece that only came into being because of a playful collaborative process of composition with the actors, and both the process and the production have been kept alive by members of the original cast and Serban's former students. The production is a total theatre of the senses, combining the chanting of 'incomprehensible' ancient languages with intensely emotional individual narratives and an energetic use of the chorus, in unconventional spaces. It is a living piece of theatre that has a forty-two-year history in more than thirty countries, although there have been significant gaps when it has not been performed during this period.[1] The period 2012–16 saw its revival as an opera in Romania and as the focus of an ambitious peace project in Central America and South East Asia. In summer 2015, there was a production in Guatemala and in 2016 in Cambodia.

The long and varied life of a collaborative composition

Great Jones was an initiative of Ellen Stewart, the founder of La MaMa Experimental Theatre Club, New York, and the company took its name from the street where the company rehearsed. *Fragments* was commissioned by Stewart to be the opening production at La MaMa's Annex Theatre, known since 2009 as the Ellen Stewart Theater. Serban and Swados will be considered as 'co-directors' or 'co-composers' since their collaboration and influence on the piece is closely intertwined, and both were actively involved in compositional procedures with the actors and musicians throughout the devising and rehearsal period. The project emerged from Swados' and Serban's work with Peter Brook in the early 1970s and may be considered as a continuation of the (re)search for a universal theatre language. The directors' aim was to find a language of sound and gesture that would allow Euripides' tragedies to speak to people with no understanding of the texts or their cultural origins, in any context and in any country; this ambition has remained at the centre of the project throughout its different manifestations. The physical and vocal language of the piece was developed in close collaboration with the actors and musicians in the original production, like Onni Johnson and Bill Ruyle, who were in Guatemala in 2015 passing on the piece with Kim Ima and George Drance. Kim and George first performed in *The Trojan Women* in 1996, and were Serban's students at Columbia University. I asked all four about the 'ownership' of the piece, and to what extent the original production was a directors' piece or group collaboration. According to Bill Ruyle, who has often been the musical director of the piece, 'Liz and Andrei certainly shaped the structure. Liz, with the music and the text, really created the structure and the form and the rhythms and all the pitch relationships but how they were actually articulated was a very collaborative process' (Drance et al. 2015). A further elucidation of the serious playfulness of this collaborative, compositional process was given by Drance, who described his work on the piece as a student with Serban:

> Andrei would always say as a director he can do nothing until the actor comes up with something, so he would ask the actor, 'What is it that attracts you? What is it that fascinates you? How do you embody this? How do you show this?' And then once the actor shows something then Andrei loves to play with it. Then he shapes it [...] so I think it always has been a collaborative piece. (Drance et al. 2015)

The matter of 'ownership' is further complicated and clarified when Drance speaks of *The Trojan Women* as part of La MaMa's collective history. Ellen Stewart insisted it was La MaMa's piece when people would call it Andrei Serban's, since the theatre always looked at ownership as something that is shared by all artists who contribute to creating a work (Drance et al. 2015). Perhaps, as Ruyle says, 'the piece owns the piece' (ibid.) and it is, as Onni Johnson says, always in a state of becoming: 'It's alive and different, it's taking on life, we're birthing it' (ibid.).

Collaborating with the directors: The individual and the tribe

Re-finding the collective experience of the tribe was a key concern of New York Theatre in the late 1960s, from *Hair* to The Living Theatre and Bread and Puppet, and it was out of this context that the Great Jones Repertory Company's *The Trojan Women* emerged in 1974. This tribal energy was closely linked to the protests against the Vietnam War on the streets, often led by Bread and Puppet's huge, tearful 'Grey Ladies', and the related political desire that came out of the student revolution of the 1960s for collaborative processes of devising performance in preference to overtly hierarchical, director-led productions. Critics often prefer to chart the careers of the individual 'auteur–directors' at the centre of this theatre – Julian Beck, Judith Malina, Peter Schumann, Joe Chaikin, Richard Foreman, Richard Schechner – rather than to acknowledge the collaborative, group work that was often at the heart of the development of these productions. The tribe, of course, has a different kind of language to the individual, an orally trans-mitted language of sound and chant charted on the page by Jerome Rothenberg's hugely influential volume of world poetry, *Technicians of the Sacred*, first published in 1968. The 'tribe', the embodied culture of *The Trojan Women*, is the director, the composer and their actor and musician collaborators in the working context of 1974, and all subsequent leaders and casts in context. The piece is the product of a continuing research experiment to find a language of sound and gesture that can clearly communicate Euripides' work across cultures, drawing on all the biographies, techniques and socio-political contexts brought to the table; it is not an attempt to recapture the 'primitive' and any confusion with this demeans its importance for contemporary practitioners.

This experiment to find a theatrical 'tribal' language also emerged from Elizabeth Swados' own feminist stance within the collaboration, with an emphasis on the extended sung or chanted vowel, found in Native American chant, as the cohering sound focus of the female chorus. This approach, reliant on close listening within the chorus of women and a vigorous extrovert style, reflects Swados' commitment to active, collaborative composition with the performers during the devising period. The Irish poet Eavan Boland discusses the key choice that she felt she was obliged to make when becoming a woman poet between the introvert, introspective *I* and the communal, collective *we*. She describes these pronouns 'crying out their different histories like street-hawkers' (Boland 2011: 23). The first-person singular is the enticing voice of most poetry since the latter half of the nineteenth century, but before she could respond to this she writes, 'the *we* interposed itself. In its strength and poise I recognized the old dignity of poetry – it's relation to the tribe' (ibid.: 23). The chants and songs of *The Trojan Women*, its 'poetry', are the result of a group of women discovering the sound of their 'tribe'.

Collaborating with the audience

When I saw *The Trojan Women* in 1976, the swirling action thrummed with the rhythm of Ancient Greek, Nahuatl (known informally as 'Aztec'), Latin and Navajo chants and songs. Not a word of English was heard. I was nineteen and unprepared for this explosion of American energy, a crucible of fierce and delicate sound and movement, which as an 'audience member' I was expected to be within, to be an 'active' witness rather than a 'passive' spectator. To capture something of the still present immediacy of my experience of the production, I shall use the present tense to describe some of the action. As Serban says, 'Theatre is made for this moment, for right now. It works only in the present' (Serban, quoted in Menta 1995: 27).

Part 1: The individual women

After a long and slightly chilly wait outdoors with a view of the stark rock of Edinburgh's Arthur's Seat, we are called by the blowing of conches into the cavernous gymnasium space, similar in scale to the La MaMa Annex. Thunderous trombone notes and a scatter of percussion accompany us into the darkness, where we are quickly immersed in turmoil. We can smell the actors and each other, and a musky, earthy scent. Women and men – who seem to be just a few years older than me – are in ragged costumes showing a lot of flesh. High on a scaffolding gantry, Cassandra (played by black actress Valois Mickens) runs from side to side, fire torches in her hands and bare-breasted, scream-singing her prophecies to a drum rhythm.

She descends close to our level and, in a shamanic frenzy, she collapses before a soldier slips a noose around her neck and drags her upwards. High up on another part of the gantry, Andromaca (Priscilla Smith) is washing her child, Astianax (Diane Lane), with water from a basin. Soldiers put the child in a cage and Andromaca, speech-singing with the quietly piercing harmonics of sound using the indrawn breath, laments as she slowly pours the water over the still child. Andromaca is pushed into a small cage behind her child but suddenly she 'escapes' and stands right on the edge of the gantry with her arms spread out. She jumps from what

FIGURE 9 *La MaMa, 1976, Cassandra (Valois Mickens),* The Trojan Women, *La Rochelle, France. Photo Alain Le Hors*

seems to be a great height into the arms of the actors standing in parallel lines. The humiliation of Helen (Joanna Peled) is the most startling destruction. She hurtles through the space on a wagon and we have to get out of the way fast. Soldiers and women cruelly taunt her with rasping, cutting sounds, strip her naked and tear off her wig to expose a shaved head. They smear her with mud before a giant bear symbolically rapes her. After he lifts her above his head and throws her down, she is 'crucified' on a pole and spat on. The experience is visceral and sensuous. As a powerless 'witness', carefully clutching my programme, I am swept along in the tide of sound and action, both disturbed and excited, with no time for reflection. To use American poet Charles Olson's terminology, this drama is 'energy transferred' (Olson 1966: 16), from where the creators of the piece got it, from the vigour of ancient languages and their experience of New York and Sao Paolo.

Part 2: The collective

The second half of the piece begins with the actors gently using bamboo poles to usher us into seating areas. A flute signals the start of the weaver scene. A woman slowly carries her loom up a ramp, stabs herself and infinitely slowly – in the fall equivalent of the Noh walk – slides beautifully to the floor.

Someone screams. The women frantically begin to climb the ramp and are beaten back by whips wielded by men. They are bound in a circle with rope and a boat is constructed. They sway in silence, perhaps beginning a journey of renewal or a new chapter of suffering. I stumble out into the cold Edinburgh night in a daze, reeling from the intense emotion, the brutality and the sensuality of the experience. American critic Harold Clurman wrote in *The Nation* that *The Trojan Women* was 'the only effective and nearly complete application of Artaud's inspiration I have thus far seen' (Clurman, quoted in Menta 1995: 26).[2] I have witnessed something that will stay with me forever and will be with me every time I begin making a piece of theatre.

Inevitably, these are fragments of a performance, but the fact that I remember the cohering visual and sound images is a tribute to Peter Brook's acid test for theatre – 'what remains?' (Brook 1972: 136). Today, I am able to bring images currently in my head to connect with these memories: a photograph of a woman of Srebrenica, smartly dressed, hanging from a tree after the murder of her son by the Serb soldiers; the lashing of a Yazidi woman by Daesh forces in northern Iraq. This forty-two-year-old production has a searing contemporary resonance, but no one in the cast or the audience in 1976, two years into the history of the project, had any idea this version of *The Trojan Women* would still be with us in 2016, with members of that original cast helping to prepare Guatemalan and Cambodian groups for a production. So what has allowed this experience, clearly rooted in the New York culture of the late 1960s and in experimental work with language focusing on an investigation of a primal feeling in speech, like Peter Brook's and Ted Hughes' 1971 *Orghast* at the Shiraz Festival (on which Andrei Serban worked), to stand the test of time?

The durability of the original collaborative composition

To use Brook's terminology again, Great Jones' *The Trojan Women* has become a living '*organism*' (Brook quoted in Smith 1975: 58) rather than an institution or a piece of history. What Serban brought back from his work with the director and his collaborators, as well as a fascination with the idea of a visceral language speaking directly through the body, was a fierce discipline different from much *avant-garde* American theatre at the time. Japanese actor and director Yoshi Oida, Brook's Noh-trained collaborator who also worked with the first cast of *Fragments* during the devising process in 1974, believes that commitment to free expression is a false idea of creative freedom: 'To reject dialogue as such can become easily one dimensional, unless part of a discipline in which other means may be discovered' (Oida, quoted in Smith 1975: 59). Oida developed the 'stick work' for Brook's *Orghast* company in 1971, manipulating sticks in a series of contrasting movements with vocal sounds, an exercise that became central to Serban's devising procedures for *The Trojan Women*. Serban himself was responsible for the breathing exercises followed by the *Orghast* actors, drawing on techniques applied from ancient Zoroastrian sources. And therein lies some of the key to the continuous rebirth of the collaborative composition that is Great Jones' *The Trojan Women*. What may, on the surface, sometimes have had the feel of a spontaneous 'hippy' happening is a meticulously scored performance making use of techniques, inspired by Serban's and Oida's work with Brook, that can be taught and repeated in many contexts.

This still evolving production of *The Trojan Women* is a negotiation and an experiment between the *I* and the *we*, between the personal and the political, the home and the city streets, the 'auteur–director' and the collective, the oral and the written text, the sung and the spoken. The production has undergone many manifestations in more than thirty countries, from street versions to opera, and in July 2015 it was alive and well in Guatemala as *The Trojan Women Peace Project* led by a team of four, including Onni Johnson and Bill Ruyle, two of the original ensemble. These performances of the piece were informed by the real experience of armed conflict of the participants and audiences, and – at least partly – they confronted and processed their own experiences through their encounter with the work. From the first, this outward-looking concept of the 'usefulness' of strange sounds, cries and a truly shocking, barbaric story has been at the heart of the project. Ellen Stewart, who commissioned the project, 'wanted to do something that a black could play that was not with a needle in the arm, or in a jail cell, or cleaning house for a white woman, or being in the morgue – that was what you saw on the stage in the 60s and 70s' (Stewart 2004: 2).

The always topical resonances of *The Trojan Women* affected Swados's, Serban's and the group's initial preparation for the piece, when they travelled to Brazil in 1974 to the Sao Paolo Festival to begin work. They were surrounded by the chaos of political problems in the city and a pressure to perform in Portuguese rather than Greek. When her mother died, Swados returned to the USA and the production could not be completed. Serban said this first work on the piece was close to '[The South American] understanding of ceremony very close to their own origins' (Serban, quoted in Menta 1995: 23). The Amazonian shaman's chant, encountered by Odin Teatret in 1976 during their 'barter' journeys, was not far from their minds as they tried to work in the disorganized city.[3] The fundamental koan of making Euripides our contemporary was already present in the first stages of composition, especially when Swados's raw experience of grief is added to the equation.

The woman composer as co-director of a collaborative composition

Serban's and Swados's compositional attempts to find sounds and text to express the narrative and emotions of Euripides' tragedies place a vowel-heavy, rhythmic language at the centre of the experience. Some women poets, like Eavan Boland, continue to speculate on whether more extensive use of extended vowel sounds is found more in women's poetry than men's, and whether this may be connected to the sounds of birth, love and grief, like the Irish keening. The only surviving woman poet of ancient Greece, Sappho, made use of three female speech genres: prayers to goddesses, laments and praise-songs for young brides. Beating the breast and tearing at clothes were typical gestures of lament. This is what the women of Troy would have been doing – collectively tearing at their clothes to the accompaniment of the elongated vowel. Euripides would have known of the speech traditions that marked the different stages of a woman's life, and alluded to them in his own rhythms and vocabulary, in the same way that Catullus made use of one of Sappho's wedding songs. André Ladinois, in *Making Silence Speak*, suggests that Greek female speech genres were also the home of subversive group protest and eroticism. The score of Great Jones's *The Trojan Women* was composed by a woman and, in the solo and chorus parts, is largely performed by women. Swados, fulfilling the role of the composer as co-director, wrote that 'sound is the medium through which I perceive life' (Swados 1988: 2). She drew on many cultures, but her family influence was the davening, reciting the prescribed liturgy of Jewish prayer, where the cantor is openly tearful or joyous, and where the belief is that prayer can change bad to good. What she created as the composer–director of *The Trojan Women* is a liturgy of grief and hope, a sound-expression of the grief and the wish for peace that goes from generation to generation, war to war. She had no doubt that this is a kind of sympathetic magic: 'It is part of the composer's belief system that music has the power to make things happen' (Swados 1988: 7). In particular, singing can create harmony, and when she created this order Swados felt 'a bit like a witch doctor' (ibid.). Her life search in music was for a precision of sound to invoke specific emotions (often buried in the unconscious), just as Meyerhold believed precise physical gestures could achieve the same. The science of this is still unproven, but, anthropologically, we can be assured of the strong connection between vowel-heavy ceremonial language and healing earth-rites. These words take us back to 'tribe' again and, in some ways, the communal singing of the piece by the predominantly female chorus and the learning of the chants has allowed members of the original 'tribe' of Great Jones's *The Trojan Women* to carry the knowledge of the production and to pass it on. 'Songs are a part of change', says American folk singer Peggy Seeger, as 'they help the people making the change' (Seeger, quoted in May 2015: 53), and, as she also says, they create 'a feeling of belonging – and that makes us harder to beat' (ibid.). The search for belonging through the visceral songs and chants of Great Jones's *The Trojan Women* was rooted in the co-directors' attempt to re-discover the power of the original performances of Euripides' tragedy.

A collaborative dialogue with Euripides and the Ancient Greeks

Serban, Swados and their early collaborators on *The Trojan Women* worked on a large scale, deliberately tapping the collective unconscious, and trying to find 'the intelligence of emotion' (Serban, quoted in Menta 1995: 21) in possible chanted and sung sounds that the ancient text may possess, while always acknowledging the mysteriousness and final elusiveness of the source. Ed Menta, in *The Magic World Behind the Curtain*, writes that they were trying to bring 'an organic connection to the experience and *energy*, for both performers and audience alike, not unlike what the theatre may have meant to our progenitors in 5th century Athens' (Menta 1995: 40, original italics).

Euripides' tragedy was written to be performed in a large outdoor auditorium in the middle of the countryside, and it was a civic duty for Athenian citizens to attend; their attendance became part of the expression of community, shared belief and heated discussion of contemporary events. *The Trojan Women* was highly topical, since at the time of its production Athens had been at war with Sparta for sixteen years. The previous year the Athenians had attacked Melos, where they killed all the male citizens and sold the women and children into slavery. Part of the Athenian population was opposed to the war and the experience of *The Trojan Women* would have surely led to fierce debate about the past, present and future actions of the state, just as it did in Guatemala in 2015. The audience in ancient Greece are known to have shown their feelings loudly and with the stamping of feet, and the original meaning of 'tragedy', a ceremonial song sung when a goat was sacrificed, may also have been present in their consciousness. Although Euripides created a topical, discursive and often philosophical work clearly distant from what we understand as a ceremony, the potency of the rite is part of the layers of memory that the Greek audience would have brought to the experience in the fifth century BCE. While it cannot be said that Great Jones's *The Trojan Women* is a rite or ceremony, it retains something of the idealism of the late 1960s as a demonstration of how people can collaborate creatively, and how knowledge can be passed orally and kinetically from generation to generation without any previous knowledge being required. In our culture, the barrier between the sacred and the profane (already dissolving at the time of Euripides) is no longer obvious. Great Jones's *The Trojan Women* may be said to recapture something of the nature of a healing ceremony, taking casts and audiences though a repeated, shared pattern of suffering, death and resurrection, to use the anthropologist Mircea Eliade's understanding of the schema of all 'mysteries' or rites of passage. The 'resurrection' or the defeat of death (as well as one possible outcome of the journey for the women in the boat at the conclusion of the piece) may also be seen in the holy waste of energy, the sheer longevity and persistence of the work, and – above all – in the repeated commitment of expressing extreme suffering in 'play' in order that different casts and audiences may take something from this into their own lives and contexts, forever collectively and collaboratively re-inventing their experience of the production. The continuing human resonance of this work as a large-scale public piece of theatre may teach us much, not only about Greek tragedy, but about how to create contemporary drama of importance to society as a whole, a dynamic response to the threat of its marginalization as a leisure activity for the privileged and well educated. Elizabeth Swados put this wider ambition for the usefulness of the piece, opening out its possibilities for its application within different societies, succinctly in a 2014 interview:

> When I think of giving up my music to all these places for them to stage and probably redo I feel that's what theatre is made for, that's what you're supposed to do, you're supposed to create something that heals, something that awakens, something that infuriates, something that entertains and pass it on in all different ways. (Swados 2014)

The 'Black Mountain' American poet Charles Olson believed that recapturing this public importance of dramatic language, the 'projective size' of Euripides' *The Trojan Women*, where it was able 'to stand [...] as its people do, beside the Aegean – and neither Andromache or the sea suffer diminution' (Olson 1966: 25) should be at the heart of the search for a contemporary drama. He writes that no equivalent works for our times can be made without understanding 'the full reverence of human voice', which begins in the breath ('man's special qualification as animal', ibid.: 25)[4] and the basic unit of language must always be considered the syllable for 'from the root out [...], the syllable comes, the figure of the dance' (ibid.: 18). He calls the line 'the threshing floor for the dance' (ibid.: 19), referring to the performing area of the Greek amphitheatres, so similar in shape to the flat threshing floors still found on the slopes of Mediterranean hills. It is 'the push of the line in the hand of the moment' (ibid.: 20), driven by percussive syllables that is palpable in the chanted language of Great Jones's *The Trojan Women*. On YouTube, there is a short video of Swados leading three minutes of incantations and chants from the production in Nahuatl, Ancient Greek and Navajo with the cast to the pulse of a single drum.[5] The collaborative discipline of the actors, the solidity of the sounds and the driving, intense work of making them in this excerpt give a stronger sense of the immediacy of the early incarnations of the production more than any of the longer, grainy video documentation.

It is in the precision of sharply enunciated consonants and stretched vowel-heavy syllables, punched out with rhythm of the breath and the beat of the drum, that Great Jones's *The Trojan Women* finds its kinetic energy. Being inside that dancing energy was the new theatre I experienced in 1976. And it is revealing to note that the actors and musicians also speak of this feeling of existing within the piece: 'Once you've lived in it for a while I think you become part of that community that really shares it' (Drance et al. 2015). Indeed, as it was described somewhat ambitiously in the programme in 1976, it is an 'epic opera', which has had a full production with trained opera singers, directed by Serban, at the Romanian National Theatre in Bucharest in 2012, reinvented for a sumptuous opera house with 100 performers in the first torch-lit section constructing a procession frieze of the conquest of Troy. While the original production is still recognizable behind the huge cast, static 'trance' tableaux influenced by Balinese ceremony and stylized costumes, Serban has once again reinvented this violent ceremony for a new audience in a new context. 'Theatre should [...] give you the feeling you're walking the wire. [Theatre] is an art destined to heal, to purify, to strengthen us. An art that helps us live' (Serban, quoted in Patianjoglu 2013: 2). Reviewing the opera, Ludmila Patianjoglu writes that 'vowels are torturing, tormenting, caressing, killing' (2013: 2) and consonants are yelled and groaned. Once again, the production has re-found the primal energy of a tribal language. And it was in a different manifestation of this energy of singing, chanting and moving together that the 2015 and 2016 work of La MaMa's *Trojan Women Peace Project* was based.

The content of *The Trojan Women* is predominantly human suffering and, in particular, women's suffering in a time of war. It is an 'open text' into which individuals and groups can project their own readings and resonances. Great Jones's version 'has space [...] for people's own connections, stories and history to resonate' (Drance et al. 2015) and its relevance, unlike many adaptations of Greek tragedy, is not diminished by referring to any specific situation or context. It refuses to date, and is always 'informed and filled with the energy of what's going on in the world, what's going where you're performing it' (ibid.). In its 2015 context, a production with theatre groups and women's groups in the towns and surrounding countryside of Guatemala City, Comalapa and Antigua, the piece helped to revive and re-establish theatre after the civil war in cities where there are demonstrations every day. The four leaders of the project said the women from the Maya communities outside the city were immediately able to make a connection with *The Trojan Women*, as part of a community devastated by the army. It is mostly the women's stories they tell in their indigenous theatre because all the men were killed, mirroring Euripides' narrative. But work on the piece in the daily workshops was not to do with a discussion of politics but a passing on of technique, song and chant in order that the new Guatemalan casts should understand it viscerally rather than cognitively. Onni Johnson feels that it is wrong for the leaders to impose a political resonance on to the piece because 'it's really up to the people that we meet to see how they want to use it' (Drance et al. 2015).

Something authentic, springing from the production forty-one years ago, was being passed on, beyond a kit of texts and gestures, and this was done orally by Johnson and Ruyle, the members of the original cast, who – in a similar way to Swados and Serban – were able to pass on 'the subtleties, the feeling, for the approach [...] it really lives with them, it doesn't live on paper' (Drance et al. 2015). There is clearly the idea here that the production is not something that can be taught from a script or a film, or even completely by the inheritors of the tradition. So far, the passing on has always involved one or more of the original directors or original collaborative cast, who, after the text and music have been learned, are able to 'bring it to a new level, so it's not just about re-learning the music, re-learning the staging but from the original company something has passed on that's more than physical language or the music about the way to do it' (Drance et al. 2015). It is hard to define the subtlety of this 'energy transferred' but the process is analogous to receiving a folk song from the singer who is the original source rather than someone who has learned it from this singer. A folk song emerges from a specific landscape, a specific time, often a specific kind of manual work, in short a 'culture'. What Swados and Serban and their collaborators created in the original *Fragments of a Greek Trilogy* was a complete culture of theatre. This is not to diminish the contributions of all those who have performed the piece or teach it subsequently. As Swados said to George Drance, after he had been working with it for some time and was still feeling intimidated by its history, 'this piece is just as much yours as it is anyone's else and I think once you've lived in it for a while [...] you become part of that community that really shares it' (Drance et al. 2015). The piece is subtly, and not so subtly, changing all the time. With the exception of its operatic incarnation, it is passed on predominantly orally, making use of individuals' often idiosyncratic notes from previous productions, and what is passed on are the narrative, chants and gestures, not the visual images which were so memorable to me, because these depend on context and the availability of labour and materials. The action morphs into something different and in Guatemala there were no torches, no slide for the weaver to come down and no bear. The physical brutality and nudity of the original production were not present, but Johnson and Ruyle believed that the essentials were all there, and the cultures of the people they were working with and the spaces where it was performed informed the depiction of the action; the monster or super-being to replace the bear emerged from their own myths and stories. The exploration of Great Jones's *The Trojan Women* remains dynamic, ever changing and ever new, defined by the nature of the collaborative contexts in which its current co-directors find themselves.

A further collaboration: A different compositional direction

Swados and Serban took the approach of inventing the sounds of the language. A different, 'archaeological' approach was taken by the director Włodmierz Staniewski in his production of *Elektra* for Gardzienice[6] in 2004. Fascinated by Great Jones's version, Staniewski invited the company to perform *The Trojan Women* in Poland, allowing performers and directors to compare approaches, and presenting the pieces in a double bill, beginning indoors with Gardzienice and then travelling outside to ruins where *The Trojan Women* was performed. Gardzienice worked from fragments of an Ancient Greek score to recreate music, and from ancient vase paintings to recreate theatrical or rhetorical gestures (chironomia), creating a multi-lingual version of *Elektra* in which 'the extremes of emotion [are] expressed in a tempestuous blend of song, sound, word and gesture'.[7] Though the results are recognizably related to Greek folk music and more obviously melodic than Swados' work on *The Trojan Women*, the effect on the audience has been described as similar to Great Jones's production, 'breaking the texts into their essences, creating a fully visceral world'.[8] Ben Spatz, who performed in the production in Poland, commented that Staniewski is concerned with an embodied technique of sound and movement, 'a distinct territory where what you care about is the integration of these aspects of technique in a single body or group of bodies' (Spatz 2015) rather than the layering of different 'texts', like digital imaging and recorded music, which creates a different kind of complexity. This stance towards the performer and the performance also makes it clear why both productions can, essentially, be performed anywhere, indoors or outdoors.

Gardzienice's performance of the sounds and movements of Greek tragedy is the result of an extended period of research and experimentation, comparable to Swados's and Serban's work from 1971 to 1974 with Brook and Great Jones. It is informative to compare a short excerpt from Gardzienice's 2007 production of *Iphigenia at Aulis* in Ancient Greek, Polish and English, also premiered at La MaMa Annex in New York.[9] Here, the rhythmic beat for the Ancient Greek text comes from the force of two blades repeatedly struck together by Agamemnon as he prepares to sacrifice his daughter. The filmed excerpt takes place during the company's expedition to the Corycian Cave on the slopes of Mount Parnassus, and sounds echo from the walls. Although the performance, at least in film documentation, seems less forceful than Great Jones's *The Trojan Women*, it sprang partly from the same wish to make the piece communicate across cultures through the use of gesture and sound. Where it differs fundamentally is in its use of the mother tongue of the host country where performances take place (English, German and Polish) to express elements of the narrative.

But by collaboratively re-examining and re-inventing the sounds of Greek tragedy, like Great Jones's *The Trojan Women*, Staniewski and the actors of Gardzienice were trying to re-find the scale, sounds and physical energy of fifth-century BCE Greek theatre for our own times in indoor and outdoor spaces radically different to the small black studio, the proscenium arch and the thrust stage. This work can inform and expand the theatrical vocabulary available to all directors and their collaborators when they aspire to re-invent Greek tragedy able to stand within the scale and challenges of our own society without, as Olson writes, 'suffer[ing] diminution' (Olson 1966: 25). The many manifestations and influences of Great Jones's *The Trojan Women* suggest that – as well as an investigation into re-discovering the visceral energy of the sounds of Ancient Greek – 'tribal' energy, meticulous technique and a vision of the auteur–director(s) as playful collaborator(s) may be at the heart of this process.

Bibliography

Barba, E. (1979) *The Floating Islands*, F. Taviani (ed.). Odin Teatret: Holstebro.

Blumenthal, E. (1976) 'Andrei Serban Makes Dead Languages Live Again', *Village Voice*, 1 January.

Boland, E. (2011) *A Journey with Two Maps: Becoming a Woman Poet*. Manchester: Carcanet.

Brook, P. (2002) *The Empty Space*. London: Penguin.

Drance, G., Ima, K., Johnson, O. and Ruyle, B. (2015) '*The Trojan Women* Peace Project'. Transcription of recorded Skype interview with the author, 15 July.

Eliade, M. (1976) *Myths, Dreams and Mysteries*. London: Collins.
Euripides (1987) *The Bacchae and Other Plays*, P. Vellacott (trans.). London: Penguin.
Euripides (1991) *Hecuba*, J. Lembe and K. Reckford (trans.). New York; Oxford: Oxford University Press.
European Centre for Theatre Practices Gardzienice (2013–15), online at http://gardzienice.org/en/ELEKTRA.html (accessed 27 July 2015).
Foley, H. (2001) *Female Acts in Greek Tragedy*. Princeton and Oxford: Princeton University Press.
Gardzienice (2012) '*Iphigenia at Aulis*, part 2'. Online at https://www.youtube.com/watch?v=CKX6nZkn7gs (accessed 26 July 2015).
Goff, B. (2012) *Euripides: Trojan Women*. London: Bristol Classical Press.
Holmberg, A. (1987) 'Greek Tragedy in a New Mask Speaks to Today's Audiences'. *New York Times*, 1 March. Online at http://www.nytimes.com/1987/03/01/theater/greek-tragedy-in-a-new-mask-speaks-to-today-s-audiences.html?pagewanted=3> (accessed 13 July 2015).
Hughes, T. (1995) *Winter Pollen: Occasional Prose*. London: Faber & Faber.
Lardinois, A. P. M. H. (2001) *Making Silence Speak: Women's Voices in Greek Literature and Society*, A. Lardinois and L. McLure (eds). Princeton: Princeton University Press.
Menta, E. (1995) *The Magic World Behind the Curtain: Andrei Serban in the American Theatre*. New York: Peter Lang.
Olson, C. (1966) *Selected Writings of Charles Olson*, R. Creeley (ed.). New York: New Directions.
Patianjoglu, L. (2013) 'Andrei Şerban's Triumph and the Power of Love'. Online at http://archive.criticalstages.org/criticalstages8/entry/Andrei-%C5%9Eerbanrsquos-Triumph-and-the-Power-of-Love#sthash.NkUCCbNx.dpbs (accessed 12 July 2015).
Rothenberg, J. (1984) *Technicians of the Sacred*. Berkeley: University of California Press.
Seeger, P. (2015) Interview by J. May, *Songlines* 110 (August/September): 52–3.
Serban, A. and Swados, E. (1974) *The Greek Trilogy*. Online film, commentary by M. Croyden, at http://www.artfilms-digital.com/=68&CategoryID=1&SubCategoryID=232 (accessed 3 July 2015).
Sidiropoulou, A. (2015) 'Adaptation, Re-contextualisation, and Metaphor: Auteur Directors and the Staging of Greek Tragedy'. *Adaptation* Volume 8.1 Issue 1 March 2015. Online at http://adaptation.oxfordjournals.org/content/early/2014/11/24/adaptation.apu037 (accessed 1 December 2014).

Smith, A. C. H. (1975) *Orghast at Persepolis*. London: Eyre Methuen.

Spatz, B. (2013) 'Citing Musicality: Performance Knowledge in the Gardzienice Archive'. *Studies in Musical Theatre* 7.2: 221–35. Online at http://eprints.hud.ac.uk/19732/ (accessed 6 July 2015).

Spatz, B. (2015) Transcription of recorded interview with the author at Coffee Kabin, Queensgate, Huddersfield, UK, 15 July.

Stewart, E. (2002) *Dionysus Filius Dei*. Online at http://www.lamama. org/archives/2001_2002/dionysus.htm (accessed 2 July 2015).

Stewart, E. and Schillinger, L. (2004) Online at http://www. wordswithoutborders.org/article/drama-queen-an-interview-with-ellen-stewart (accessed 12 July 2015).

Swados, E. (1973) 'Peter Brooks Workshop, Elizabeth Swados leads'. Online at https://www.youtube.com/watch?v=xw8XvWGv7FM (accessed 28 July 2015).

Swados, E. (1974) '*Trojan Women* clip'. Online at https://www.youtube. com/watch?v=c9sWweGh03Q (accessed 28 May 2015).

Swados, E. (1988) *Listening Out Loud*. New York: Harper & Row.

Swados, E. (2014) Interview, 4 June. Online at https://www.kickstarter. com/projects/lamama/trojan-women-peace-project-phase-one/ posts/864417view on Kickstarter (accessed 20 July 2015).

Taplin, O. (2000) *Greek Tragedy in Action*. London: Routledge.

Willis, A. (2005) *Euripides' Trojan Women: A 20th Century War Play in Performance*. DPhil thesis, University of Oxford.

7

Theater of War: Ancient Greek drama as a forum for modern military dialogue

Sophie Klein

Introduction

The ancient tragedies of Aeschylus, Sophocles and Euripides delve into timeless themes, such as honour, justice, loyalty and the value of human life. Their stories take on additional layers of meaning when performed for audiences that have had personal contact, either directly or indirectly, with the horrors of combat. This is the central idea behind Theater of War, an innovative project developed by Bryan Doerries, artistic director, translator, and co-founder of Outside the Wire, a 'social impact company' based in New York. Theater of War presents scenes from Sophocles' *Ajax* and *Philoctetes* to military communities worldwide. It uses the ancient dramas as catalysts to open up candid conversations among modern-day soldiers and civilians about the physical and psychological scars of war. Performances combine staged readings, panel discussions and town hall-style talkbacks to expose and explore the connections between the ideas expressed by the plays and the audience's own experiences.

To date, Theater of War has presented over 300 performances of *Ajax* and *Philoctetes* in venues as varied as the Pentagon, the Mayo Clinic, Caesars Palace, Arlington National Cemetery, Disney World and Guantanamo Bay. Over 60,000 active-duty service men and women, veterans and members of their larger communities have attended these events. Doerries (2014a) has remarked,

> if there's one thing I've learned from listening to audiences respond to tragedy all over the world, it's that people who have come into contact with death, who have faced the darkest aspects of our humanity, who have loved and lost, and who know the meaning of sacrifice, seem to have little trouble relating to these ancient plays. These are their stories.

This chapter presents an overview of the Theater of War project and explores some of the ancient principles behind its modern productions of *Ajax* and *Philoctetes*. The chapter is divided into three parts: the first focuses on Doerries' vision and goals for the project, the second examines the ways in which he implements them in performance, and the third presents a case study describing a production of Sophocles' *Ajax* that took place at LIU Post in New York on 12 December 2014. The aim of the chapter is to identify and discuss the ways in which Doerries' performances tap into and recreate key dimensions of these fifth-century Athenian plays for a contemporary military audience.

The Theater of War project: Directorial vision and goals

Outside the Wire was founded in 2008 by artistic director Bryan Doerries and producing director Phyllis Kaufman. The company's mission is to use

> theater and a variety of other media to address pressing public health and social issues, such as combat-related psychological injury, end of life care, prison reform, political violence and torture, domestic violence, and the de-stigmatization of the treatment of substance abuse and addiction.[1]

Some of the plays they have presented include Sophocles' *Philoctetes* and *Women of Trachis* (end-of-life care), Aeschylus' *Prometheus Bound* (prison reform), Seneca's *Thyestes* (political violence and torture), Tennessee Williams' *A Streetcar Named Desire* (domestic violence), Euripides' *Bacchae*, Eugene O'Neill's *Long Day's Journey into Night* and Conor McPherson's *Rum and Vodka* (alcoholism, substance abuse and addiction). Other projects use Aeschylus' *Persians* to explore the topics of xenophobia and racism, Stephen Belber's *Tape* to discuss sexual assault in military communities and Stephen Mitchell's translation of *The Book of Job* to investigate how communities come together to heal after natural disasters.

The Theater of War project, in particular, focuses on the impact of war on soldiers and their communities. It presents scenes from Sophocles' *Ajax* and *Philoctetes* developed with specific audiences in mind, namely active-duty military men and women, veterans, family, friends and healthcare professionals. Taking into account these discrete points of view, the performances aim to provoke powerful responses and prompt meaningful dialogue about the enduring issues raised by these plays.

Each Theater of War event is structured in three parts: a staged dramatic reading of select scenes, a panel discussion and a town hall-style conversation with the audience afterward. The entire event takes approximately two hours, including the performance and the post-performance talkbacks. Doerries (2015a) is keen to emphasize that 'discussion is the most important element of what we do. It's not an afterthought. It's the objective.'

The performances themselves are barebones staged readings. There is no formal set, only the setting of the event itself – an army base, a veterans' hospital, a prison, a homeless shelter, a college auditorium. Three to five actors sit at a table with scripts, microphones and water bottles in plain view. They wear modern, everyday clothing; no distinctive costumes or other signals set them apart from anyone else. The house lights remain on for the entire performance, further blurring the boundaries between the actors and the audience. The entire room, then, becomes part of the playing space and everyone present participates in the perfor-mance. As Meineck (2009: 174) has remarked, this decision allows 'actors and audience to connect in a way that is usually impossible in the modern theatre. The acts of watching and being watched [become] essential to the shared experience that unfold[s], and [are] an important factor in facilitating the remarkably free expression that follow[s].'

The panel typically includes 'an active duty soldier who has experienced at least one deployment to the current conflicts, a veteran who has experienced at least one deployment to any past conflict, a spouse or another family member, and a mental health professional and/or a member of the military chaplaincy'.[2] Doerries meets with the panellists before the performance and asks them to listen closely to the scenes, identify any particular lines or moments that stand out to them, and reflect upon how these might relate to their own experiences. After the reading, he invites them to join the actors on stage and share their reactions to the play.

During the final segment, Doerries moderates a town hall-style conversation with the audience. He asks broad, thought-provoking questions such as 'How do we honour Ajax's great accomplishments without honouring the violence that took place at the end of his life?' He also encourages the audience to share unprompted observations and to ask their own questions. In this way, he creates a space in which they can collectively process the ideas and emotions provoked by the play. As McDonald (1992: 13) observes, 'conflict and questioning are vital to ancient tragedy ... Good drama asks questions. It does not matter if these questions are unanswerable, at least they must be asked.' The event ends when the last audience member finishes speaking.

Outside the Wire has developed a raft of other projects from questions raised during these discussions. One such project is The Female Warrior Program, which presents five scenes from Sophocles' *Ajax*, featuring a female actor in the title role and a male actor as her husband, Tecmessor. This format shifts the focus on to female soldiers, in particular, and opens up a discussion about the specific challenges that they and their families face upon their deployment and return from war.

Doerries sums up his goal for the Theater of War project as follows: 'to comfort the afflicted and to afflict the comfortable'. He seeks to unite members of a community through the experience of shared discomfort. In this way, he not only produces powerful modern theatre, but he also *re*produces a salient feature of ancient tragic performances. As Segal (1996: 149) notes:

It is a deeply held assumption among the Greeks of the archaic and classical periods that the sharing of tears and suffering creates a bond of common humanity between mortals ... Sharing these 'woes of life,' their *kêdea* (*Odyssey* 15.399), creates a bond between human beings, for they thus recognize what can happen to all humans as suffering mortals, δειλοῖσι βροτοῖσι (*Odyssey* 15.408; *Iliad* 24.525) ... Drama effects a concrete, public sharing of grief through the collective response of the chorus, and more broadly through the community of spectators in the theatre.

Ultimately, each Theater of War event aims to recognize the heroism and sacrifice of our service men and women, and also to promote increased understanding of – and compassion for – the physical, emotional, and psychological struggles that they face on the battle- and home fronts.

Bringing the plays to life: Translation, direction and discussion

Doerries is involved in every aspect of the project, from translating the scripts to directing the performances to moderating the discussions afterwards. He often takes on an acting role in the readings as well. He cultivated these interests as an undergraduate at Kenyon College in Ohio, where he majored in Classics and began to experiment with translating and staging ancient drama. He went on to earn a master's degree in theatre directing from the University of California, Irvine, and to serve as the director of programmes at the Alliance for Young Artists and Writers in New York. His work with Outside the Wire draws together his backgrounds in – and passions for – classics, theatre and community outreach. For this reason, he has been called 'part professor, part carnival barker' and 'a tireless evangelist for the Greeks and the gains that tragedy can provide to a community in pain' (Mason 2014: 59).

His translations of the tragedies are bold, elegant and, above all, accessible. They aim to break down the barriers of language, time and culture that too often separate modern audiences from the full dramatic force of ancient plays. Since Theater of War performances are staged readings, they rely on the strength of the words as opposed to spectacle. Doerries' translations, therefore, strive to render the text as clear and evocative as possible, enabling the audiences to visualize the action and relate to the characters, stories and feelings. Several audience members have described the experience as 'watching a movie in their minds'. The following passage illustrates an example of the stripped-down and emotionally charged language:

> AJAX: But what will I say/ to my father, Telamon, / when he sees my face?
> How will he even bear / to look at me when I / explain how I disgraced / our family name for / which he fought so hard?
> His heart will break / right then and there.
> Should I scale the walls / of Troy and face the army / by myself, show them what / I'm made of, and then die?
> No, that would only / please the generals.
>
> I must do something / bold to erase all doubt / in my father's mind / that his son was any- / thing but a coward.
> When a man suffers / without end in sight / and takes no pleasure / in living his life, day / by day wishing for / death, he should not / live out all his years.
> It is pitiful when men / hold onto false hopes. / A great man must / live in honor or die / an honorable death.
> That is all I have to say (Doerries 2015b: 47–8).

Doerries adapted the Greek text with the Theater of War audiences in mind; his translations are shaped by their perspectives. His philosophy is that 'the audience is more knowledgeable about the play than [he is]' (Doerries 2014b). They have lived through the epic experiences and emotions that he is trying to convey. To that end, his translations are constantly in flux. Since the success of a performance relies on the reciprocity between the translation and the audience, every performance is an opportunity to connect with the audience and fine-tune the script further based on the actors' and audiences' feedback. While the working script continues to evolve, his literary translations of four Greek tragedies – *Ajax, Philoctetes, Women of Trachis* and *Prometheus Bound* – were published in September 2015 (Doerries 2015b).

As director, Doerries works closely with the actors to help them understand and inhabit their roles. Over the years, the company has built up an impressive group of core performers, ranging from film and television stars – such as Adam Driver (*Star Wars: The Force Awakens, Girls*), Jesse Eisenberg (*Batman v Superman: Dawn of Justice, The Social Network*), Paul Giamatti (*John Adams, Sideways*), Jake Gyllenhaal (*Nightcrawler, Jarhead*), Frances McDormand (*Olive Kitterage, Fargo*) and Martin Sheen (*The West Wing, Apocalypse Now*) – to local actors and students. It currently has close to 200 actors in its base, all of whom are passionate about the project. Many have expressed to Doerries that they see it as an opportunity to be of service.

The rehearsals are minimal, often only a couple of hours in advance of a performance. The most common note or direction that Doerries gives his actors is to 'make them wish they'd never come'. He asks them to push their portrayals of anguish and suffering as far as possible in order to unnerve the audience and 'generate a sense of connection and community through shared discomfort'. The other piece of advice he frequently gives them is to 'think of the first performance [that they] do for a military audience as the "dress rehearsal," because the real direction will come from the audience. What audience members say will shape [their] next performance far more profoundly than anything [he] could say during rehearsal' (Doerries, 2015a).

Doerries made the decision to present the plays as staged readings rather than full productions. This decision was motivated by two main ideas. To begin with, Doerries believes that these plays were designed to be *heard*, first and foremost. He posits – and proves – that the words are powerful enough to create and sustain the plays' tragic momentum, without the use of spectacle. In this regard, he aligns himself with Aristotle who famously subordinates the visual elements of tragedy to the verbal (cf. Taplin 1978: especially 1–8 and Hall 1996: 297, among others). At *Poetics* 1453 b3–7 – and similarly at 1462 a11–18 – the ancient author asserts:

> The effect of fear and pity can arise from theatrical spectacle, but it can also arise from the intrinsic structure of events, and it is this which matters more and is the task of a superior poet. For the plot-structure ought to be so composed that, even without seeing a performance, anyone who hears the events which occur

will experience terror and pity as a result of the outcome (translation Halliwell, 1987, 45).

Furthermore, Doerries believes that, for Theater of War's purposes, stagecraft can conflict with the immediacy of the issues and emotions raised by the plays. The audience brings in preconceived notions of 'Greek tragedy', often involving highly stylized masks and movement, and any such signposts of antiquity can detach them from the story and diminish their experience of it. He wants the plays to feel timeless and relevant, not like museum pieces or academic artifacts. A staged reading, then, strips a play down to its most elemental parts. It allows the audience to focus on the *words*, above all else, and project their own experiences and emotions on to the characters.

Another important directorial decision that Doerries made was to feature prominently a panel as part of the performance. The panel serves a number of key functions. Most importantly, it brings together – and shines a spotlight on – a representative sample of the population for whom the play is being performed (cf. Longo 1990 and Hesk 2007, among others). Like the original productions of these plays, the Theater of War performances speak to men and women whose lives have been touched by war in some way. By inviting these individuals up on stage and asking them to participate in the performance, Doerries puts the community at the centre of the theatrical experience, both literally and metaphorically.

Moreover, by sharing their reflections on the characters and events of the play, the panel effectively functions as an extension of the chorus. They watch the story unfold and voice their reactions to it, thus modelling responses for the larger audience of the play. As Foley (2007: 355) observes, 'the chorus mediated not only spatially, but temporally and formally between audience and actors ... It could help to direct or channel the emotional response or expectations of the audience'. Notably, like its ancient Greek counterpart, this modern 'chorus' is also composed of soldier-citizens (cf. Winkler 1990). The military roles that the panellists play in real life add authority and nuance to their commentary. In this way they both represent the community and, to quote Goldhill (2007: 50), 'mobilize the *voice of the community* – with the full weight of what community means in democracy and in the shared cultural world of the ancient city'.

In his final role as moderator, Doerries guides the post-performance discussions with a great deal of skill and sensitivity. He never asks anything so clinical as 'How did this make you feel?', but rather he grounds all of his questions in specific lines or moments from the plays. Doerries (2014b) has observed that the plays 'unlock something in the audience' and 'give individuals with no background in classics or formal training in Sophoclean argumentation permission, vocabulary, and structure with which to speak about these issues'. He asks similar questions from one event to the next and relays answers that previous audiences have come up with. In this way, he expands the discussion beyond any one performance and connects different audiences through shared conversation, as well as discomfort.

Sophocles' *Ajax*

This final section describes a performance of Sophocles' *Ajax* that took place on Friday 12 December 2014 at the '1st Annual Long Island Symposium Dedicated to Supporting Military Members, Veterans, and Families' at LIU Post in New York. The cast included critically acclaimed theatre, film and television actor Jay O. Sanders (Broadway: *Hamlet*, *Pygmalion*, *Saint Joan*; film and TV: *Edge of Darkness*, *The Green Hornet*, *JFK*) in the title role, Tony Award winner Maryann Plunkett (Broadway: *Saint Joan*, *The Crucible*, *Me and My Girl*) as Tecmessa, and Doerries himself playing the chorus. The audience was composed primarily of active-duty soldiers, veterans, family, friends and mental healthcare professionals. The event lasted approximately an hour and a half.

The performance was held in an intimate college auditorium. As usual, there was no formal scenery beyond two tables, preset with microphones and water bottles and, in this case, draped with light-coloured cloths. The actors sat at one table, scripts in hand. The other table remained vacant, but visible during the performance. The panellists would sit here afterward.

The event began well before the performance officially started. Sitting in the audience, several veterans struck up conversations with one another. They identified what branches of the military they had served in and traded stories about where they had been deployed. The occasion itself, then, set the stage for the performance. It played an important role in fostering connections between audience members and cultivating a sense of community.

Walking among the audience, Doerries formally opened the event by welcoming everyone and explaining what was about to happen. Dressed in a suit and carrying a microphone, he channelled a kind of talk show host. He emphasized the fact that the event was a 'participatory' experience and that the goal was to create a space for discussion and start a conversation about what the play brought up in us. He announced that this was the 282nd performance of the project worldwide since 2008, and that more than 60,000 veterans and their families had seen it. He promised to share the ideas that we came up with that day from one community to the next.

Addressing a central question of the project, Doerries explained why he had chosen to present these dramas: 'Ancient Greek war plays have something very powerful to say today. Veterans have something to say in response. They are individuals who have lived lives of mythological proportions.' Framing the story in this way, he proceeded to set up the context for the scenes we were about to see: the action takes place in the ninth year of the Trojan War – one long deployment. The Greeks' best soldier, Achilles, whom everyone thought was invincible, has recently died. His death is a major blow both to the morale and the strength of the army. Additionally, there is no time for his comrades to mourn his passing or process their grief. Ajax, one of Achilles' great friends and second only to him in strength, integrity and loyalty, is especially upset by this loss and the way it is being handled.

Doerries continued to explain how the greatest honour in ancient warfare was to receive the armour of an honourable man. Over time, however, the process by which the armour was given out had become politicized. The Greeks decided to hold a contest to see who would win Achilles' armour, and that contest would be based on who could make the best speech. Odysseus, a hero better known for his intellect than for his military prowess, wins. Ajax is humiliated and soon begins to lose his sense of self. When Doerries recounted this particular aspect of the story, audible murmurs could be heard among the crowd.

In a rage, Ajax plots to kill the Greek generals. The goddess Athena intervenes and redirects him toward the camp's animals instead. In his delirium, Ajax believes that he is slaughtering the men who have dishonoured him and, in so doing, he dishonours himself. Ajax's men hear a rumour about his behaviour and debate whether to stay with their leader or to abandon him in his time of need. The performance picked at this point in the story. We would see two scenes: one in which Ajax confronts his men, his wife and his son about his tragic fall (c. line 348) and the other in which he reflects upon his life before falling on his sword (c. line 815).

There was no curtain, no lighting or sound cues, no boundary markers between the playing space and the audience. From any given seat, it was possible to see fellow audience members – and their reactions – in one's peripheral vision. A brief moment of silence followed Doerries' introduction, and then the actors began. Shattering the silence, Ajax let out a gut-wrenching groan, sending a wave of electricity through the crowd.

We watched as the hero processed the horrible deeds he had done in the fog of war and divine madness. He reflected on the shame he suffered and the disgrace he had brought upon himself, his men, and his family. His words revealed the utter defeat, powerlessness and vulnerability that he felt. Doerries' translation, enhanced by the actors' sensitive interpretations, conveyed these emotions in stark, direct and heartbreaking terms:

AJAX: Do you see what / I have done? I was / the bravest in battle, / never lost my wits, / and now I've killed / these harmless barn- / yard animals with / my hands! What a joke / my life has become, / my reputation, my / sense of honor!
… Darkness, / my light, / black abyss, / take me / down to / live in / oblivion, / for I am / no longer / worthy to /
live among / gods or men.
Athena, / grey-eyed / goddess, / daughter / of Zeus, / will torture / me until / I'm dead.
Nowhere / to run, / no escape.
My greatness / dies on this / heap of beasts.
I defeated / myself with / delusions.

TECMESSA: It's hard to hear a strong / man say such weak words!

AJAX: You surging straits, / roaring with waves, / you caves, / you groves / along the coast, you / have held me at Troy / for

many long years, / no longer, no longer, / when I have ceased to /
fill my lungs with air.
I speak to those who understand! (Doerries 2015b: 40–4)

As Ajax contemplated the consequences of his actions, he meditated
upon the many roles that he had played, namely soldier, father,
son and husband. He thus identified who he was and the value
of his life in relation to his community. Blinded by his sense of
honour, he was unable to see any solution to the problems that he
had created for those who depended on him the most. Tecmessa
pleaded with her husband. She begged him to think of the terrible
fate that awaited their family if he followed through on the terrible
plans he was considering. She underscored the fact that her life was
inextricably bound to his:

TECMESSA: I have nowhere else to go, / no one to whom I can
turn.
My parents are dead / you destroyed my / homeland. You now /
are my homeland, my safety, my life.
Nothing else matters but you.
I ask you to remember / all the good times / we had and to treat /
me kindly, for a noble / man always remembers / those who
gave him / pleasure and protects / them from danger. (Doerries
2015b: 50)

In this way, Tecmessa called attention to the ways in which war
reaches beyond the battlefield and extends to the home front. This
message was rendered all the more powerful in light of the fact
that the actress who played Tecmessa was married to the actor who
played Ajax in real life.

Doerries himself played the part of the chorus, which represented sailors and soldiers who had served under Ajax. The chorus'
interactions with the hero revealed the close relationship between
the general and his men. Their words betrayed their fear for their
leader and for themselves without him:

CHORUS: I've grown so home- / sick over these months /
encamped on the out- / skirts of Troy, worn / down by the
tortures / of time, waiting here / to die and someday / set foot
on the black / dust of Hades' shores.

And now I must care / for incurable Ajax, / his mind infected / by divine madness.
He was the one you [Salamis] / sent overseas to win / the war with overwhelming / force.
Now he is alone.
Caught up / in thoughts, / he unnerves / his friends, / as we watch / his greatest / acts of bravery / slip through his / fingers, only / to be forgotten, / erased from history / by the generals.
(Doerries 2015b: 57–8)

The chorus thus reinforced the deep bond that develops between fellow soldiers, the duty they have to care for their own, and the self-sacrifice that this responsibility often demands.

The second scene portrayed the moments leading up to Ajax's suicide. His final thoughts centred on his family and community: he begged Zeus that his brother Teucer would be the one to find him, he prayed that the sun god Helios would announce his death to his parents; he fondly recollected his childhood home and his friends. The actor playing Ajax managed to convey a profound sense of isolation during this monologue, despite the fact that he was still sitting beside his wife and staring out at a room full of people. His famous speech concluded as follows:

AJAX: No more talk of tears. / It's time. / Death, oh Death, / come now and / visit me …
But I shall miss / the light of day / and the sacred / fields of Salamis, / where I played as / a boy, and great / Athens, and all / my friends. I call out to you, / springs and rivers / fields and plains, / who nourished me / during these long
years at Troy.

These are the last / words you will / hear Ajax speak …
The rest I shall say / to those who listen / in the world below.
(Doerries 2015b: 76)

The actors never once looked at one another. They directed all of their words out toward the audience, visualizing their addressees in the very space where we were sitting. In this way, they drew us into the world of the play and included us in the conversation in a direct and powerful way.

Following this scene, Doerries summed up the rest of the play for the audience. He discussed how Ajax's wife and brother arrive too late to stop the hero from killing himself, how they process their grief in terms of 'survivor's guilt', and how Ajax's former enemy Odysseus becomes his champion and convinces Agamemnon to allow him an honourable burial. He suggested that Odysseus does this because he 'is moved by admiration for [Ajax's] greatness rather than by hatred for his smallness'.

Before turning the event over to the panellists, Doerries posed the first discussion question to the audience: 'What was Sophocles, a general as well as a playwright, trying to say to his community?' Having planted this seed, he then invited the panellists to come up on stage and reflect upon the performance they had just witnessed.

The first panellist was a physician who specialized in the treatment of PTSD in veterans. He remarked that he was very touched by the vignettes, and, in particular, one of the chorus's lines following the discovery of Ajax's body: 'How could / I have been / so blind, so deaf / to your cries, / while the red / blood gushed / from a hole / in your chest?' (Doerries 2015b: 80). To him, these lines served as a tragic reminder that we need to pay close attention to our soldiers and the battles they continue to fight when they return home from war. The panellist shared that, too often, he sees veterans struggle to reconnect with friends and family that are 'blind' and 'deaf' to their suffering. Drawing on the chorus' words, he encouraged the audience to reach out to veterans and make an effort to better understand the horrors they have gone through in order to help them heal.

The next panellist was a young woman who had served two tours in Iraq and Kuwait in the National Guard. She spoke of her personal experience with combat and her struggle to reintegrate into her community afterward. When she stumbled in her speech and began to cry, the audience immediately rallied to support her, filling the auditorium with applause. When her voice returned, the panellist said that she identified in particular with one of Ajax's lines: 'I speak to those who understand' (Doerries 2015b: 44). To her, these words captured the unique bond that exists between soldiers, based on shared military experience. She reiterated the necessity to expand the circle of 'those who understand' to include both military and non-military personnel.

The next panellist, who was serving his twenty-fourth year in the Marine Corps, spoke about his concern for the wellbeing of his troops. In particular, he addressed the challenges that he faces 'bringing them back down to earth before sending them out again'. A key aspect of his job is to help his men move past the gore and carnage they have just witnessed in order to get back into a mission. He reiterated many of the points raised by the previous panellists, namely that too often soldiers suffer in silence, and that they need to be able to confide in one another. Speaking to both the soldiers and the civilians in the room, he encouraged them to reach out to veterans and let them know 'we're here for you'.

The final panellist, a young veteran in his thirties, admitted that the play brought up 'uncomfortable' feelings. He spoke about the structure and sense of purpose that the army had given him while he served. Now, as a veteran, he had to figure out who he was apart from it, what to do next, and 'what his life was worth'. He commented in particular on Ajax's line 'what a joke my life has become' (Doerries 2015b: 40), which echoed stages in his own process of self-reflection.

The common message of all four panellists was a plea to the community to *listen* to its soldiers, to make an effort to understand what they have been through and to stand beside them in support. By sharing their personal stories and their honest reflections, the panellists added eloquent social commentary, realism and pathos to the play and the issues it raised.

Following the panel talk-back, Doerries opened the conversation up to the larger audience. He returned to the question that he had posed earlier: 'What was Sophocles, a general as well as a playwright, trying to say to his community?' The audience volunteered a range of thoughtful answers. They posited that Sophocles was trying to 'enlighten the community to the atrocities of war', 'discuss the cost of heroism' and 'address the responsibility of civilians to carry the military'. The discussion focalized on the theme of fraternity among soldiers, in particular, the culture that they share and the difficulty that they often have letting outsiders in. Building on the panellists' comments, the audience reinforced the need for greater communication and empathy among soldiers and civilians.

Afterward, Doerries relayed some of the responses that other communities had come up with. A veteran from a previous audience suggested that 'despite the fact that Ajax loses his best friend, becomes unglued, and takes his own life, perhaps Sophocles told his story in order to "boost morale" among the soldiers in the audience'. When Doerries asked him to explain how this tragic tale could 'boost morale', the veteran replied, 'Because it's the truth.'

The next question focused in on the unique burden that military spouses bear. Through the figure of Tecmessa, the audience considered whether it is better to be happy and ignorant of a partner's pain or to share in their suffering. Speaking from their own experience, they discussed the different types of pain that come from knowing and not knowing what a spouse has been through.

Doerries then asked one final question: 'If Ajax were someone you knew, loved, cared about, sworn to protect, and you knew he was alone on a beach and you had a chance to be with him, what would you say or do?' The audience responded with a great deal of candour and compassion. One individual replied: 'I'd tell him that I love him and that I'm sorry that he's going through this, I'm here to listen, I care.' Another said: 'I'd say "You matter to me: I may not know how you feel, but I will walk with you for as long as it takes."'

When the last audience member finished speaking, Doerries thanked them all for participating in the conversations and sharing their thoughts and experiences. He concluded the event with a benediction: 'If you related to anything that was said on stage or in the audience today, know that you are not alone, in this room, in this country, across time.'

Conclusions

Doerries' innovative directorial approach provides a vivid illustration of how a theatrical production can derive power from a targeted understanding of its audience. Every aspect of the Theater of War project is designed with military communities in mind, with the goal of fostering communication and compassion among soldiers and civilians. Doerries accomplishes this with a carefully orchestrated combination of performance, panel discussion and town hall-style talkback. His poignant translations and minimalist productions of *Ajax* and *Philoctetes* highlight the plays' timeless themes and facilitate the audience's ability to project its ideas and emotions on to the characters. By featuring a panel, Doerries creates a modern-day chorus that both represents and models responses for the larger target audience. By sharing their impressions, coloured by their first-hand experience with some of the plays' tragic themes, the panellists enrich the audience's reception of the performance and its messages. Their candour, in turn, encourages other members of the audience to step forward and tell their own stories, effecting a kind of communal catharsis. It is the concinnity of these elements that distinguishes the Theater of War project as a uniquely effective platform, both for a dramatic rendering of the ancient plays and a nuanced discussion of their implications in the modern world.

Bibliography

Doerries, B. (2014a) Short Bacchae Piece, 9 September.

Doerries, B. (2014b) Interview, 12 December.

Doerries, B. (2015a) Correspondence, 11 March.

Doerries, B. (2015b) *All That You've Seen Here is God: New Versions of Four Greek Tragedies: Sophocles' Ajax, Philoctetes, Women of Trachis and Aeschylus' Prometheus Bound.* New York: Vintage Press.

Doerries, B. (2015c) *The Theater of War: What Ancient Greek Tragedies Can Teach Us Today.* New York: Alfred A. Knopf.

Foley, H. P. (2007) 'Envisioning the Tragic Chorus on the Modern Stage'. In C. Kraus, S. Goldhill, H. P. Foley and J. Elsner (eds), *Visualizing the Tragic: Drama, Myth, and Ritual in Greek Art and Literature: Essays in Honour of Froma Zeitlin.* Oxford: Oxford University Press, 353–78.

Goldhill, S. (2007) *How to Stage Greek Tragedy Today.* Chicago; London: University of Chicago Press.

Hall, S. (1996) 'Is there a *Polis* in Aristotle's *Poetics*?' In M. Silk (ed.), *Tragedy and the Tragic: Greek Theatre and Beyond.* Oxford: Clarendon Press, 295–309.

Halliwell, S. (1987) *The Poetics of Aristotle: Translation and Commentary.* Chapel Hill: University of North Carolina Press.

Hesk, J. (2007) 'The Socio-Political Dimension of Ancient Tragedy'. In M. McDonald and J. M. Walton (eds), *The Cambridge Companion to*

Greek and Roman Theatre. Cambridge: Cambridge University Press, 72–91.

Longo, O. (1990) 'The Theater of the *Polis*'. In J. J. Winkler and F. I. Zeitlin (eds), *Nothing to Do with Dionysos? Athenian Drama in its Social Context.* Princeton: Princeton University Press, 12–19.

Mason, W. (2014) 'You Are Not Alone Across Time: Using Sophocles to Treat PTSD'. *Harper's Magazine,* 57–65.

McDonald, M. (1992) *Ancient Sun, Modern Light: Greek Drama on the Modern Stage.* New York: Columbia University Press.

Meineck, P. (2009) 'These are Men Whose Minds the Dead Have Ravished': 'Theater of War/The Philoctetes Project'. *Arion* 17.1: 173–92.

Segal, C. (1996) 'Catharsis, Audience, and Closure in Greek Tragedy'. In M. Silk (ed.), *Tragedy and the Tragic: Greek Theatre and Beyond.* Oxford: Clarendon Press, 149–72.

Taplin, O. (1978) *Greek Tragedy in Action.* Berkeley: University of California Press.

Winkler, J. J. (1990) 'The Ephebes' Song: *Tragōidia* and *Polis*'. In J. J. Winkler and F. I. Zeitlin (eds), *Nothing to Do With Dionysos? Athenian Drama in its Social Context.* Princeton: Princeton University Press, 20–62.

PART THREE

Directorial
Re-Visions

8

Jan Fabre's *Prometheus Landscape II*: [De]territorialization of the tragic and transgressive acts of arson

Demetris Zavros

A voiceover explains all the Health and Safety procedures in place at the theatre venue.

Lights off: Two performers on either side of a rather corpulent alter-Prometheus [Bound] light their cigarettes with a match – the first little act of arson.

Belgian director Jan Fabre has been producing work in a variety of artistic disciplines including drawing, painting, sculpture, performance art, opera, theatre, dance and film. Fabre has constantly problematized the boundaries of each one and challenged their communicative devices as well as the limits of what is widely considered acceptable and tasteful. His first attempt at the myth of Prometheus (*Prometheus Landscape I*) was a result of a ten-day workshop in Berlin in 1988. In his very illuminating paper for the Twelfth International Symposium of Ancient Greek Drama (Cyprus Centre of the International Theatre Institute 2012), Freddy Decreus explains that this first 'landscape' was very loosely based on Aeschylus' tragedy but delves into an investigation of the tragic through the creation of a liminal space/experience in several different ways.[1] In his second attempt, *Prometheus Landscape II* (2011), Fabre directed as well as wrote part of the text; 'We Need Heroes Now' was inspired by a group of protesters (photographed at Ground Zero the day after the history-altering events of 9/11) who held a banner with the inscription 'We need heroes now'. The second part of the text for the performance ('I am the all-giver') was written by Jeroen Olyslaegers (based on Aeschylus' *Prometheus Bound*).[2]

The myth of Prometheus – the selfless hero who is tortured in eternity for helping mortals to progress through his gift of fire which stands both for hope and technology (Ruffell 2012: 35) – has been used throughout the centuries as a symbol of rebellion against tyrannical and autocratic regimes. Aeschylus' tragedy itself has been discussed and staged in relation to philosophical, political, religious and technological interpretations over the centuries, and has also been a favourite of practitioners who identify their work within the field of less traditional approaches in the [performing] arts. It is ground-breaking in the rather anti-Aristotelean demands of its spectacular staging, its rather episodic structure (composed of speeches/dialogues between the 'visiting' characters and the 'bound' hero) and its unconventionally minimal plot.

This chapter will examine Fabre's contemporary directorial adaptation of the Greek tragedy in relation to the notion of 'minorization' suggested by Gilles Deleuze in his essay on the theatre of Carmelo Bene, One Manifesto Less (1979).[3] Deleuze's suggestion of a 'critical theatre' in the staging of a classic will provide a context of investigation alongside other related notions that Deleuze and Guattari put forth in several of their writings (especially in the two volumes of *Capitalism and Schizophrenia*). *Prometheus Landscape II* builds on as well as differentiates itself from the first 'landscape' in some very important ways that might prove instrumental in the discussion of Fabre's directorial adaptation of the Greek tragedy.

However, I will argue that while they employ different strategies, both performances aim to create a theatre that re-imagines the tragic in such a way that it delves back into its very roots in order to find its contemporary essence.

'Critical theatre': Minorization, deterritorialization and subtraction

Fabre is not interested in a museum theatre based on a reconstruction of the original tragedy any more than he is in a 'museum of the everyday' (Bene quoted in Deleuze's essay, Murray 1997: 243). His staging is not contemporary in that it 'represents' everyday life outside the theatre any more than it represents the fictional cosmos encapsulated in the tragedy. He, like Carmelo Bene (albeit in different ways, as I will argue), amputates elements of power and in essence re-imagines the 'theatrical matter' but 'also the theatrical form, which ceases to be a "representation" at the same time that the actor ceases to be an actor' (Deleuze in Murray 1997: 241).

Deleuze discusses the notion of 'major texts' and explains that there is a double operation entrenched in our traditional approach: one of 'magnification/ normalization'. He supports that everything that is given a 'major' status (whether it be an event, a text, a person, a mythic persona or a 'heroic feat') simultaneously undergoes a process of normalization. 'One pretends to discover and admire but in fact one normalises' (ibid.: 243). He calls for an alternative, antidote treatment of classic (major) texts that 'would recover the active force of the minority' – a 'critical theatre'.

Fabre is what Deleuze calls an 'operator' rather than a director or author. He uses the Aeschylean text and 'minorates' it through a process of subtraction and 'what is subtracted, amputated or neutralised are the elements of power, the elements that represent or constitute a system of power' (ibid.: 241). Crucially, the elements of power in theatre are connected to the issue of coherence in terms of both subjectivity and representation. There are some differences in the way Fabre approaches the notion of 'subtraction' but these do not negate the minorization process. Instead, as I will argue, Fabre's minorization opens up a wider continuum in the experience

FIGURE 10 *Fabre's* Prometheus Landscape II. *Photo Wonge Bergmann*

of the performance, which alludes to the strata as well as their deterritorialization and makes the audience implicitly involved in the minorization process.

Fabre's adaptation and directorial approach is a very careful operation; a setting of 'fires' that aims to free the 'major' text from its tendencies to normalization. He does not disregard nor a priori denounce the Aeschylean dramatopoiesis of the myth, but puts it in a spin, makes it stutter, makes it slip. Fabre 'lodges' himself on the tragedy and explores and experiments with the opportunities it offers, on all different levels. The tragedy is used as the territory to be deterritorialized through the opening up of its 'anatomy' into a 'landscape', a landscape that is allowed to work like a desiring machine, a Body without Organs, a constitutive force that doesn't aim to represent the fictional cosmos of the tragedy but uses the existing 'model' in order to free it from its binding strata and its inherent (and normalizing) systems of power.

Landscape and theatre: As a body without organs

Fabre's approach to the tragedy is divorced from Aristotelian hierarchies from the start. He proposes to create a 'landscape' of the tragedy, a notion that is, at first instance, connected to the visual component (*Opsis*), an element that Aristotle rated last in the art of tragedy. In her compelling argument about contemporary directorial adaptation processes in terms of metaphor, Avra Sidiropoulou notices that 'the conceptualisation of space has been a paramount agent of revising the classics. In fact, for most directors, the re-imagining of space is the most obvious starting point in the adaptation process' (2014: 9). While we could certainly not dismiss Fabre's connection/alliance to the 'visual',[4] which is abundantly infused in his unique directorial language, the notion of the *landschaft* here is used, I believe, as an agent of transcoding and transmutation on all levels rather than a visual metaphor.

As Una Chaudhuri notices in *Land/Scape/Theater* (2002: 12), the initial binary of 'landscape as environment and landscape as discourse' that existed in the systematic study of environmental sciences on the one hand and the humanities on the other is super-seded today and the post-structuralist dismantling has resulted in a variety of new (and often a lot more performative) understandings of the term (including Thrift's related 'non-representational theory' in the field of human geography).

According to Chaudhuri, the first use of the notion of landscape in theatre can be credited to Gertrude Stein in her 'Landscape Plays' (collected in her 1932 *Operas and Plays*). Stein crucially centralizes the notion of 'composition' (as well as the sense of distance and perspective) in the text over a sense of narrative or representation of reality. Ever since, several different artists – ranging from Heiner Müller, *Verkommenes Ufer Medeamaterial Landschaft mit Argonauten* (1982) to Heiner Goebbels, 'Text as Landscape'[5] and his *Shadow/Landscape with Argonauts after Poe and Mueller*; Cage, *Imaginary Landscape IV* (1952), to name but a few – have utilized the notion of the landscape in their creative endeavours. Fabre himself has explored the notion in his Performance art work at least since 1978 with *My Body, My Blood, My Landscape* (1978) and later with *Sanguis/Mantis Landscape* (2004).

In 'From Logos to Landscape: Text in Contemporary Dramaturgy' (1997) Lehmann discusses an emerging theatre practice (since the 1970s) that opposes the antiquity-old logocentric approach to theatre. In this paradigmatic shift from *logos* to *Opsis*, Lehmann notices that *logos* in theatre is inextricably bound to the concept of structure, or a certain 'architecture' that prioritizes telos, unity, 'coherence in view of reason', order, causality. A non-logocentric form of theatre then would not only bring the *opsis* into a more prevalent position, but would re-invent the notion of structure or form that this new theatre practice would be based on. He sees the origins of this new theatrical space in Kristeva's *chora* (developed from Plato's '*khora*' in *Timaeus*) and states that through this notion theatre's connection to its choral dimension is re-affirmed but criti-cally in the 'rediscovery of theatre as *chora*' we find a space where fixed meaning and unity are no longer the building blocks. While both of Fabre's attempts at the myth can be considered under this line of investigation, *Prometheus Landscape II* approaches the choratic in a different way from the first landscape – one that can be rethought in light of Deleuze and Guattari's investigation.

Ronald Bogue traces the lineage of Deleuze's discussion of the 'sensible' and the 'aesthetic' on several pre-existing lines of thought, including Lyotard's figural as well as Maldiney's essentially phenomenological theory, which is also based on Erwin Straus's distinction between perception and sensation (Bogue 2003: 116). Deleuze takes on Lyotard's notion of the figural (as opposed to the figurative) as that which 'disrupts the clichés of coded representation [...] but also makes possible "matters of fact," figures that bypass the brain and work directly on the nerves' (2003: 130).

Straus differentiates between perception, which he relates to a geographical understanding of space, and sensation, which is something he relates to the notion of *landscape*. Based on Straus's discussion of sensations, Maldiney identifies 'a primary generative chaos, in which world and self are indistinguishable' as well as systolic contractions that 'create a separation of "here" and "there"', and diastolic ones where 'we do not possess the world but are possessed by it, filled by the interplay of light and dark, appearance and disappearance, whose rhythm instils an alteration of abandon and retreat' (Bogue 2003: 141).

In such a landscape, we gain access to the *Mitwelt* of an unfolding self-world that knows no clear differentiation of subject and object. Deleuze and Guattari relate *Mitwelt* to 'The Body without Organs', a concept that they borrow from theatre visionary Artaud. It pervades their general philosophical dictum and it works against the three strata that they consider the more pervasively binding: organism, significance and subjectification. The BwO is defined as 'the totality or plane of ... prehuman, prelinguistic and profound differences', which Western thought has tended to consider as deviations or distractions from existing categories of representation (Colebrook 2002: 16).

Deleuze and Guattari's BwO and the related notions of territorialization and deterritorialization can easily be related to Maldiney's 'primary generative chaos' and diastolic/systolic movements. 'Deleuze relates the *Mitwelt* to the BwO and the forces that determine 'provisional organs' on its oscillating surface. This, I argue, is essentially how Fabre approaches the minorization process of the tragedy through his 'theatre as landscape': every provisional organ of the performance of the dramatic text, i.e. every theatrical means and process normally used to re-create the fictional cosmos encapsulated in the dramatic text (as well as the phallogocentric ideologies that it represents), is reconfigured as 'a locus of deformation, a figural chaos, but also a graph or diagram for the development of a canvas whose function is to harness forces' (Bogue 2003: 130).

While he admits to differentiating between the different art forms and the 'languages' they speak,[6] in re-imagining the tragedy into a 'landscape' Fabre is inevitably creating another in-between, a hybrid, a liminality and a deterritorialization of the theatrical text. And in this in-between Fabre 'forms alliances' (to use the Deleuzean terminology) between different milieus of different types of forces and intensities. Landscape and geography, diastole and systole, representation and its deformation by the lines of flight (that are already inherent in the mythic text) are all part of the performance and are made to co-exist in the experience of this rhizomatic in-between, the Tragic Body without Organs.

The notion of the 'landscape' (and its aesthetic, performative, socio-political and philosophical implications) could be conceived as an exteriority to the dramatic frame, the 'major' Aeschylean text (like any war machine ought to be according to Deleuze and Guattari).[7] In essence, Fabre 'minorizes' the tragic text into a landscape that not only invites pure exteriorities existing but 'curbed'[8] within the mythical frame, but in this very careful and intricate operation he instigates and supports a new concept of the 'tragic' itself and the audience's experience of it. Fabre minorizes the 'major text' through a polarization of some of those ingredients that are already implicit in it, both in terms of subject matter and form of expression.

Minorization and organs/markers of power

Deleuze and Guattari's two-volume *Capitalism and Schizophrenia* is an attack on the regulating and normalizing processes that pervade both the capitalist system and psychoanalytic exegeses of human behaviour. And on the level of subject matter, one can but notice that their aims are rather congruent to Fabre's in this performance. In the second volume, *A Thousand Plateaus*, Deleuze and Guattari explain that the State is defined by 'the perpetuation or conservation of organs of power. The concern of the State is to conserve (2007: 394). The two heads of the State, the two poles of political sovereignty, its double articulation, is the magician-*king* and the jurist-*priest*' (388, my italics).[9] Fabre's 'war machine' works on the level of the subject matter (anti-capitalist, anti-psychoanalytical, anti-phallocentric) as well as the theatrical form and its communicative structures (post-dramatic, non-logocentric, non-representational, rhizomatic, etc.).

The ways in which different institutions have regularized and normalized bodies and behaviours and the body in revolt is a recurring theme in Fabre's work. Fabre celebrates the 'war machine' and sets it against the State apparatus through a variety of expressive and communicative devices, but more usually than not, he presents the normalization and its effects as a territory which is transgressed by the bodies in revolt. In *As Long as the World Needs a Warrior's Soul* (2000),

> [h]e shows the regulating processes of sexual discourses and their suffocating effect on disciplined and normalized bodies, bodies that are molded and fixed to 'fit' into a class, a genus, a species. Yet, Fabre traces countermovements of the body in revolt and rebellion. (Stalpaert 2005: 180)

In *Prometheus Landscape II* he looks at any form of normalization that falls under the phallogocentric curbing of desire and the policing of the body (entrenched in Judeo-Christian notions of guilt and *ressentiment*) as this surfaces from a re-imagination of the tragedy. In the process he questions not only how we have misused the gift of fire by overregulating 'safety' over our 'bound imagination' (as instigated by Hephaestus), but also the notion of the hero itself (Velle 2011).

Fabre's 'We need heroes now' opening antiphonal prelude to Olyslaeger's text is a questioning of our need for a hero as much as an admission of our conditioned yearning for one. And in the aftermath of 9/11 the 'desperate' longing for a hero acquires multiple meanings:

> Where is our hero
> Who would give his all for us?
> Even his life
> To make his uniqueness count
> To give his mortality worth and meaning
> To escape from oblivion. (Fabre, 2011)

By whose standards are heroes defined and where do we draw the line between a selfless heroic feat and a monstrous criminal act of egotism? This question will be revisited later in the performance when Bia (Violence) and Kratos (Power/Force/Strength but also 'State' in Modern Greek) will transform from childlike figures (breaking the silence with their playful laughter and marching snare drumming) into painful emulations of expressions of a not-so-distant fascist totalitarianism with Hitler salutes and moustaches.

The second performer in Fabre's prologue unfolds a continuous waging of war against the psychoanalytical approach and the inevitably failed effort to 'understand' human nature (Decreus 2012: 140). The ever-growing list of aphoristic 'Fuck Yous' in the contrapuntal speech duet can be retrospectively read as a revolt against all those who demonized desire by categorizing it, symptomatizing it and medicating it – all those who understood 'BwO phenomena as regressions, projections, phantasies, in terms of an *image* of the body' (Deleuze and Guattari 2007: 182).

But while in *As Long as the World Needs a Warrior's Soul* as well as some of Fabre's other performances – *Je suis sang* (2001), *L'Histoire des Larmes* (2005) – the regulatory normalization is both presented and dismantled on stage through references to oppressive mechanisms we recognize from everyday life, in *Prometheus* the *careful investigation* into the Aeschylean tragedy is what gives rise to the deterritorialization of the text through lines of flight and creates conjunctions, connections with mythical, theatrical and extra-theatrical milieux. Fabre uses the dramatic text and wages a war against those organs of power that effectuate the normalization and policing of desire by exploring 'form' (and communicative devises used) almost inextricably from content (performance subject matter), through the re-imagination of the chorus and the polarization of the visual.

Landscape and the re-imagination of the chorus

The notion of the choratic becomes essential in the re-imagination of tragedy into a landscape. My argument is that Fabre re-imagines the function of the chorus through the notion of the landscape in such a way that it pervades the whole of the performance. And the two landscapes differ in the way the choratic is displaced as well as the way they negotiate the balance between the diastolic and systolic forces that pervade them through their relationship to the strata of the tragedy.

The chorus in Aeschylus' tragedy is comprised by the Oceanides (daughters of the god Oceanos) and their function in the tragedy exceeds conventional expectations. According to Ruffell, they deter from offering 'abstract reflections around the themes of the play' (2012: 42) and they act as characters who offer their opinion and advice; they are there to support Prometheus and they remain loyal to him until the end of the tragedy (even after the final threatening words of Hermes which are directed at them). The chorus of Oceanides does not feature in Fabre's work but it is displaced at different levels in the creation of the landscape.

Olyslaeger's text 'I am the all-giver' is a series of nine monologues separated by fragments of popular song relating to fire, heat and desire. Every song at the end of an 'episode'[10] is a little act of defiance/arson and a 'poor' monodic anti-*choros* that is always interrupted, silenced abruptly with fire-extinguishing material. On a surface level, the choral *stasima* are almost displaced in a monody of popular song – a song of the populace – which is put out incessantly. But the choral (along with traditional notions of the functions of the chorus in Greek tragedies) is re-imagined in more ways than one. This staging is no longer concerned with a separate investigation of the ubiquitous enigma of the function of the chorus in the same way that it has repeatedly troubled contemporary theatre directors; it is a choratic approach to the tragedy as a whole.

In the first *Landscape* (1988), according to Decreus, 'the chorus of Prometheus characters (in different constellations, from one to seven) tried to find their place in "the ever unfinished book of the mortals", as the text mentioned, blaming the gods to be mainly "charlatans"' (2012: 137). What Decreus describes as 'the chorus of Prometheus characters' I would call a choratic multiplicity (or Deleuze's 'dividual') based on and simultaneously de-centring and de-subjectifying the heroic figure. The connection between this 'acoustic landscape' (and the connection that Decreus notices to Lehmann's much later discussion of the 'post-dramatic') and Bogue's description of Debussy's attempt to create a new type of choral writing is pertinent here.[11] In essence, in the first Prometheus, Fabre conceptualizes the choral attribute of the tragedy in such a way that it permeates, floods and opens up the performance into a choral acoustic/visual landscape, and this affects the language used ('the language was completely emaciated, the choirs were reduced to stuttering sounds' [Van den Dries in Decreus: 136]) as well as the way the landscape is conceived and organized.[12]

In the second landscape, however, Fabre reconceptualizes this choratic treatment of the tragic text in a way that he deterritorializes the text by initially retaining a closer connection to it. This does not mean that he departs from the Deleuzean 'imperative' for non-representation/deformation; in fact he is using a closer relationship to the territory, the strata, to effectuate the deterritorialization in the creation of his Landscape as a Body without Organs. In effect, he also broadens the continuum of a pool of connections and meanings and significations and affects that are inherent in the presentation of the myth.

So, while in the first landscape the choratic opened up the heroic character into a BwO that resembles the 'Dividual', in the second landscape, Fabre retains the differentiation between the central character and the rest of the composition very clearly, but only in order to prioritize and make more evident the in-between. And it is in this space in-between that everything exists in a constant process of 'ceaseless variation', on a continuum between signification and affect that constantly changes in a play between diastole and systole, a deformation of the provisional organs that comprise the language of 'clichéd representation'.

'Minorization' through a polarization of the visual: 'Excess' and the continuum of reference and abstraction, representation and affect

Prometheus Bound is a tragedy that relies on *Opsis* almost as a revolt against not only Aristotelian principles, but against contemporary staging standards. The viewers were almost invited to become complicit voyeurs of the suffering of the main character on stage. As Ruffell explains, 'the emphasis on the act of viewing, the object of viewing and on emotional response in the viewer all encourage the audience (spectators, *theatai*) to reflect upon their own actions' (Ruffell 2012: 102).[13] And it is not suggested that the 'act of seeing' is something alien to Greek tragedy (Ruffell gives Sophocles' *Ajax* and *Oedipus Tyrannus* as clear examples), but that this tragedy differs 'in the emphasis on the quality of the spectacle of one character, which is unusually extensive and blunt' (2012: 102).[14]

Ruffell suggests that the 'stark visual symbol' of Prometheus pinioned in the centre of the stage (echoing 'the Athenian punishment of *apotympanismos*' [2012: 85]) helps promote the core dramatic idea and the tension created between him and the characters/ visitors who interact with him in the course of the tragedy. Fabre essentially polarizes the visual aspect (the 'stark visual symbol') of the central image inherent in the staging of the Aeschylean tragedy in a way that its use exceeds its dramaturgical and representational logic. This polarity/centrality of the heroic symbol is adopted in a way that the heroic figure is not prioritized as the 'centre' against the less important landscape that surrounds it (in the form of the binary that pervades traditional forms of landscape painting as well as the Aeschylean tragedy), but as one that is questioned and problematized through its own position as well as the choratic multiplicity that surrounds and engulfs it.

Fabre does not literally subtract the hero as a 'marker of power' (to follow Deleuze's suggestion) from the performance nor the visual arrangement he composes. Neither does the visual composition of his 'landscape' resemble the famous example of Breughel's *Landscape with the Fall of Icarus*, where the tragic hero is given an almost inconsequential role in a world that seems to pursue its own concerns as usual. So how is it that this marker of power is destabilized? Decreus notices that the notion of transcendence and the perpetual failing of 'man' to fulfil the image which he was made in ('In His image') as well as Western philosophy's split between the ideal and the material world (from the platonic Cave to later re-incarnations that pervaded Western philosophy and thought) are also part of the myth's semiological baggage. Prometheus dares to cross these two separate worlds and bring to earth that which was heavenly. The representation of the Promethean model in a way that resembles the 'Vitruvian man' is evidence to the fact that

[...] Fabre's answer no longer considers man the golden ratio (*sectio aurea*) nor the golden offspring of some overaged gods. His reversed humanism misses the age-old confidence in a finished state or definitive mission of the human (esp. Western) race and is therefore bound to create a new, and hence, personal, mythology. (Decreus 2012: 132)

Fabre has questioned and problematized this binary (high/low, heaven/earth, god/human) in a few of his works.[15] Yves De Maeseneer suggests that Fabre has also looked at destabilizing notions of transcendence through a special type of 'disfiguration' in his work with angels – *Wall of the Ascending Angels* (1993), *Angelos* (1997). The 'hero' and the suspended 'angels' he created for a few of his works might be traditionally connected to notions of soteriology, but, in both cases, the artistic work supersedes the transcendental model in which these notions are embedded. Fabre is not prophesying a 'provincialist regression into a mythical past' (De Maeseneer, 2003: 382) with situating the heroic figure at the centre of the stage. While Fabre admits that he likes to use 'models' (angel, Christ, [mythic] 'hero'), he uses them in a way that negates their supernatural, theological, mythical origins and transcendental qualities and focuses on beauty,[16] as a part of immanent reality. In the same way that De Maeseneer suggests that 'against today's aestheticisation, Fabre reveals the fragility of Beauty by stressing the materiality of art' (ibid.: 384), in this contemporary staging of the Promethean myth, he reveals the tragic fragility of Beauty by stressing the corporeality in theatre at the same time that he destabilizes 'recognition' through the process of 'ceaseless variation'. It is by using excess in the place of 'surveyability', unity and representation that he restores the 'tragic' dimension of theatre as a space of liminality – a space of multiplicity.

Fabre seems to follow the Deleuzean imperative to '[c]reate the 'continuum' of every utterance (1997: 246) far beyond its immediate linguistic associations. The centralization of the visual (especially in its connection to the opening antiphonal prelude 'We need a hero') takes on and produces a multiplicity of significations and affect. Prometheus increasingly appears to become grotesquely intrusive in the composition of the landscape; the once ultimate 'model' of heroism becomes painfully romantic, irrelevant and superseded. This 'major marker of power', itself previously considered a symbol of rebellion, spreads open into a continuum at the same time that 'fire' (and desire) are shown to be constitutive as well as destructive.[17] And this continuum contains the symbolic reference as much as its silencing, the glorification of its beauty as much as its deconstruction, its critique, its refutation and even its Brechtian distancing.[18] This 'landscape' doesn't preclude in its amputation of power markers any more than it offers ready-made solutions to the questions it poses in the introduction. It puts the marker on a spin and allows the audience the potential, the choice to operate the subtraction alongside the director, the author of the new text and the performers. And the concretization of the symbolic reference to the heroic mythical figure in the use of the central image is of course but one extremity on the continuum that the landscape encapsulates.[19]

The rest of the 'characters' themselves (recognizable to varying degrees on stage)[20] are porous identities, already becoming molecular rather than holding on to their molar wholeness. With the exception of the elevated 'hero', the others spring instantaneously from a more indistinct choratic multiplicity. Characters appear as instances of individuation in an everlasting perpetually changing chorus in variation; a chorus of bodies moved by the constitutive power of desire, endlessly at war with the State apparatus, which tries to silence their song with buckets of sand and gradually oversized fire extinguishers. The bodies of the performers appear always in excess of the representation of characters at the same time as that reference is made implicitly or explicitly known. This is the sense of the choratic whence actors are constantly in flux between the characters they assume and the BwO they spring from and fall back on to, a choral body that doesn't sing with their voices but encapsulates the Dionysian energies that gave rise to the 'goat song' to begin with.

It is this game of diastole and systole that creates the rhythm of the performance and Fabre works very precisely as a director/ operator who constantly negotiates the balance of those forces in the unfolding of the landscape in time. The structure of the performance approximates a rhizomatic 'form' more akin to the non-arborescent model that Deleuze and Guattari are proposing in *A Thousand Plateaus*. Each 'plateau' of this landscape might spring from a specific mythic character but is allowed to take flight and deterritorialize in such a way that endless points of connections

– 'circuits, conjunctions, levels and thresholds, passages and distributions of intensity' (2007: 177) – exist between the 'plateaus' themselves (as well as other milieus and 'planes of consistency', inside the theatre and out). And this rhizomatic and molecular structure of the performance allows for intensities and energies that are marginalized within the tragedy itself to enter the new landscape (Athena, Dionysus, Epimetheus and Pandora). Pandora as a force of desire is 'curbed' in the Hesiodic myth but arguably even more so in the Aeschylean tragedy. In Hesiod's *Theogony*, Pandora is very much related to female sexuality and an array of miasmatic associations inferred through the ideological prism of Greek patriarchy. Fabre and Olyslaegers re-introduce her into the landscape and give her the last word. She is 'the all-giver'.

'Io' is one of those characters that we can recognize from the tragedy and she comes in direct opposition to the elevated heroic figure. Io's presence and monologue too offer a critique on a patriarchal society that has been permeated by the 'ethics' of a phallogocentric order – the State with its religious, moral and legalizing institutions, which normalize desire. Yet it is in her performance and the transgressive excess of her physicality that she punctures the institutionalized code of representation in a theatre that is driven by the rules of moderation and 'safety'[21] on all different levels.

The gadflies that pursue and torture her take on the form of religious figures who ritualistically inflict very precise stings with sharp axes[22] and absolute coldness. The corporeal excess that is forced out of her every pore in the same way that spit escapes her mouth in the intensity of the moment is nothing but real. The stage becomes a space of a suffering female body (one that doesn't have to be dressed 'in men's clothes in order to enter the pantheon of heroes', as we hear in Fabre's prologue), an Artaudian 'tree-body' or 'pure body' as Van den Dries defines 'the body in its most pure and material form' that 'can only be achieved through pain and suffering, a process of disintegration and disruption' (Crombez and Gronau 2010: 41). There is a purely intense materiality in the production of her sounds and how this corporeal excess and the attack on the senses affects the audience. And it is interesting that this happens through a mediation of the voice[23] that engulfs the audience's bodies (ears among other organs) with its amplified seismic vibrations. Every spasm, every moan and growling drenched in the anxiety of 'pain' or the anticipation of a blow, every scream, every pause joins her every word and they are all exerting axe-like blows to our own participatory senses. There is no escape for either us or her. Her act of arson is both a matter and a form of expression. The landscape furthermore proves to be a multiplicity once more; the audience a distanced observer as well as an immersed wanderer.

Fabre's [Tragic] Body without Organs: An 'encounter'

We see what Deleuze refers to as 'a figure of the minority consciousness' not only through the excessively affective corporeality in the performance of 'Io' (and the other performers) as opposed to the static concreteness of the heroic symbol, but also through the liminality inherent in the process of becoming. When rhythms and intensities are allowed to exceed the strata of dramatic representation, the sign is in a process of 'becoming' rather than a state of assignment and recognition; desire as a possible vector of deterritorialization (or a line of flight) becomes a constitutive force in the encounter as the Body-without-Organs of the performer becomes another landscape whereupon the war machine wages their battle against the elements of power in the theatre; those that insure 'both the coherence of the subject in question and the coherence of representation on stage' (Deleuze in Murray 1997: 241).

In *Non-Representational Theory: Space, Politics, Affect*, Thrift questions the nature of the sign as a relationship between the signifier and the signified and supports that an alternative, more productive understanding would conceive of the sign coming 'into being *when thought is thrown into crisis* because the reassuring world of representation has broken down' (Marks in Thrift 2007: 115, my italics). As Laura Cull clearly explains, Deleuze also argues that objects of recognition

'do not disturb thought' insofar as they provide thought with 'an image of itself'; they reaffirm for thought, in other words, what it already thinks it knows. For Deleuze, instances of recognition do not involve genuine thought. We only 'truly think' when we have difficulty in recognizing something. (Cull 2009: 250)

Theatre can be experienced as 'an encounter rather than as an act of recognition' in the same way that the sign comes into being when thought 'is thrown into crisis'.

Fabre is using the 'landscape' as a way of allowing the original text to produce what Deleuze calls a 'fundamental encounter' (2001: 139) by revitalizing and subverting the codes of clichéd representation in a process of polarization and disfiguration, which nevertheless retains its connections to the strata that it deterritorializes and thus allows for a space of ceaseless variation to exist in the in-between. By creating a liminal space in the co-existence and the continuum between information and affect, through the minorization of the dramatic text into a BwO, he puts our minds in a state of crisis, which is already always constitutive of genuine thought.

The ritualistic manner in which the performance is stylized pays tribute to its origins and opens up the continuum between the pre- and the post-tragic, essentially always extracting those transgressive energies and intensities that belong to the 'tragic' proper; the lines of flight that exist (however 'curbed') within the myth and the dramatic text take over in diastolic movements of disfiguration *but not* incomprehensibility exactly because of the fact that Fabre doesn't 'wildly deterritorialize' with no connections to the strata.[24] Deleuze and Guattari make it clear that dismantling 'the organism' does not mean obliterating it:

> You have to keep enough of the organism for it to reform each dawn; and you have to keep small supplies of signifiance and subjectification, if only to turn them against their own systems when the circumstances demand it [...] and you have to keep small rations of subjectivity in sufficient quantity to enable you to respond to the dominant reality. (2007: 178)

The mind is made to participate into the transgressive and transformative act of approaching its limits because it is presented with a carefully organized/composed space that uses those 'organs' that were hitherto in the service of 'drama' in the tragedy as loci of deformation; however, in this continuum of ceaseless variation that creates the 'canvas whose function is to harness forces', Fabre does not completely obliterate the tragedy into an incomprehensible 'abstraction'; he uses it to re-invent the experience of the tragic. Discussing both of the landscapes, Decreus supports that in both instances the tragedy loses aspects of its tragic dimension because it is 'no longer conceived as a climactic plot and text [...] The dramatic action did not come to the expected end, but lingers on, without the traditional *Katharsis* and *peripeteia*' (2012: 142). I want to suggest that while the dramatic dimension is lost due to the minorization process that results in the rhizomatic staging, a 'new' sense of the tragic arises and along with it a possible reconceptualization of the all-important notions of catharsis and *peripeteia*: Fabre's 'tragic' is connected exactly to the 'lingering on'. He doesn't stage conflict in a way that it relates to action/plot, agon, reversal, etc. The conflict exists in the experience of the crisis that we undergo when representation and recognition no longer constitute the dominant mode of approaching theatre, and it is not so much as lack that we experience this as much as a constitutive potentiality.

Fabre's directorial adaptation is an example of those 'contemporary performances of ancient plays' that Erica Fisher-Lichte supports 'trigger a state of liminality' as well as one where the audience reception 'is always an active, creative and transformative process' (2010: 39–40). And this transformative process is inextricably linked to a re-imagination of catharsis. In 'A Future for Tragedy? Remarks on the Political and the Postdramatic' Lehmann supports that 'tragic experience is bound to a process where we are taken to the edge of normative and conceptual self-assurance, [...] [an] entering the twilight zone, where the sustainability of cultural norms which we adhere to is put into doubt' (2013: 99). The tragic seems to already always be connected to a state of liminality that is produced through a simultaneity, either in the inseparability of *phobos* and *eleos* (fear and pity) in the classic conception of the tragic or the unity of empathy and distance or the Hegelian *erschuttert/befriedigt*. Of course, here we are not discussing the creation of 'a deeper unity of the colliding opposites' that is imperative in the Hegelian ideal (2013: 92). It is in fact the disharmony that exists in the simultaneity that may prove productive and constitutive, a disharmony, then, that is not conceived as a 'lack' of harmony but as an affirmative force of production and creation. This conversion of the negative is what Nietzsche calls transmutation – 'the no stripped of its power, transformed into the opposite quality, turned affirmative and creative' (Deleuze 1983: 191). This is the ultimate way that the notion of 'catharsis' can be conceived of in Fabre's re-imagination of the tragic, not as 'moral sublimation and medical purging' in which the tragic is seen as 'the exercise of depressive passions and "reactive" feelings' (1983: 200), but as a non-teleo-logical process of affirmative and constitutive nature – one that opens up new ways of perceiving the world around us.

By decentring character, narrative, representation and recognition from the core of the performance, Fabre reaffirms the transgressive quality of the tragic as well as its affirmative and constitutive qualities. In this case, the 'constitution and loss of the self' are experienced, as the crisis of the mind in reception (of the 'unrecog-nizable' in terms of cognitive identification) is not (only) categorized as aesthetic but becomes a vital force of new cognitive explorations. This is yet an alternative way of looking at how the tragic still persists in its post-dramatic 'reincarnation' through this process of minorization. In this new reimagining of the tragedy, the closest we come to catharsis is through a process of purging our bodies of strictly cognitive and/or phenomenological ways of spectating and is a continuous process of re-configuring the brain in order 'to create new connections, new linkages, or vital "transmitters"' (Rajchman 2000: 136). The audience of Fabre's performance experience the simultaneity and multiplicity inherent in the diastolic forces of the 'landscape' and in doing so they almost learn to experience anew. They participate in the dismantling of the 'here/there', spectators to a theatrical event and wanderers/wonderers in the landscape, 'distanced' observers who 'lose themselves in it'.[25] In this sense Fabre also reinvents the narrative-related *peripeteia* into an experience that is more akin to the *peripatetic*.[26]

Fabre's 'minorization' of the tragic text is not only proof that tragedy is not dead (as heralded by Steiner [1961]), but it is re-imagined in such a way that it (re)connects to a choratic space; a space that is open enough to include its pre-dramatic roots as much as the reference to the banal, the everyday and the popular. This is the true power of Fabre's re-imagination of the tragedy: it does not obliterate the essence of the tragic in its critical reading and minorization of the Aeschylean text. It offers a new contemporary experience of the tragic as a new, transgressive, constitutive and affirmative in-between.

Bibliography

Amy, M. (2004) 'Measuring the Clouds: A Conversation with Jan Fabre'. *Sculpture* 23.2.

Artaud, A. (1976) *Selected Writings*, S. Sontag (ed.), H. Weaver (trans.). Berkeley: University of California Press. (555–74).

Bogue, R. (2003) *Deleuze on Music, Painting, and the Arts*. New York: Routledge.

Colebrook, C. (2002) *Gilles Deleuze*. London: Routledge.

Cull, L. (2009) 'How Do You Make Yourself a Theatre Without Organs? Deleuze, Artaud and the Concept of Differential Presence'. *Theatre Research International* 34.3: 243.

Cull, L. (2012) *Theatres of Immanence*. Houndmills UK: Palgrave Macmillan.

De Maeseneer, Y. (2003) 'Un Ange Passe ... A Conversation Between Theology and Aesthetics: The Case of Jan Fabre'. *Literature and Theology* 17.4: 374–87.

Decreus, F. (2010) 'Does a Deleuzean Philosophy of Radical Physicality Lead to the "Death of Tragedy"? Some Thoughts on the Dismissal of the Climactic Orientation of Greek Tragedy'. In E. Hall and S. Harrop (eds), *Theorising Performance: Greek Drama, Cultural History and Critical Practice*. London: Duckworth, 123–36.

Decreus, F. (2012) 'Jan Fabre's *Prometheus Landscape I* (1988) & *II* (2011), or How to Deal with Pain and Suffering in a Postdramatic, Postragic and Rhizomatic Landscape? Wisdom from Suffering Pain, Frenzy and Their Treatment in *Ancient Greek* Drama.' 11th International Symposium of Ancient Green Drama. ITI Cyprus, Nicosia, 6 July 2012.

Deleuze, G. (1983) *Nietzsche and Philosophy*. New York: Columbia University Press.

Deleuze, G. (2001) *Difference and Repetition*, P. Patton (trans.). London; New York: Continuum.

Deleuze, G. and Guattari, F. (2007). *A Thousand Plateaus*. Minneapolis: University of Minnesota Press.

Di Pietrantonio, G. (2009) *Jan Fabre: Homo Fabre*. Brussels: Fonds Mercator.

Fischer-Lichte, E. (2010) 'Performance as Event, Reception as Translation'. In E. Hall and S. Harrop (eds), *Theorising Performance: Greek Drama, Cultural History and Critical Practice*. London: Duckworth, pp. 29–42.

Fuchs, E. and Chaudhuri, U. (eds) (2002) *Land/Scape/Theatre*. Ann Arbor: University of Michigan Press.

Goebbels, H. (1997) 'Text as Landscape'. *Performance Research* 2.1: 61–5.

Lehmann, H. (1997) 'From Logos to Landscape: Text in Contemporary Dramaturgy'. *Performance Research* 2.1: 55–60.

Lehmann, H. (2006) *Postdramatic Theatre*. London: Routledge.

Lehmann, H. (2013). 'A Future for Tragedy? Remarks on the Political and the Postdramatic'. In J. Carroll, S. Giles and K. Jürs-Munby (eds), *Postdramatic Theatre and the Political*. London: Bloomsbury Methuem Drama, 87–109.

Murray, T. (1997) *Mimesis, Masochism, and Mime*. Ann Arbor: University of Michigan Press.

Rajchman, J. (2000) *The Deleuze Connections*. Cambridge, MA: The Massachusetts Institute of Technology Press.

Ruffell, I. (2012) *Aeschylus: Prometheus Bound*. Series *Companions to Greek and Roman Tragedy*. London: Bristol Classical Press.

Sidiropoulou, A. (2014) 'Adaptation, Re-contextualisation, and Metaphor: Auteur Directors and the Staging of Greek Tragedy'. *Adaptation* 8.1: 31–49.

Stalpaert, C. (2005) 'The Reconfigurative Power of Desire. Jan Fabre's *As Long as the World Needs a Warrior's Soul*'. *Arcadia International Journal for Literary Studies* 40.1: 177–93.

Stalpaert, C. (2009) 'A Dramaturgy of the Body'. *Performance Research* 14.3: 121–5.

Thrift, N. (2008) *Non-Representational Theory*. Abingdon: Routledge.

Truniger, F. (2013) *Filmic Mapping*. Berlin: Jovis.

Van Den Dries, L. (2010) 'Artaud and Fabre'. *Ritual and the Avant-Garde*, T. Crombez and B. Gronau (eds), special issue of *Documenta* 28.1: 36–45.

Velle, M. (2011) '"And Fuck You All Second Rate, Third Rate And Fourth Rate Psycho-Fuckers": Jan Fabre's "Prometheus Landscape II", or the Tragic Hero Dismantled'. In J. Nelis and F. Decreus, *Receptions of Antiquity*. Gent: Academia Press, 227–31.

Zavros, D. (2008) *Music-Theatre as Music: A Practical Exploration of Composing Theatrical Material Based on a Music-Centric Conceptualisation of Myth*. PhD thesis, University of Leeds.

9

Dionysus the destroyer of traditions: *The Bacchae* on stage

George Sampatakakis

The stage history of Euripides' *Bacchae* is significantly uncharacteristic of the reception of Greek drama. While Greek tragedy from the Renaissance onwards was considered a part of the European cultural heritage and was broadly adapted and staged (Burian 1997), Dionysus remained unwelcome until the beginning of the twentieth century. Euripides' descent from excellence – mainly in the anti-Euripidean nineteenth century (Michelini 2006: 3–10) – was due to his illustrations of *passions* (Schlegel 1894: 376) allegedly inappropriate for the educational mission of the classics and, consequently, for a decent audience, given also that the *Bacchae*, a play where male-ordered state is destroyed by frenzied women and an effeminate Eastern god, could not possibly be seen as properly Greek before the twentieth century. Even when Euripides' tragedies were used as model-plays for French and German neo-classicist writers, the ethics of the tragic heroines was drastically Christianized in order to comply with either Louis XIV's decorum, or Goethe's eclectic humanism.

On the contrary, the Dionysus of the *Bacchae* represents the 'unaccountable and the illogical' and, as a result, 'was anathema in the first part of the nineteenth century because it fitted so awkwardly with the whole sane and sanitized view of an ancient Greece based on simplicity and controlled reason' (Walton 2008: 192). Despite the intellectual climate, Euripides' *Medea*, for example, was broadly staged in the nineteenth century (Macintosh, 2000), precisely because an actor-specific play could not be regarded as inappropriate for the star-system theatre. Nonetheless, there are two serious parameters that should be taken into consideration regarding the absence of the *Bacchae* until its first modern re-performance in 1908. Firstly, in considering a very specific problem of exclusion, there should be a specific agenda of theatre, which has prevented the performance of the *Bacchae*, and, equally, there should have emerged a new function that the performance should fulfil when the 'ban' is raised. Nietzsche's redefinition of Dionysus as the perfect *coincidentia oppositorum* (Henrichs 1993: 27–31) that represents the hysterical and violent powers of the world, as well as voluptuousness and sensuality, played an important role in promoting the popularity of Dionysus, the Destroyer of theatre norms.

Secondly, when different socio-cultural needs necessitated a change in applied methods or systems of acting and directing, at the time when *Bacchae* became the model-tragedy for Cambridge Ritualists, this same play seemed to cover the gap in the tragic repertoire between the actor-specific plays and the new function of the theatre of the director. And this is my central proposition: the *Bacchae* is a play for the theatre of the twentieth and twenty-first centuries, that is to say for the theatre of the *mise-en-scène* beyond psychological characterization and closer to the modern ritualization of theatre. Additionally, with regard to the play's popularity after the 1960s, Fischer-Lichte (2014: 4–12) underlines the topicality of the play's analogies to modern history regarding mainly the outburst of politically motivated violence. In my view, this can be explained further by the play's own plot-pattern. The *Bacchae* has a structural typicality (destruction of order/rebirth of new order), which was readily available for artists to be used as a political metaphor: Dionysus came to Thebes to destroy the aristocratic state of Pentheus, liberating the oppressed and threatening stable social normalities. As a result, a new political structure was established after the transgression and subsequent broadening of borders.

In a different vein, Fischer-Lichte (2014: xiv) relates the popularity of the *Bacchae* to the process of globalization and its socio-cultural consequences, namely the productive transgression and subsequent re-definition of borders between different cultures following the increasing number of encounters between their members. Nonetheless, one can adopt a very critical stance against the characterization of Dionysus as the 'God of Globalization' in a 'global village' where 'one culture meet[s] those of others, and they adapt to each other' (225), since the destruction of an oppressive establishment is inevitable in the *Bacchae*.

The aim of this chapter is to map out indicative stage usages of the *Bacchae* according to a typology of theatre directing, which spans from mere archaeological reconstructions to post-modern utilizations (Pavis 2007: 206–11). For most directors, the *Bacchae* provided a certain topicality of subject matter from which some present-day analogies emerged, thus historicizing the play. The aesthetic result of this process varies not only because it is historically and culturally specific, but also because a personal style is always involved. There have also been many cultural usages of the *Bacchae*, in fact usurpations (Sampatakakis 2015: 398–9), like Kathakali-*Bacchae* or Beijing Opera *Bacchae*, exactly as any classical Western play was tested, sometimes by trial and error, in Eastern performance traditions. Not surprisingly, we have seen the Bacchae dancing like ecstatic Sufis (Kneehigh Theatre, Truro, 2004), or singing superbly like a gospel choir (National Theatre of Scotland, Edinburgh Festival, 2007). In any case, the performance history of a play is the history of its transformations, unrestrained from any allegedly incontestable or inalienable meaning; it is a history documenting the death of authenticity.

Archaeological reconstructions and the desire for authenticity

At the beginning of the twentieth century, the prevailing demand was that classics must be reinterpreted for the stage in the spirit of our time, and the *Bacchae* was meant to play a decisive role in determining the new function of performance. On 10 November 1908, during a matinee performance at the Royal Court in London, an audience witnessed the resurrection of Euripides' *Bacchae* after a silence of two and a half millennia.[1] All surviving evidence suggests that the Royal Court production, directed by William Poel, was not readily conceived as a revival, but rather as a reconstruction of Greek theatre aesthetics. This was mainly due to the intellectual support and authority of Professor Gilbert Murray, who was the driving force behind the Royal Court production, suggesting to Lillah McCarthy, who played Dionysus, the *Bacchae* for her matinee performance. But Murray's dramaturgical advice was somewhat artistically restrictive, as shown in his correspondence with the director and the actress.[2]

Murray suggested that the actress and the director should first look at the vases in the British Museum in order to get an authentic vision of the Greek dress (MSS 14.37, 14 October 1908), and also proposed a way to understand Dionysus as a proto-Christian martyr (MSS 10.37, 10 October 1908):

> Try to imagine what the story of some persecuted Christian saint or missionary would be. Pentheus is a tyrant and a persecutor, Dionysus a holy and sanctified being; but when this holy being has his will, his full revenge, he seems infinitely worse than his prosecutor.

Judging from the surviving photographs in London's Theatre Museum, Dionysus was portrayed as a guiltless martyr with a pervasive Carravagian innocence of a woman loosely holding the thyrsus, and the critic of *The Times* (19 November 1908) supports this view:

> It can be imagined how compelling a figure Miss Lillah McCarthy looks with the ivy and grapes in her hair, and the flame-coloured tunic under her tiger-skin, a strange Eastern god full of grace and beauty, and of a subtle perfume-like charm.

Still, the emotional passivity of the spectacle was eased off by a stylized way of dramatic delivery with invasive rich sounds (MSS 14.106, 14 October 1908).

The proscenium-stage that was draped in purple, with steps in front (McCarthy 1934: 294), proved extremely restricting, and Poel had to separate the chorus into four Sirens (Chorus in the

programme) and three dancing coryphées (Dancers) so as to avoid
a traffic jam:

> I have four stately women with deep-toned voices whom I call
> 'the Sirens' and will wear a dull grey Hellenic costume. Their
> duty is to take the more solemn passages and to strike the note
> of irreversible fate. Then I have three Coryphées in pale helio-
> trope who will dance and sing the gayer chorus speeches. (MSS
> 14.212, 25 October 1908)

Undeniably, the production was of a 'highly static nature'
(Macintosh 2007: 158) with the chorus only moving once during
the performance.

Furthermore, Poel had some extremely interesting ideas about
the play, aiming to contrast the visual with the acoustic effect, so
that the spectator could experience the pre-expressive pitilessness
of a pagan spectacle:

> If the play comes out as I would like it to come out, I want the
> audience to be looking at a Greek vase full of repose, dignity,
> and grace – and then by means of the story and the word to
> grasp *through the brain and not through the eye* the Pagan
> pitilessness of it all. (MSS 14.212–13, 25 October 1908, my
> emphasis)

Poel's work seems to move against the visual sensationalism of
naturalist theatre towards a more logocentric idea of theatre where
the text is verbalized according to the dramatic character, and
intended not only for aesthetic reception, but also for ideological
consumption. The main drawback was that the text was irrevocably
trapped into a visual environment that aimed to emit an authentic
Greekness, despite the 'Christian' tones of the translation (Perris
2012: 31). But by the time Poel started to achieve a wider artistic
interest in the play, outside Murray's authentic Greek vision, the
latter had already prohibited a third performance on the ground
that 'It was not Greek and it was not Euripides' (MSS 15, 9
November 1908).

During the twentieth century there were several productions that
maintained a nostalgic reference to archaic aesthetics, strangely
combined with an extreme psychological realism. This was not

necessarily an aesthetic, but a cultural demand, fomenting ethnic fantasies and introversions (mainly in Modern Greece). The 1962 National Theatre's Modern Greek première of the *Bacchae* in Epidaurus proves, in conclusion, that realist approaches were mainstream for more than half of a century: 'Paxinou in Agave's part is overwhelming; she forces the spectator to participate in her horrifying lament by expressing all of its human truth, devastated nonetheless by her fortune' (review in the newspaper *Kathimerini*, 19 June 1962).

Theatricalization, ritualization and new structures

Sex and revolution

The Performance Group's *Dionysus in 69* (The Performance Garage, New York, 1968), directed by Richard Schechner, is monumental, precisely because in this production 'the god of theatre performed the dismemberment of the theatre in its old, traditional form so that it could be reborn in a new shape and function' (Fischer-Lichte 2014: 46). In Schechner's production the text of the *Bacchae* was appropriated according to his theories about an Environmental Theatre that would challenge aestheticist theatre and the conventional 'expectation–obligation network' (Schechner 1968: 43) between the spectacle and the spectator. As the director pointed out:

> Environment can be understood in two different ways. First, there is what one can do with and in a space; secondly, there is the acceptance of a given space. In the first case, one *creates* an environment by transforming a space; in the second case, one *negotiates* with an environment, engaging in a scenic dialogue with a space. (Schechner 1968: 50)

As Fischer-Lichte (2014: 31) notes, a new type of acting emerged in as much as 'performing meant undergoing a rite of passage that might lead to a new individual identity', creating thereby 'in-between identities' (33), given that, first, the actor's identity was not concealed behind a dramatic character and, second, the performers wrote their own lines, even if the Euripidean text was underlying the script of the performance. In fact, the script organized the actions of the performers, as if they were participating in a secular ritual that retells the story of Dionysus linearly, incorporating the sexual and anti-war aesthetics of the 1960s. Most importantly, Schechner (1994: 40) sought to *break down* the performance into a *social event*, where the spectators were expected to join in at one point or another, as if they were participating in 'a kind of new Mass' (43), thus experiencing a type of communality.

The Environmental director worked with a very concrete method in creating the *mise-en-scène*, mainly as a way to incorporate *found* elements (personal stories, life experiences, fantasies, workshop material) into the given text. This was primarily a de-aestheticization technique of including *real life* into drama, not in terms of thematic analogies, but in terms of the play's *temporal coexistence* with the real world (Schechner 1994: 290–1). The steps followed included: (1) free workshop; (2) introduction of the text, in order for the Group to acquire an awareness of certain themes; (3) introduction of the project (an agreement on which things are brought in and which are kept out according to the themes and the environment); (4) construction of the environment and attribution of roles; (5) organization of a script; (6) open rehearsals to test out the performance; (7) construction of a *score*, that is, the concretization of 'the exact physical actions, musical tones, and rhythms that embody the themes and moods of the production' (ibid.: 290–5, 294).

One of the main functional elements of the performance was the creation of an iconography based on nakedness, violence and rituality, all anchored to contemporary pop aesthetics and politics (hippies, Vietnam, May 1968, sexual revolution). Early in the performance the birth of Dionysus was enacted in a birth ritual modelled after the adoption ritual of the Asmats of New Guinea. Five naked men lay side by side on the floor, while five women stepped over them with open legs, leaning slightly forward so that their bodies formed a tunnel representing the birth canal. Inevitably, the ritual assumed the severe erotic connotations of a liberated community in action.

The death ritual was also indicative of the aesthetics of the performance. In a reversed version of the birth ritual, women with splayed legs were holding up their blood-stained hands, thus creating a death canal for Pentheus to enter. In this manner, 'Pentheus was symbolically swallowed by the community that [...] he had tried to dominate' (Fischer-Lichte 2014: 42). But iconography for Schechner, even if symbols looked tribal in inspiration, was politically inclined, a version of Brecht's de-familiarization effect (Schechner 1994: 310, my emphasis):

> Just after the women kill Pentheus [...], they freeze. The grimaces of the murdering mothers are not different from the agonies of the murdered sons. It is hard to tell whose blood is whose. The whole grizzly scene is from *Vietnam* or *Auschwitz*. After a freeze of about five seconds the women drop the limbs of the men and rush into the audience bragging of 'this great deed I have done'.

Dionysus in 69 remains a revolution in itself, as it was the first production to feel the sexual suggestions inbuilt in the text. Only after this performance did a 'gay' Dionysus and the exposure of the naked body become fashionable, almost mainstream, for the *Bacchae*. Accordingly, the Performance Group played an essential role in promoting the American movement for sexual liberation and freedom of speech:

> PENTHEUS: What specifically do you want me to do?
>
> DIONYSUS: Specifically, I want you to take off my shirt and my pants and my underwear. Then I want you to caress my body all over. I want you to caress it very slowly and carefully. And then I want you to caress my cock until it gets hard. And then I want you to take my cock in your mouth and caress it with your lips and your tongue and your teeth. I want you to suck on my cock. Bill, I want you to suck my cock. (Schechner 1970: n.p.)

Dionysus in 69 was an all-powerful spectacle that shockingly challenged theatrical traditions, leaving, for some, a 'horrifying imprint' (DeBroske 1968: 13), thus making a strong political statement against all types of conventionalism and conservativism:

> The breakdowns of lovingness into viciousness call for control. If that control suppresses them both we have a conservative

society or theatre. If it stimulates and uses them, a fascist society or theatre. In this show, the gently permissive cool lovingness of the hippie [...] has created [...] a fascist type of universe, a situation structured by oppression and repression, by the stimulation of basic emotions coerced into fake non-liberative [...] expression, in the service of a collective enterprise of propaganda [...]. (Brecht 1969: 163)

Ritualization and cultural imbalances

Several years later, political readings remained mainstream. Theodoros Terzopoulos' arena was always post-traditionalist Europe, in which classical texts were emancipated from the terrorist assumptions of authenticity (Rabkin 2002: 324–8), and his *Bacchae* (Delphi, 1986) was a political statement against Modern Greek aesthetic normalities. Terzopoulos is a director of Brechtian descent with heavy influences from Meyerhold's constructivism. In his theatre the body of the actor is the main priority. At the outset, Terzopoulos accepts the hypothesis that the actor's body exists in a condition of resistance unable to recognize repressed abilities and memories, a condition properly termed by Grotowski (1969: 17) as 'passive readiness'. This key phase in Terzopoulos' method sets out the fundamentality of the body in recovering pre-expressive behaviour in order to create a new theatrical self. This strategy aims at the de-culturation of the body from its daily signification by means of a de-familiarization of the movement, and anti-realist abstraction: the daily body is restored into an artificialized body, which uses constructed Gestus as signs of a symbolic code that possesses 'some of the ceremonial quality of a religious rite' (Artaud 1976: 221).

The stage of the production consisted of a cyclical platform fastened to the ground by centrifugally attached pieces of rag that together produced the effect of a spinning, air leaving space. The entire spectacle was spatially constructed so that it was impossible to escape from the circle, an organic part of which were the actors themselves. The kinesiology of the performance demanded a symphonic movement keeping for every actor a certain agreement with the collective. In the opening scene, Dionysus (A. Sakellariou) was depicted as a warrior dancing the military dance of *bunomai*.

His hand was cleaving the air horizontally in a mimesis of both epileptic abandonment and the Japanese *bugaku* dancer. The movements were broad and strong amid slow, solemn simulations of battle movements: he was beating the sand-covered floor with his feet in a semi-squatting posture, both pointing his spear to the audience in a ritualistic march, and stretching each foot out slowly to the front. What is more, Dionysus was geometrically paired off with Pentheus (D. Siakaras), who danced the antistrophic dance. As in the ancient Japanese *bugaku*, the dances followed each other in pairs, that is, the dance on the left was followed by the dance on the right, the dance of Pentheus being the 'answer dance' (*kotaemai*).

Pentheus from the beginning until the end was presented as powerless and exposed to the authority of ecstasy. Directly noticeable was that female traits in Dionysus' and Pentheus' appearance were invisible. All emphasis was laid on the power imbalance between the expressive body of the God and the impassive body of the disbelievers. Agave, on the contrary, was designed as a cacophony detached from the circle, virtually motionless and vertical only. The Gestus of speechlessness during the recognition scene, where she holds the head of Pentheus (in fact an empty head-mask) in front of her own forehead, was emotionally effective. Agave seemed to have completely lost the perception of her own identity, a fact that was theatricalized first in her *aphonia*, and second in the visual confusion produced by the coexistence of two faces with one pair of eyes. *Spastic* or *paralytic aphonia* is a condition that causes vocal stuttering, as voice comes out in the form of bursts with vocal spasms, due to emotional stress (Angell 2009: 161). The vocal chords only move back and forth rapidly in response to air pressure from the lungs and, if this movement is extensive enough to set air above the vocal folds, vocalization occurs. Amazingly enough, this is what we saw in Terzopoulos' Agave: the spasms of the affected subject in her struggle to make a meaning out of an identity-threatening experience, that is, the involuntary and inconceivable infanticide, 'no longer obeying the principles of a logocentric staging and representation' (Decreus 2012: 300).

Terzopoulos' references to political and cultural histories (Greek civil war, folk rituals) voiced the otherness within Greek historicity. Instead of the heroic grandeur, the glamorous 'continuity', or the archaic emblems, Terzopoulos digs out the most violated bodies of history. The internalized violence of cultural defeat was thereby portrayed as an inseparable part of Greekness, disturbing at once the historic harmony of *Sprechchor*, or the splendour of a frozen Greek civilization.

The aesthetics and 'technologies' of ritual often include destabilization of established cultural structures and transition to new orders. The productions discussed above prove quite undeniably that the ritualization of the *Bacchae* was crucial in transforming theatre-directing into an art form that both criticizes sociopolitical normalities and generates new aesthetic and cultural possibilities.

Historicization and productive 'unfaithfulness'

Colonial endeavours

Soyinka's Yoruba *Bacchae* (London, 1973) is indeed an ideological adaptation of the Euripidean tragedy. The Nigerian Nobel Prize holder politicized the text drastically, offering thereby a humanist allegory. Soyinka introduced some changes, which mainly refer to the issues of slavery and revolution as a liberation of the oppressed, as well as the problem of establishing a new social structure through the ritual sacrifice of the head of the state. Soyinka's 'counter-hegemonic moves' centre his adaptation in Yoruba culture and politics (Okpewho 1999: 38). These are immediately identifiable in the image of the skeletal remains of the crucified slaves, suggestive of the mass executions that took place on Bar Beach after the Biafran civil war. Historicization is also noticeable in the attitudes of Pentheus and Cadmus, who could be echoing the military leaders of Nigeria, from whom Soyinka had fled. Nonetheless, the writer created a more humanist image of Dionysus, and, in substituting Ogun for Dionysos, he transformed the ending into a Eucharist communion rite during which Pentheus' head is transmuted into a fountain of blood (that is transubstantiated into wine), thus depicting the unification of the community as a result of the tyrant's sacrifice. But this optimism is not left uncomplicated due to the discordant resonance of Agave's lamentation.

This is indeed a productive adaptation strategy which again uses the plot-pattern of the *Bacchae* (destruction of order / rebirth of a new order) as a political statement on social possibilities:

> Pentheus really dies like Christ for the good of humankind; his head becomes a fountain of blood turned into wine, a 'barbaric banquet' (Soyinka 1974: x) reminiscent of the Catholic Mass. This ritual allows each celebrant to be unified with each other and with their god. It is an ending that links the Greek Dionysos with Ogun and Jesus and links Dionysian rites and Christian rituals with carrier and scapegoat purifications for the New Year in Nigeria. Although Soyinka justifies this choice as a way to underscore the play's totality – 'a celebration of life, bloody and tumultuous, an extravagant rite of the human and social psyche' (x) – he has created a ritual that has no antecedent in Europe or Nigeria. Perhaps this is a fitting humanistic intercultural move on the playwright's part. (Nouryeh 2001: 166)

The actual production of the British National Theatre in 1973 failed to accept the primarily African investments of the text, namely the Egungun aesthetics: '[i]n the production the African was almost completely left out' (Fischer-Lichte 2014: 62). Moreover, the National Theatre production can be perfectly seen as a post-imperialist piece of salvage ethnography: '[t]he cultural revolution brought about by the play itself provoked a counter-revolution performed by the production. It denounced the transformative, liberating, and communal feast celebrated in the play as a barbaric ritual of some "primitive tribes" to be laughed at with a mixture of amusement and disdain' (ibid: 64).

The death of traditional theatre in Europe

Klaus Michael Grüber's *Bacchae* (Berlin, 1974) was one of Schaubühne's first post-Brechtian attempts to stage Greek plays and to rediscover the long-lost connection with Greek antiquity. The actual performance did not take place at the Schaubühne am Halleschen Uffer theatre, but at an exhibition hall (Phillips-Pavillon) on the Berliner Fairground. The first political statement of the *Antikenprojekt* was already made obvious by displacing the performing space of an ancient play to a multinational company's exhibition space: Greek tragedy was ready for renegotiation under new socio-economical conditions. Accordingly, Grüber 'not only broke with the conventions of staging classical dramas prevalent from the 1950s onwards, but he also defied those norms newly established after the 1960s by the so-called *Regietheater* [...] that was accused of demolishing the classics' (Fischer-Lichte 2014: 100). In doing so, the director presented the past as un-authentic in the sense that 'what remains are only fragments, play texts torn out of their original context, which cannot convey their original meaning' (Fischer-Lichte 1999: 16).

The very shape of the stage – a wide right-angled white area with four glass apertures on the back wall, as if a screen or a canvas – duplicated too the effect of fragmented vision. The play was seen projected upon a white 'screen' on the back of which alien images mingled with the 'ancient' visitors: the man with the tuxedo holding a champagne glass, the two horses, the operators of the road-sweeping machine. Thus, a major iconographic confusion was produced in so far as strains of past images (a Dionysus, a Pentheus), identified as such by their lines, were adjusted upon an updated backdrop as something extremely far off and ill-matched. Or, as Remshardt (1999: 37) argued, 'Unruly Nature and technological Order flanked Civilization'.

In the opening scene, Dionysus (M. Köning) holding a red high-heeled shoe was pushed on to the stage on a hospital gurney under the music of Stravinsky's *Apollon musagète*. A diseased image imported from the past, he was naked, except for a G-string in the form of male genitals, the same that Pentheus wore. Dionysus, looking confused and misplaced, began the Prologue stuttering, then repeating the words *Ich ... ich ... ich*, until he finally found his way to the unfamiliar text: *Ich ... ich ... ich ... bin Dionysos?* Caressing the red shoe, he started masturbating until he finally fell down off the trolley. And during his first encounter with Pentheus (B. Ganz), the elusive god was kissed in the mouth by the curious young ruler.

The Parodos is considered to be monumental in European theatre aesthetics. The chorus, all dressed differently, made their entrance from the opening side wall amid blowing wind and flying leaves. They came to inspect and rectify the 'new' space with surgical concentration and calmness: they ripped off the wooden floor boards, started a fire, dug out water, ivy, grapes, wool, a mask, and suddenly, following this neo-Dionysian picture of miracles, two men – Cadmus and Tiresias – were born from earth covered with mud and clay. In this way, the chorus came to reveal a new world that was suppressed under the wooden floor of civilization, a world that was earth-born exactly like the ancestor of Thebes, the earth-born Echion. But miracles are unsuitable for the civilized world, so the road-sweeping machines came to clean up the mess.

It is obvious that Grüber was not interested in interpreting the play, but in theatre itself as an *unmistakably performative art* and interventionist "political" institution' (Fischer-Lichte 2014: 110, my emphasis). The reaction to the production was split between the leftists' and the right wingers' reception, as is usually the case in radical political productions. Reinhard Baumgart in the *Süddeutsche Zeitung* (16/17 February 1974) was *frightened* by the lack of pathos in Grüber's *Bacchae*, given that pathos, the basic element of theatre, conveys either *Ausdruck* or *Leiden* both absent from the performance. Günther Rühle (1974: 14) questioned the truthfulness of the spectacle, in as much as the performance looked like 'exercises for the actors who don't care about the audience', according to Georg Hensel (quoted in Remshardt 1999: 41). But a more careful reviewer, Benjamin Henrichs, offered a good response: the production 'does not argue or narrate the play as an argument, but only takes it as a point of departure for very primitive theatre dreams that seem impermeable to argumentative attacks' (quoted in Remshardt 1999: 42).

Trying to characterize the relationship between text and performance in Grüber's production, Fischer-Lichte (2014: 109), instead of the previously used terms 'deconstruction' and 'dissolution' (Rühle, 1993: 208), chose the term *sparagmos*: 'something seemingly whole is torn apart and the question is how the scattered pieces can be restored to the former – or a new – wholeness'. Accordingly, the Greek play could be critically experienced by the spectators as a sign of the 'fundamental strangeness and inaccessibility of the distant past' (Fischer-Lichte 2014: 111), and perhaps its invalidity, since the images of the past lacked any type of *Werktreue* quality (Kaiser 1975: 14).

The Marxist Bacchae

Tadashi Suzuki is another director who politicized the *Bacchae*, training his actors according to his own personal method of acting. The essential purpose of Suzuki's method is for the body to revert to its previous 'cultural' self, 'before the theatre [had] acquired its codified performing styles' (Suzuki 1995: 155). The body is the carrier of culture, and essentially culture *is* the body. Suzuki's cultural optimism with regard to the actor's body rediscovering its lost, traditionally Japanese, self contradicts his pessimism regarding the teleology of history. Liberation from the chains of non-animal civilization is replaced in performance by a pessimistic restoration of those forces that deprived the actor's body of its cultural self, namely oppressive political and cultural establishment. Fischer-Lichte (2014: 169) sees this as

> the double-edged character of Suzuki's theatre – the attempt to develop a theatre aesthetics rooted in the human body as the common ground of all cultures [...] while exposing the cyclical nature of political history as a repeated clash of cultures leading to death and destruction.

Suzuki's *Bacchae* (Tokyo, 1978) was performed as a play-within-a-play, following Brecht's technique in the *Antigonemodell* (1948), where the story of Antigone was used in order to present 'the role of force' and resistance 'in the collapse of the head of the state' (Brecht 1978: 210). The basic story of the *Bacchae* was used as a fantasy-solution expressing the hopes and aspirations of the oppressed people by making Dionysus the symbol of a Liberator God for all those deprived of their freedom. In a desperate and futile attempt to take revenge on their tyrant, a group of slaves performed the *Bacchae*. But at the end, the tyrant comes back from the dead in a 'nightmarish vision' of the 'brutal fact' repeated ever since the beginning of history: the festive liberation is cruelly crushed down by a despot (SCOT 1985: 13), as history proves the teleology of cruelty. For Suzuki, the conflict between Dionysus and Pentheus was not a battle between god and man, but the drama of conflict between two communal value systems that exist on the same social axis.

As a Japanese director, Suzuki was not interested in staging a Western play in the *Shingeki* way (that is, staging it in the manner following European lines). Instead, the director composed and staged his own original piece by enculturating a Western play with the use of traditional Japanese techniques. Suzuki's adaptation technique is reminiscent of two kinds of compositional devices common to Japanese literature: *honkadori* ('taking a foundation poem') and *sekai* ('world') (Goto 1989: 108). Greek tragedy, the foundation text, is projected upon modern times, that is, any despotic regime in the case of the *Bacchae*. The influences of Noh and Kabuki can also be observed in movements and gestures in Suzuki's productions: larger-than-life motionless poses, effortless glide, valorous samurai-like stretching of the legs, rhythmic circular movements and marches that intensify the essence of an emotion.

There have been numerous versions and re-adaptations of Suzuki's *Bacchae* from 1978 to 2008 (McDonald 1992: 59–73, 1994; Carruthers and Takahashi 2004: 154–79; Sampatakakis 2005: 211–20; Fischer-Lichte 2014: 159–85). The 1981 Toga production with the ruthless Japanese Dionysus (S. Kayoko) confronting an American Pentheus (T. Hewitt) is imperative for the stage reception of the play. Suzuki is not a utopian and he knows perfectly well that history has the power to recycle itself. That was obvious in his *Bacchae*, where Pentheus/Man/West survived the *sparagmos* and was resurrected at the end to reinstate the civilization of oppression: *This is too much to suffer from women*, Suzuki's American Pentheus contested.

Directing the classics from the 1960s onwards meant using the text as *Material*, thus broadening the range of hermeneutic possibilities. The activation of a new meaning through the injection of present-day aesthetic and cultural elements (not necessarily in the sense of thematic analogies) gave rise to an uncontrollable dimensionality of the classics, permanently rejecting their unproductive confinement to textual fidelity. Accordingly, the *Bacchae* played a key role in promoting this new function of theatre as a self-governed performative art.

Post-modernism or not?

The premiere of Matthias Langhoff's *Bacchae* (1997), commissioned by the National Theatre of Northern Greece, with the rampant audience of Thessaloniki shouting 'Outrage!' at the Theatro Dassous is from one perspective indicative of chauvinistic panic. Langhoff came to Greece and built up a new topos of Thebes, a topos where culture is non-existent, bringing this time from the West the ambitions of a Dionysus destroyer of the local household. The exposed male genitals, the lesbian chorus, the colonist Agave who speaks dodgy Greek, the street-market aesthetics of souvenirs, all constitute references that critically challenged Modern Greek normality.

Langhoff's *Bacchae* is a production where the 'authentic' meaning and the expected 'authentic' elements of the text were drastically replaced by new ones, so that the only available term one could think of is *post-cultural* and, in a sense, post-authentic:

> This 'national' relationship you have with the Greek classical authors is not valid for me. I'm outside all this, because I'm not familiar with this relationship. And I see the *Bacchae* without this 'background', like a clean play, like a clean story. (Langhoff 1997)

And as Pavis points out, the postcultural applies 'to the postmodern imagination, which tends to view any cultural act as a quotation or restructuring of already known elements' (Pavis 1992: 20–1).

The director employed a very concrete method based on the montage of contradictory Kitsch images, mainly drawn from Modern Greek culture. The resultant iconography was produced by means of an ironic, in fact parodic, gaze on Modern Greece as a source of low folk-aesthetics:

> It is obvious that I am against what is called 'good taste', because this concept does not exist. It is just a 'cultural phobia'. But I cannot say the same thing for aesthetic values. My education is associated with the visual arts and I have good knowledge of European culture. Therefore, in each of my productions one element comes from here, and the other comes from there. (Langhoff 1997)

The performance started with the bull-like naked Dionysus (M. Hadjisavvas) in a doggy position 'landing' onstage with an ugly three-horned mask covering his head. As he recited the

Prologue, he slowly started to stand on his two feet imitating in a way the 'evolution' from the four-legged animal to the standing *Homo erectus*. As he was taking the mask off, the new topography of Thebes appeared. A butcher's shop with hung pieces of meat occupied the left side, while an elevated platform imitated the scenery of a Greek *kafenio* (coffee shop) on the right. What was immediately noticeable was the lack of attractiveness. Dionysus' allusive beauty was replaced by an image of a beer-bellied naked Dionysus with messed hair and snake-skin painted face, who after the Prologue wore a hideous turquoise suit. Langhoff's portrayal of Dionysus' masculinity is a metaphor of a culture-specific attitude. The butch Dionysus inside the butcher's Thebes looked like a neo-Greek 'toughie' inside a transvestite culture. His snake-skin face and his turquoise suit resulted from a major post-cultural amalgamation of opposites in the sense that there was no distinguishable culture in this hybrid of Dionysus. However, the animality of the face and the 1980s tastelessness of the suit, as well as the transition from the naked bull-god to the clothed macho stranger, both connoted an image of a trans-cultural Greek masculinity: the old and the new in a synthesis of opposites potentially cancelling each other out. Thebes was further identified as Hellenic, inbetween classical antiquity and Byzantine Orthodoxy, by the folkloric symbols of the small Orthodox oil-lamps, the icons hung with offerings and the big Brechtian placard writing 'KITHAIRON WATER'. Accordingly, Langhoff argued: 'There is a peculiar osmosis between archeologists and the Greek Orthodox Church. Both attempt to restore the sacredness of these ruins, yet through the prism of Orthodoxy' (*Ta Nea*, 18 August 1997).

Langhoff's chorus was another kitsch-pastiche creation and highly indicative of his 'idiosyncratic style' (van Steen 2013: 511). The ecstatic Bacchants were replaced with a group of female cleaners holding buckets, with dirty, crazy-coloured robes, hairdresser's bandanas and athletic shoes, resembling the Eastern European immigrants that Modern Greeks were so keen on hiring as house-maids. Pentheus (N. Karathanos) was portrayed as a Neo-Nazi tyrant, bullying even the blind seer. Teiresias was poignant, but he looked weak as a drunken blind beggar playing the accordion. Cadmus looked like an aged middle-class gentleman starved of any emotional qualities, and when the Messenger brought the horrifying news of Pentheus' death the audience's attention was distracted by the 'rituals' of the chorus, who covered the hanging meat with the remains of Pentheus' blooded wedding dress. Distractive polyphony is one of Langhoff's main directorial strategies combined with a personal aesthetics of montage, which gives priority to powerful images of 'violence', and 'not lyricism' or 'psychological consideration' (Aslan 2000: 215). This is perhaps an equivalent of Brecht's *Einzelgeschehnis* (individual occurrence), in which every actor is an occurrence in the director's description of the story, although 'the description does not centre on any individual character's objectives, nor has a through-line of motivation been developed to link the various beats together' (Rouse 1995: 232).

The reception of Langhoff's production (Sampatakakis 2005: 227–30) by mainstream critics is reminiscent of the aesthetic traditionalism and ethnocentrism of Greek reviewers. As Patsalidis and Sakellaridou noticed:

The problem with the reception of his reading is that Greek audiences and critics did not see his work as a form of fair appropriation but rather as expropriation and exploitation, as an example of an arrogant 'neo-imperialism' hastily disguised as an aesthetic pursuit [...]. What mattered most to local critics was not the fact that Langhoff used the text of Euripides, but that he trivialized it, draining it of its source culture through an arbitrary, ill-informed, non-negotiated, and essentially one-sided mode of transportation. (1999: 16–17)

Despite the 'generic ambiguity' (Foley 2010: 137), in fact aesthetic polyphony, of the modern productions of the *Bacchae*, the play was not popularly offered for post-modern utilizations. Nonetheless, Langhoff's production challenged traditionalist perceptions of the *Bacchae* by presenting a unique culture-specific spectacle with no intention to either repeat the play linearly on stage, or historicize it. Such productions are self-referential *szenische Schreiben*, which acknowledge the text as an inevitable product of the process of staging (Balme 1999: 142), and the performance as an idiosyncratic aesthetic construct that forcefully celebrates the art of the director.

Dionysus, the destroyer and the *Kunsttrieb*

Dionysus, Dionysus, not Thebes, has power over me.
(*Bacchae*, 1037–8).

Friedrich Nietzsche (1995 [1872]: 5–7) envisioned Dionysus, the God of Destruction and Rebirth, not simply as a symbolic concept, but as a natural *Kunsttrieb* (artistic impulse), a philosophical claim that proved so properly valid for contemporary theatre. The most distinguished and influential performances of the *Bacchae* played a critical role in promoting a new function for theatre as an autonomous performative art, permanently rejecting the 'dictatorship' of faithfulness and the established aesthetic canons. Theatre aesthetics would not have been the same without *Dionysus in 69*; directing the classics would not have been so productively destructive without Grüber and Terzopoulos; cultural usurpations of the classics would not have been so widely legitimate without Soyinka and Suzuki.

Bibliography

Angell, C. A. (2009) *Language Development and Disorders: A Case Study Approach*. Sudbury MA: Jones & Barlett.

Artaud, A. (1976) *Selected Writings*, S. Sontag (ed.), H. Weaver (trans.). Berkeley: University of California Press.

Aslan, O. (ed.) (2000) *La poétique de Matthias Langhoff: Karge et Langhoff, Matthias Langhoff: Un metteur en scène européen*. Paris: CNRS Éditions.

Balme, C. (1999) 'Robert Lepage und die Zukunft des Theaters im Medienzeitalter'. In E. Fischer-Lichte et al. (eds), *Transformationen*. Berlin: Theater der Zeit, pp. 133–46.

Brecht, B. (1974) *Brecht on Theatre: The Development of Aesthetics*, J. Willett (ed. and trans.). London: Methuen.

Brecht, S. (1969) 'Theatre Reviews: *Dionysus in 69*, from Euripides' *The Bacchae*, The Performance Group'. *The Drama Review* 13: 156–68.

Burian, P. (1997) 'Tragedy Adapted for Stages and Screens: The Renaissance to the Present'. In P. Easterling (ed.), *The Cambridge Companion to Greek Tragedy*. Cambridge: Cambridge University Press, 228–83.

Carruthers, I. and Yasunari, T. (2004) *The Theatre of Suzuki Tadashi*. Cambridge: Cambridge University Press.

DeBroske, S. (1968) 'Dionysus 69: Nudity, Guts and Truth'. *Washington Square Journal*, 21 November.

Decreus, F. (2012) 'The Reptilian Brain and the Representation of the Female in Theodoros Terzopoulos' *Bacchai*'. *Logeion* 2: 284–303.

Fischer-Lichte, E. (1999) 'Between Text and Cultural Performance: Staging Greek Tragedies in Germany'. *Theatre Survey* 40: 1–29.

Fischer-Lichte, E. (2014) *Dionysus Resurrected: Performance of Euripides' 'The Bacchae' in a Globalizing World*. Bristol: Wiley-Blackwell.

Foley, H. (2010) 'Generic Ambiguity in Modern Productions and New Versions of Greek Tragedy'. In E. Hall and S. Harrop (eds), *Theorizing Performance: Greek Drama, Cultural History and Critical Practice*. London: Duckworth, 137–52.

Goto, Y. (1989) 'The Theatrical Fusion of Suzuki Tadashi'. *Asian Theatre Journal* 6: 103–23.

Grotowski, J. (1969) *Towards a Poor Theatre*, E. Barba (ed.). London: Methuen.

Henrichs, A. (1993) 'He Has a God in Him: Human and Divine in the Modern Perception of Dionysus'. In T. A. Carpenter and C. A. Faraone (eds) *Masks of Dionysus*. Ithaca: Cornell University Press, 13–43.

Iden, P. (1982) *Die Schaubühne am Halleschen Ufer: 1970–1979*. Frankfurt am Main: Fischer.

Jäger, G. (1974) '... wie alles sich für mich verändert hat: *Die Bakchen* des Euripides in Berlin und Wien'. *Theater Heute* 15: 12–21.

Kaiser, J. (1975) 'Werktreue: warum und wie?' In *Theater 1974 Berlin*. *Theater Heute*, 12–20.

Langhoff, M. (1997) 'Eimai enantion tou kalou goustou'. *Ta Nea*, 18 August.

Macintosh, F. (2000) 'Medea Transposed: Burlesque and Gender on the Mid-Victorian Stage'. In E. Hall, F. Macintosh and O. Taplin (eds), *Medea in Performance 1500–2000*, Oxford: Legenda, 75–99.

Macintosh, F. (2007) 'From the Court to the National: The Theatrical Legacy of Gilbert Murray's *Bacchae*'. In C. Stray (ed.), *Gilbert Murray Reassessed*. Oxford: Oxford University Press.

McCarthy, L. (1934) *Myself and My Friends: Lillah McCarthy*. London: Butterworth.

McDonald, M. (1992) *Ancient Sun Modern Light: Greek Drama on the Modern Stage*. New York: Columbia University Press.

Michelini, A. N. (1987) *Euripides and the Tragic Tradition*. Madison, WN: University of Wisconsin Press.

Nietzsche, F. (1995) *The Birth of Tragedy from the Spirit of Music*, C. F. Fadiman (trans.). New York: Dover [1872].

Nouryeh, A. (2001) 'Soyinka's Euripides: Postcolonial Resistance or Avant-Garde Adaptation'. *Research in African Literatures* 32: 160–71.

Okpewho, I. (1999) 'Soyinka, Euripides, and the Anxiety of Empire'. *Research in African Literatures* 30: 32–55.

Patsalidis, S. and Sakellaridou, E. (eds) (1999) 'Introduction, *(Dis)Placing Classical Greek Theatre'*. Thessaloniki: University Studio Press, pp. 13–24.

Pavis, P. (1992) *Theatre at the Crossroads of Culture*, L. Kruger (trans.). London: Routledge.

Pavis, P. (2007) *Contemporary Mise en Scène: Staging Theatre Today*, J. Anderson (trans). Oxford; New York: Routledge.

Perris, S. (2012) 'Our Saviour Dionysos: Humanism and Theology in Gilbert Murray's *Bakkhai'*. *Translation and Literature* 12: 21–42.

Rabkin, G. (2002) 'Is There a Text on This Stage? Theatre, Authorship, Interpretation'. In R. Schneider and G. Cody (eds), *Re: Direction: A Theoretical and Practical Guide*. London and New York: Routledge, pp. 319–31.

Remshardt, R. E. (1999) 'Dionysus in Deutschland: Nietzsche, Grüber, and *The Bacchae'*. *Theatre Survey* 40: 31–49.

Rouse, J. (1995) 'Brecht and the Contradictory Actor'. In P. Zarrilli (ed.), *Acting (Re)considered: Theories and Practices*. London; New York: Routledge, 228–41.

Rühle, G. (1982) *Anarchie in der Regie?* Frankfurt am Main: Suhrkamp.

Rühle, G. (1993) 'Grüber et l'Antiquité'. In G. Banu and M. Blenziger (eds), *Klaus Michael Grüber*. Paris: Éditions du Regard, pp. 207–13.

Sampatakakis, G. (2005) *Bakkhai-Modell: The Re-Usage of Euripides' 'Bakkhai' in Text and Performance*. Unpublished PhD thesis, University of London.

Sampatakakis, G. (2015) 'Review of Erika Fischer-Lichte, *Dionysus Resurrected: Performances of Euripides' 'The Bacchae' in a Globalizing World'*. Chichester: Wiley-Blackwell, 2014. *Logeion* 4: 387–97.

Schechner, R. (1968) '6 Axioms for Environmental Theatre'. *The Drama Review* 12: 41–64.

Schechner, R. (1969) 'Speculations on Radicalism, Sexuality, and Performance'. *The Drama Review* 13: 89–110.

Schechner, R. (1970) *Dionysus in 69*. New York: The Wooster Group.

Schechner, R. (1994) *Environmental Theater*, 2nd ed. London and New York: Routledge [1973].

Schlegel, A. W. (1894) *A Course of Lectures on Dramatic Art and Literature*, 2nd ed., J. Black (trans.). London: Bell.

SCOT (1985) *Suzuki Company of Toga*. Tokyo: The Japan Performing Arts Center.

Silk, M. S. and Stern, J. P. (1981) *Nietzsche on Tragedy*. Cambridge: Cambridge University Press.

Soyinka, W. (1974) *The Bacchae of Euripides: A Communion Rite*. New York: Norton.

Suzuki, T. (1986) *The Way of Acting: The Theatre Writings of Tadashi Suzuki*, T. Rimer (trans.). New York: Theatre Communications Group.

Suzuki, T. (1995) 'Culture is the Body'. In P. Zarrilli (ed.), *Acting (Re)considered: Theories and Practices*. London and New York: Routledge, pp. 155–60.

van Steen, Gonda (2013) 'Bloody (Stage) Business: Matthias Langhoff's Sparagmos of Euripides' *Bacchae* (1997)'. In V. Liapis and G. W. M. Harrison (eds), *Performance in Greek and Roman Theatre*. Leiden: Brill, 501–15.

Walton, M. (2008) 'Dionysus: The Victorian Outcast'. *Victorian Review* 34: 185–99.

Unpublished material

The Gilbert Murray Papers, in the New Caledonian Library, Oxford, MSS 10/53–4, 58–61, 63–4, 70–71, 74–5, 96; 13/220; 14/2–3, 8, 37, 106; 15/22, 35–7.

10

Ariane Mnouchkine's *Les Atrides*: Uncovering a classic

Dominic Glynn

As sociologist Jean Duvignaud once put it, there is something incredibly odd about meeting up in a dark room to watch a group of people play out a text written several centuries ago (1965: 56). This is precisely what theatre aficionados do week in, week out: they pack in to auditoriums, black boxes, outdoor venues and improvised halls alike to witness, and thus participate in, the performance of 'classics'. These classics are curious cultural artefacts indeed, deemed as they are to be both 'transcendent and time-bound' (Greenblatt 2000: 3). In other words, such texts dug out of the annals of literary history bear the hallmarks of a specific place and time in the past – which implies that they need to be translated into the present – yet are also deemed to somehow speak to us today, now. Implied also is that they spoke to us yesterday, and the day before yesterday. Yet, as a number of eminent literary theorists and historians have shown, works are labelled classics as a result of perpetual ideological power struggles.[1] This means a history of interpretation – of re-interpretation even – exists; hence Alain Viala's adage that to study a 'classic' is to study history (1993: 30).[2]

Each country and each language has its own sense of literary heritage and comes up with its own list of classics, and a select few works – the plays of the Ancient Greek tragedians, notably – have achieved 'universal classic' status.[3] They form constantly revisited territories, commented on in classrooms all over Europe and frequently staged, at least in adapted forms. In the words of Christian Biet, the fragmentary texts of Ancient Greece have become 'highly respectable monuments that have been revered, mythologised, commented [on] and rewritten' over time (1997: 7). Or, as Marie-Claude Hubert says in her *Histoire de la scène occidentale*, 'What is left of ancient Greek theatre today except for a few fragments' (2011: 7). In order to be able to engage with these primary texts, it is therefore – literally almost – necessary to 'uncover meaning' by working through a millennia-long history of interpretation. Director Daniel Mesguich says as much when he highlights the differences between staging new writing and working on a classic:

> To direct a classic means not only staging a *visible* text of course (the literal, printed, text), but also in a way – and this is where lies the difference with contemporary texts) – to direct a second *invisible* text which is made up of the memory of the visible text, its *history*, its *dust* (notes, commentaries, exegesis, productions, even the effects of successive intimidation it has brought, etc.).

This is what occurred with the production cycle that I have been invited to remember critically here – Ariane Mnouchkine's *Les Atrides* (1992–5). So it is that I shall investigate, in this chapter, the underlying tension between contemplating a work from afar and up close. By charting the company's history and by looking at the textual excavations operated in translation before moving on to highlighting distantiation techniques, I will consider how Mnouchkine engages with the invisible text of Aeschylus and Euripides' works in a global era.

The rise of the Théâtre du Soleil

Les Atrides, along with the revolutionary cycle *1789–1793* and the Shakespearean cycle, *Les Shakespeare*, counts as Ariane Mnouchkine's greatest achievement as a director. Given that Mnouchkine is considered one of the most important theatre directors in the world of the last fifty years, this is quite some statement. Indeed, such is Mnouchkine's renown that she is not only highly regarded in France, where she plies her trade, but on the international stage. Simply listing the names of her productions provides an outline of key moments in recent theatre history – French history first and foremost, but the history of Western theatre more generally also. In 2014, the golden jubilee year of her company, the only company she has ever worked with, the Théâtre du Soleil, French daily *Le Monde* ran a feature where people who had attended the company's shows over the last fifty years recalled their experiences; the overwhelming number of responses and flood of affection for the company displayed in the short accounts reveal how it has today become an institution.[4] However, if the company has survived for so long, it is because it has managed to carve out a space for itself outside the public-private dichotomy that characterizes the French theatre scene. It is precisely for this difference, which is somewhat akin to that cultivated by Peter Brook, both outside traditional structures but without seeking to be marginal, that the company is revered.

As a result, there are a number of values and features that have underpinned the company, if not from its inception in 1964, at least for a long time. Chief among these is the communitarian approach and collective spirit that means that everyone takes part in all the different activities. Another is the fact that since 1970 the company has been based at the Cartoucherie de Vincennes, a former armament factory in the woods on the outskirts of the city of Paris. A third stems from the fact that the Soleil is the successor to a student society named the ATEP (Association Théâtrale des Étudiants de Paris), founded by Mnouchkine and others in 1959. The ATEP was intended to be the rival of the Théâtre Antique de la Sorbonne, which had been formed in the later 1930s by a certain Roland Barthes. Yet like Barthes, the members of the society were profoundly influenced by Brecht, as can be attested by the fact that the inaugural lecture was delivered by Jean-Paul Sartre on the theme of epic versus dramatic theatre (1973: 147). Also Roger Planchon, whom Barthes and colleagues at the journal *Théâtre Populaire* considered the true inheritor of Brecht, was the society patron. To this day, Ariane Mnouchkine has remained indebted to Brecht's work and *Les Atrides*, in particular, provided epic storytelling.

A fourth point is that since the early 1980s Mnouchkine has utilized the visual imagery of non-Western performance traditions in her productions. Mnouchkine's first experience of theatre in Paris was at the international festival held at the Théâtre des Nations. Judith Miller notes that 'she indeed went there to Giorgio Strehler's version of Pirandello's *Giants of the Mountain* eleven times, as well as to have her first taste of Kathakali theatre' (2007: 5). Even more intriguingly, she may have been able to see perform a working-class company that could be said to have provided the blueprint for the organization of the Théâtre du Soleil, namely Joan Littlewood's Theatre Workshop.

Mnouchkine's work with the Théâtre du Soleil has been all about collaboration. Each member of the company is expected to contribute to all tasks, from washing the floors to giving input on costume design. Actors are encouraged to try playing different parts, and it is only relatively late on that Mnouchkine decides who is best suited for a specific role, based on what they have shown her in improvisations and rehearsed performances of different scenes. These characteristics have contributed to making Mnouchkine's work stand out from the rest of the field of production in France. It is also worth considering that *Les Atrides* represents arguably the last of the momentous productions by established directors such as Peter Brook (the *Mahabharata* in 1985) and Antoine Vitez (*Le Soulier de Satin*), which Christian Biet and Christophe Triau have labelled 'sum total shows' (2006: 726) – in other words, productions that encapsulate the whole of these directors' practices, but also in a sense the whole of directing history. This is how *Les Atrides* was inscribed within a discourse on history and within a field of production. Mnouchkine's production of *Les Atrides* was both French – marked by a particular way of doing theatre in France, and more specifically in opposition to a particular way of doing theatre in France – and international. The question, as we now hone our analysis specifically on the production – on the 'figure on the carpet', so to speak – is how it articulated such opposing tensions.

Textual excavations

When attempting to stage Greek tragedy, the question of translating the work(s) from the past both literally and metaphorically arises early on in the process. For *Les Atrides*, Ariane Mnouchkine enlisted a team of scholars and literary advisers to provide the company of the Théâtre du Soleil with access to the plays that formed the cycle, namely Euripides' *Iphigenia at Aulis* and Aeschylus' *Oresteia*. Chief among these advisors were renowned Hellenists Jean Bollack and Pierre Judet de la Combe. The two philologists' association with the project came as a result of Ariane Mnouchkine having read their two-volume commentary of *Agamemnon*. In the preface to *Libation Bearers* Mnouchkine comments appreciatively on their approach to scholarship, saying that they understand that research is a sinewy path, strewn with potential errors and pitfalls (Mnouchkine 1992: 7). In another publication, Judet de la Combe returns the compliment when he reflects on her approach to working on these Ancient Greek texts:

> Mnouchkine chose to associate scholarship with her project intimately, so that her findings in the wording of the translation and in the staging of the plays could always be related to precise and argued decisions concerning the meaning and the syntax of the words. (Judet de la Combe 2005: 275)

As a result of their close association, Mnouchkine relied on Jean Bollack's translation of *Iphigenia at Aulis*, and worked with them to provide the translations of *Agamemnon* and *Libation Bearers*. As for the *Eumenides*, it was the work of Hélène Cixous, who had already collaborated with the Théâtre du Soleil on two previous productions, namely *L'Histoire terrible mais inachevée de Norodom Sihanouk, Roi du Cambodge* (1985) and *L'Indiade ou l'Inde de nos rêves* (1987).

The published versions of these translations were accompanied by notes provided by Bollack and Judet de la Combe and over time they have come to be regarded as significant versions (Mnouchkine's translation of *Agamemnon*, for instance, was the set text for the baccalaureate's theatre studies option in 2010). Also, such a close relationship between scholars and practitioners is testimony to the excavation process that Mesguich referred to above. Most significantly, though, it paved the way for an astonishing dramaturgical decision, which was to stage a cycle that added Euripides to Aeschylus.

In Aeschylus' trilogy *The Oresteia* (458 BCE), the opening play, *Agamemnon*, stages the triumphant return of the eponymous general after the Trojan War and his subsequent murder at the hands of his wife. However, by opening *Les Atrides* with Euripides' *Iphigenia at Aulis* (406 BCE), Ariane Mnouchkine provided the back-story and posited the sacrifice of virgin daughter Iphigenia as the founding act that provoked the cycle of retributive murders in the Atreus family. Moreover, by virtue of this addition, Mnouchkine brought into focus how the myth comprises different versions of the story. Indeed, in the course of the cycle, two contradictory descriptions of the sacrifice are provided.

The first description, given by a messenger at the end of *Iphigenia at Aulis*, argues that the act was not only desired by the gods, but also carried out in accordance with the ceremonial rites. To underline the legitimacy of the sacrifice, the messenger quotes the priest's address to the gods textually 'Accept this offering that we render thee [...] The unsullied blood from a fair maiden's neck' (L1574–6). He also emphasizes that the victim was consenting, this time by quoting Iphigenia:

at thine hest I come,
And for my country's sake my body give,
And for all Hellas, to be led of you
Unto the Goddess' altar, willingly. (L1532–5)

He then reveals how, miraculously, the goddess for whom the sacrifice was intended substituted Iphigenia in extremis with a heifer (L1592–3). However, as Nicole Loraux has explained, despite the messenger's insistence on interpreting the substitution as a tiding of joy, the fact that the maiden is replaced by an animal not normally sacrificed in ancient Greece somewhat undermines his claims that all is in order (1985: 66).

Such a sense of unease about the validity of the act is taken to a whole new level in the second description, which paints a very different picture of the event. The chorus at the start of *Agamemnon* tells 'a much more brutal tale than we have heard in Euripides'

(Bryant-Bertail 2000: 192). Indeed, the old men reveal that orders were given to seize Iphigenia 'as if it were a kid' (L231–2), but that she resisted: 'she lay fallen forward' (L234). As a result, her father asked for her to be silenced, else she might curse his name: 'and with guard on her lovely mouth, the bit's strong and stifling might, to stay a cry that had been a curse on his house' (L236–7). In comparison with the messenger's account, the chorus's testimony places greater emphasis on the visual and thus seems all the more believable. The old men were present at the scene, but refuse to comment on events they did not directly witness: 'What next befell, I beheld not, neither do I tell' (L248). Of course, the chorus is remembering the event ten years after its occurrence; however, in comparison, the messenger's account, which was delivered to reassure the on-stage audience made up of the grieving mother and a chorus of maidens, appears fabricated.

On a meta-theatrical level, by bringing together two versions of a same myth, Mnouchkine revealed how both form part of our heritage. Iphigenia both dies and is saved as her sacrifice is re-membered by the tellers of stories in these two founding works of the European stage. On a diegetic level, Iphigenia's father Agamemnon appears all the more shifty and I concur with Jean-Pierre Vernant and Pierre Vidal-Nacquet's reading of the *Oresteia* that he is revealed to be guileless and guilty of ambition:

> Now we know what Iphigenia's sacrifice was really about: less about obeying Artemis's orders, less the heavy duty of a king who does not want to wrong his allies, than the guilty weakness of a person of ambition conspiring with the divine Triche, has decided to kill his daughter. (Vernant and Vidal-Naquet 2001: 40)

In the dramaturgical thread that Mnouchkine wove, a gap opened up between Agamemnon and the rest of society as represented on stage by the chorus and off stage by the audience. She was in effect accentuating a feature of Greek tragedy that Jean Duvignaud saw as key, whereby the dramatist isolates the protagonist and provides justifications that render his death admissible if not desirable (1971: 45). Moreover, it forms part of a Brechtian estrangement matrix, for, as Maurice Blanchot noted, Brecht's practice was characterized by the adding of what he calls 'intervalles' – gaps, discrepancies (though the literal translation 'interval' has a particular resonance here also) – and the same might be said about Mnouchkine's work.

Revealing distance in pre-performance

If on a dramaturgical level, Mnouchkine sought to heighten the audience's awareness of discrepancies by playing with these gaps, in the framing of the production, she highlighted the distance between the audience and the works. First, in the pre-performance rituals of *Les Atrides*, the director and performers' roles in bringing these mythological stories to the stage were brought into focus. Unlike in other performance venues, where actors and audience 'cannot see each other, are present at the same time, but are not together (neither in the same space, nor engaged in the same activity)' (Biet and Triau 2006: 407), at the Cartoucherie de Vincennes, Mnouchkine's home base, the performers are visible from the beginning. As Marvin Carlson points out, Ariane Mnouchkine invites 'audiences to arrive before the performance and come "backstage" to witness the actors' preparations' (1989: 134).

Such an experience can be uncomfortable for those unaccustomed to it, as for Robert Bethune, who described the experience of watching the performers prepare for *Les Atrides* as a disturbing cross between 'Madame Tussaud's and of windows in the red-light district of Amsterdam' (1993: 180). Other audience members at *Les Atrides* had a quasi-religious experience, as John Chioles who describes attending the production as akin to being asked to join 'the priesthood' (1993: 27). However, it seems to me that both the above critics were somewhat bewildered by the experience and missed the key point that a wedge was being driven between actor and character. Indeed, in many Western playhouses, audiences are expected to suspend their disbelief and view the actors as embodiments of their character, yet this is impossible in the Cartoucherie where the actors are seen preparing. As a result, the character is held at a distance from the actor. The mystique of metamorphosis that Brecht railed against in Western acting cannot take place (Brecht 2000: 822). Rather David Williams' analysis of the rift that occurs between actor and character in Peter Brook's work, which provides the actor 'with the objectivity, lucidity and compassion of a narratorial commentator or puppeteer' is appropriate to describe what happens in Mnouchkine's practice too (1991: 189).

What is more, driving a wedge between actor and character was part of an overall attempt to drive a wedge between the audience and the fable. The omnipresence of Ariane Mnouchkine prior to the performance, from checking the audience's tickets to serving food and directing people where to sit, served to show how the director was positioned in the space between the fable and the audience. As Sallie Goetsch notes: 'If Mnouchkine's engagement with Aeschylus and Euripides was mediated by translations, our experience of *Les Atrides* was even more carefully and explicitly mediated by Ariane Mnouchkine' (1994: 77). However, the most ingenious means of opening up a space between the audience and the story in *Les Atrides* was an installation. En route from the reception hall to the performance space, the audience passed next to what appeared to be archaeological digs. Trenches were filled with life-size statues of people and horses lined-up in rows, which bore a resemblance to the warriors of the Chinese terracotta army, but also to the costumed actors, for as the chorus entered at the start of *Agamemnon*, it seemed as if 'the crowd of statues had returned to life and found their way to the stage' (2000: 180).

The trenches allowed the audiences to participate in, or at least view, the excavation of the texts, digging them up from the past. They served as a metaphor for the excavation work that Mnouchkine had undertaken in order to translate the works in the first place. Also, instead of churning out pots and vases with depictions of scenes from the *Oresteia* as one might expect, the digs playfully underlined how ancient Greek society was as removed from us as Emperor Quin's mausoleum. Indeed though references to non-Western traditions might be taken as indicators of the universal scope of the myth, they mainly highlighted distance for European audiences between the material and themselves.

Mixing devices to challenge assumptions: New trends

Such distancing effects created in pre-performance by allying different cultural references were explored in the *mise-en-scène* also. For instance, rather than figuratively representing a tableau of ancient Greece, the set referred back to combat sports anchored in Roman and Spanish cultures. Ochre walls enclosed a large space that resembled an arena not unlike that of the Coliseum or of a Spanish bullring. Or to quote Guy Dumur: 'the fully lit stage is surrounded by a decrepit wall, pierced through with openings like at the plazas de toros' (1990: 58–9). The critic for *Libération*, René Solis, provides a remarkably similar description: 'the space has kept not so much the shape but the ochre colour of the arenas as well as the outer wall with, at regular intervals, spaces in which to slip away from the beast' (1990: 36), as does Robin Thornber in *The Guardian*, who labels the space a 'bare timber bear-pit or bullring' (1991: 15). The dramatic intensity of the space described is striking and fate takes on the role of the bull, which the protagonists stand up to, while the chorus darts behind to hide. Although the space may have had little in common with traditional representations of Ancient Greece, it appealed to what Mnouchkine defines as the permeability of the audience (Mnouchkine 1990: 36). Thus audience members could read into the agonistic space their own political interpretations. Thornber, for instance, was drawn to see via the arena images of 'a bloodied village square that could be anywhere from Bosnia to Iraq'.

Mnouchkine's mixing of Roman and Spanish references may not have come under much criticism, but her forays into the visual languages of Asian performance traditions have often been criticized. When in the 1980s her productions started to reveal an interest in non-Western traditions, a number of critics took this to be an indicator of a decline in the Théâtre du Soleil's political activities. Gautam Dasgupta saw this as part of a global trend: 'as political enthusiasm waned worldwide in the late seventies, the Théâtre du Soleil's productions came to be seen and appreciated largely for their prodigious aesthetic experimentations' (1982: 82). As for Brian Singleton, who attended Mnouchkine's cycle of Shakespearean dramas, *Les Shakespeare* (1981–4), he believed that the audience on exiting the theatre 'leaves behind the feudal power struggles of Shakespeare, the Asian primary source cultures and the interculturalist theatre forms, pigeon-holing this as a purely aesthetic experience' (1995: 324).

Singleton's comments about Mnouchkine's earlier production cycle may be applied to *Les Atrides*, yet my own reading of her use of non-European performance traditions is rather different. I follow John Rockwell, who in his review of *Les Atrides* for the *New York Times* suggested that Mnouchkine conducts her experiments from the perspective of a 'lifelong Parisian' who has 'created a unique style that blends world theatrical cultures in the service of Western classics and contemporary epics' (1992: 2). Mnouchkine's work needs to be viewed through the prism of the French cultural scene and her use of motifs, patterns and signs borrowed ostensibly from the East open up spaces for critical reflection precisely because they are other. Or as Eugenio Barba explains in the Preface to his *Dictionnaire de l'anthropologie théâtrale*, 'by encountering what appears foreign to us we change our way of looking and learn participation and distantiation at once' (2008: 13). This is indeed the analysis that Sarah Bryant-Bertail provides of Ariane Mnouchkine's work, describing her use of intercultural references as a 'commitment to a historically responsible theatre [which] has taken her along a Brechtian route through a Verfremdung achieved by borrowing from Asian theatre' (2000: 174).

Costume in *Les Atrides*, for instance, implicated the heroes in a world of brutality in which murder was performed almost ritualistically. Thus, in *The Libation Bearers*, the women of the chorus were dressed all in black with a red cummerbund, golden jewellery and headgear, their faces painted white in similar fashion to Kabuki actors, whilst heavy black eye liner brought out startled looks in their eyes. Some also had tears of red painted on their faces and wore very bright red lipstick, which drew attention to their mouths as conveyers of bloody news. The heightened expressiveness of the choral bodies saw them 'whirling and chanting like Javanese dancers at some tribal feast, they become enthusiastic celebrants of Orestes' blood-sacrifice while lamenting the necessity of such an "action sauvage"' (Billington 1991: 15). To quote Judith Miller, 'the shaking, convulsing bodies of the chorus transmitted to the public the emotional impact of the play's horrific actions: infanticide (*Iphigenia*), parricide (*Agamemnon*), matricide (*The Libation Bearers*), vengeance (*The Eumenides*)' (2007: 38).

As the previous descriptions attest, it would be wrong to claim that Mnouchkine attempted to replicate a particular Eastern tradition. For Eileen Blumenthal, she 'crossbreeds the Greek scripts with south Indian Kathakali dance drama', but I would suggest that this form was rather the starting point for creating her own theatrical language (1992: 16). Mnouchkine's own remark, 'the more I am Balinese, Javanese or Indian, the more Greek I am', reveals precisely such an intention of creating an intercultural language that mixes several traditions together. In this regard, Bernard Dort's description of her work as a 'Far-Eastern collage' is appropriate (1988: 54). Thus, the actors were encouraged to favour a hybrid style of performance borrowed from different sources.

Conclusions

Gisèle Sapiro's *Translatio*, a study of the translation market in France, opens with the following question: has globalization been favourable to international cultural exchanges and the mixing of cultures or has it been the illustration of economic imperialism accompanied by cultural hegemony (Sapiro 2008: 7)? When considering theatre practices that seek to set up a dialogue between cultures, this question is it seems inescapable, even though, as Patrice Pavis explains in *Le Théâtre au croisement des cultures*, these practices might wish to do so (1990: 123). Ariane Mnouchkine's theatre is characterized by its universal aspirations. As David Bradby explains, the most beautiful moments in Mnouchkine's productions are the product of a passionate vision that fights against separatism, partitioning, tearing apart and the cruelty that has been all too apparent in recent human history in favour of universal humanism (2008: 464). Thus, she highlights distance and difference between individuals, groups and cultures, but also that connections exist by engaging with works that are so well known that they need to be framed in a different light.

Ariane Mnouchkine excavated the texts from the past in order to show both that they were relevant today, and yet that they have become locked in discourses of previous centuries' interpretations. As such, her production has unleashed a wave of critical rethinking of the plays by classicists and drama scholars alike. Scholars associated with the Archive of Performances of Greek and Roman Drama at the University of Oxford (Fiona Macintosh, Oliver Taplin), for instance, have discussed at length how Mnouchkine forced scholars of classical reception to reconsider the choral body.

However, her attempts to break out of the shackles led to a difficult intercultural equation to resolve: how can we make these ancient texts seem both other and fascinating, without making contemporary others appear alienated from ourselves? Today, directors are faced with even further challenges to make visible the primary text, as people hide away behind computer screens or block out the rest of the world with their MP3 players, the notion of a collective or community has evolved. To provide an experience that goes against the grain is one way of asserting the need to meet up in the public place to be moved together and to think together. And in the digital era where new canons are being created, the telling of stories has changed, adding a further layer of dust to be brushed off in the excavation-cum-production process.

Bibliography

Barba, E. (2008) 'Préface'. In *Dictionnaire d'anthropologie théâtrale*, Eugenio Barba and Nicola Savarese (eds). Montpellier: L'Entretemps.

Bethune, R. (1993) 'Le Théâtre du Soleil's Les Atrides'. *Asian Theatre Journal* 10.2: 179–90.

Biet, C. and Triau, C. (2006) *Qu'est-ce que le théâtre?* Paris: Gallimard.

Billington, M. (1991) 'Franc and Fearless on the Parisian Stage'. *Guardian*, 31 December, p. 15.

Blumenthal, E. (1992) 'French Theatre: Molière Post-Modernised'. *Wall Street Journal* (Eastern Edition), 14 May, 16.

Bollack, J. and Judet de la Combe, P. (1982) *L'Agamemnon d'Eschyle: le texte et ses interprétations I–II*. Lille: Presses Universitaires de Lille.

Bradby, D. (2008) *Le Théâtre en France de 1968 à 2000*. Paris: Champion.

Brecht, B. (2000) *Écrits sur le théâtre*. Paris: Pléiade.

Bryant-Bertail, S. (2000) *Space and Time in Epic Theatre: The Brechtian Legacy*. Rochester, NY: Camden House.

Carlson, M. (1989) *Places of Performance: The Semiotics of Theatre Architecture*. Ithaca: Cornell University Press.

Chioles, J. (1993) 'The Oresteia and the Avant-Garde'. *Performing Arts Journal* 15.3: 1–28.

Dasgupta, G. (1982) 'Richard II, Twelfth Night'. *Performing Arts Journal* 6.3: 81–6.

Dort, B. (1988) *La Représentation émancipée*. Paris: Actes Sud.

Dumur, G. (1990) 'Les Atrides parmi nous', *Nouvel Observateur*, 20 December, 58–9.

Duvignaud, J. (1965) *Sociologie du théâtre. Essai sur les ombres collectives*. Paris: PUF.

Duvignaud, J. (1971) *Le Théâtre et après*. Paris: Casterman.

Goetsch, S. (1994) 'Playing Against the Text: Les Atrides and the History of Reading Aeschylus'. *Tulane Drama Review* 46.1: 75–95.

Hubert, M.-C. (2011) *Histoire de la scène occidentale*. Paris: Armand Colin.

Miller, J. (2007) *Ariane Mnouchkine*. London, Routledge.

Mnouchkine, A. (1990) 'Entretien avec René Solis'. *Libération*, 2 January, 36–7.

Mnouchkine, A. (trans.) (1992) *Agamemnon*. Paris: Editions Théâtrales.

Pavis, P. (1990) *Le Théâtre au croisement des cultures*. Paris: José Corti.

Rockwell, J. (1992) 'Behind the Masks of a Moralist'. *New York Times*, 27 September, 2.

Sapiro, G. (2008) *Translatio: Le Marché de la traduction en France à l'heure de la mondialisation*. Paris: CNRS.

Sartre, J.-P. (1973) *Un théâtre de situations*. Paris: Gallimard.

Singleton, B. (1995) 'Mnouchkine and Shakespeare: Intercultural Theatre Practice'. In H. and J.-M. Maguin (eds), *Shakespeare and France*. Lewiston, NY: Edwin Mellen Press.

Solis, R. (1990) 'Mnouchkine à la grecque'. *Libération*, 2 January, 36.

Thornber, R. (1991) 'Les Atrides', *Guardian*, 18 January, 15.

Vernant, J.-P. and Vidal-Naquet, P. (2001) *Mythe et tragédie en Grèce ancienne*. Paris: La Découverte.

Viala, A. (1993) 'Introduction: Qu'est-ce qu'un classique?' *Littératures classiques* 19: 11–31.

Williams, D. (1991) 'The Great Poem of the World: A Descriptive Analysis'. In D. Williams (ed.), *Peter Brook and the Mahabharata: Critical Perspectives*. London and New York: Routledge.

11

Re-imagining *Antigone*: Contemporary resonances in the directorial revisioning of character, chorus and staging

Sue Hamstead

Seemingly small directorial decisions can have immense implications for the interpretation of Sophocles' *Antigone*. Omit just one particular speech from the eponymous heroine and it is possible to present her as unswervingly dedicated to honouring the gods, whereas with that speech we are forced to acknowledge much more ambiguity in her attitude. Tone of voice alone is enough either to show Kreon[1] as reasonable and sympathetic, at least initially, or at the other extreme to turn him into a ranting dictator. Bring on Antigone's body at the end and the audience is obliged to remember the disastrous intransigence that brought such devastation down on Kreon's house, but leave it where she died and her role can almost be forgotten and Kreon's tragedy allowed to become a much more personal affair.

It has been argued of this play that it is really Kreon's tragedy. Antigone leaves the stage for the last time about two-thirds of the way through and from then on the focus is turned to Kreon: with the loss of his son and his wife, the end is devoted to telling his story. However, the figure normally deemed to inhabit the moral centre of the play and who usually attracts the most attention is Antigone, and frequently in adaptations her part will be expanded. The current drift, though, seems to be something of a reversal giving Kreon more of the limelight: there is more effort to see things from his point of view. Moreover, a trend in foregrounding of minor characters facilitates a multiplicity of perspectives and stresses the interconnectedness of the whole family.

There are always far too many new productions of the play around to do all of them justice in one chapter. I will therefore concentrate on just a few of the more thought-provoking offerings in order to allow more in-depth discussion of them. Of particular interest is their exploration of the normally more peripheral family relationships. The selections are: the National Theatre production of 2012 based on Don Taylor's translation and directed by Polly Findlay; the University of Leeds 2013 adaptation by George Rodosthenous with text by Ashley Scott Layton;[2] the Pilot Theatre adaptation of 2014 written by Roy Williams and directed by Marcus Romer; the Barbican production of 2015 based on Anne Carson's new translation and directed by Ivo van Hove. Represented are a mix of translations and adaptations. They differ considerably in approach, but common trends are detectable, and they therefore offer a good cross-section of modern perspectives on this evergreen tragedy. For convenience, they will generally be referred to from here on by the name of the director.

Setting: Providing a context

The main setting chosen for the play is often an indication of the director's (or sometimes the writer's) preoccupations. For Sophocles the stage building represented the royal palace and all the action takes place just outside. The varying choices of the productions under consideration are all attempts to create a centre of operations in which the reimagined characters can best serve the director's purpose.

When Taylor directed his own translation for the BBC in 1986, the setting was not in any strict sense a reproduction of ancient Greece, but the impression was of long ago; certainly, there was no recent technology in evidence. Findlay may use Taylor's words, but the setting she devises is completely new. Taking her cue from the war that has only just ended as the action of the play begins, she gives us Creon's bunker (Soutra Gilmour's design). The year is indeterminate but the set dressing has a 1970s feel; critic Charles Spencer's description is of 'reinforced concrete walls, glass-box offices and drab desks covered with secret files and tape recorders' (Spencer 2012). With this Findlay totally transforms the whole texture and tenor of this version. Instead of the lofty buildings and open areas, the room available is closely delimited and its use feels oversubscribed. The principal players plus the ten members of the chorus make this a crushingly claustrophobic space where tensions will almost inevitably run high and interpersonal relationships are pushed to breaking point.

For the Rodosthenous production, there is war in the background, but it is an election that has just made Creon the new Prime Minister. The main setting is the 'exclusive wedding boutique'[3] where Antigone is to be fitted for her bridal gown. So Sophocles' outdoor space, properly only inhabited by males, has been exchanged for a very feminine indoor space. In this place it is Creon who intrudes, but that does not make it any less alien to Antigone. It foregrounds her impending marriage to Haemon, a prospect she seems not to anticipate with any sense of joy: she is bad-tempered and expresses displeasure in all the items of her bridal outfit that are shown to her. Although there is no attempt to ignore the politics, this choice of setting is surely designed to signify the importance of the intra-familial relationships that are to be fleshed out. Indeed, the jokes shared among those working in the establishment concerning the inbred nature of their royal family seem designed to accentuate this angle.

In the Williams script, the main setting is a nightclub (Williams 2014: 4), but nothing so specific can be discerned in Romer's manifestation of it. The set dressing has a harsh, industrial feel: tall pillars, huge wire-mesh gates at the back, behind which Tig (Antigone) will be imprisoned. With the help of just a few properties wheeled into place and taken away again, the same set is used to represent indoor or outside space as required. The environment is – in keeping with the dialect employed – indicative of the underworld of gang warfare in which (the slightly renamed) Creo is the key player. The gang members are referred to as soldiers, and the staff of the club – including Tig and Esme (Ismene) – are also working for Creo. The scale of operations, then, is much reduced: Creo is very much king of his patch, but he does not rule a country. So his standing is diminished in absolute terms, but he perhaps has more power over his gang than the Sophoclean Kreon had over his citizens. What it achieves is to bring the action into a recognizably modern setting and to intensify the almost mafia-like familial dimensions.

At the Barbican, van Hove employs a setting that is more abstract with few properties. Video is used to provide a backdrop, as Trueman describes: 'wind-blasted city' for Kreon and 'wintry desert' for Antigone. For the most part, however, there is no attempt to locate the action in a recognizable physical space. The actors largely remain in view, stepping into and out of roles as required and only rarely exiting the stage altogether. At the front and below the level of the main part of the stage there is a sofa which is at times used by actors not involved in the current scene. The effect – in its encouragement of reflective detachment on the part of the audience – could be almost Brechtian,[4] but as we shall see, at moments of high emotion the action intrudes into this space demanding of spectators their emotional engagement.

Opening scene: Establishing the tone

There is a tendency in modern productions to include some kind of prologue to introduce the action and fill in the background, possibly on the assumption that the story is unfamiliar to modern audiences whereas the ancient Greeks would have known what was happening. But that assumption can be misleading. Sophocles especially seems to have been fond of beginning his plays *in medias res*, his objective being, I would suggest, to stimulate interest. His audience members might have known the title of the play they were about to experience, but that would have revealed very little as regards its contents. As Sommerstein has emphasized, there was 'no such thing as "the myth" in the sense of a fixed canonical story; there were only variant versions of it, and all the audience knew for certain was that the variant they were going to see would in at least some ways be entirely new' (Sommerstein 2002: 16). In particular, in the case of Antigone, there is no sure evidence that this story existed prior to Sophocles,[5] so an explanatory prologue would completely change the effect of the opening. In the case of the versions under discussion, although prologues are added, they are not necessarily explanatory, and so manage to retain the sense of unease and uncertainty that Sophocles promoted.

Thebes had just survived an attack by a foreign army, but with Oedipus' sons both dead as a result, no one can be quite sure of what will happen next: such elements are frequently absorbed into modern retellings by the addition of a prologue. However, what is then displaced is the centrality of the two sisters, Antigone and Ismene, who opened the proceedings for Sophocles. In the world of ancient Greek tragedy, once the chorus had entered, it was usual for it to remain on stage for the rest of the play. So, the prologue was a tragedian's easiest way of staging a private – in this case conspiratorial – meeting. It is often pointed out that – for contemporary Athenians – women were contravening societal expectations merely by being outside unaccompanied (see e.g. Easterling 1987: 22–3), but, since convention dictated that the stage would always represent outside space, the practical solution was to relax this rule. Sophocles' choice nonetheless is significant. Antigone quickly indicates her intention of deliberate transgression: she will bury her brother in defiance of the new leader Kreon. Her plan is in fact doubly transgressive because, following the death of her brothers, Kreon has become her closest male kinsman and consequently her legal guardian; she is therefore opposing both the head of state and the head of her family (see Blundell 1995: 114).[6] So Sophocles had begun his work with a muted but shocking act of defiance. The question for the modern adapter is how to reproduce the exhilaration of this opening. One of the favoured alternatives is to stage the event that in the play's timeframe has just happened, the event that sets in motion the whole action of the play: the doubly fatal fight between Polyneikes and Eteokles, the two brothers of Antigone and Ismene.

Rodosthenous does exactly this. The advantage is in the impact it makes: the eruption of violence in front of us is a definite attention grabber. In this case, however, it is not an attempt to explain the background and put the audience at ease. For those not familiar with the story there is still mystery: no advance explanation is given as to who these men are and why they are fighting. There are no lines spoken during the clash; instead there is a soundtrack of dramatic music. The effect is to pique the curiosity of those who are newcomers to the tale; they must await its unfolding for the assailants to be identified. The sisters' entrance is further displaced by Creon's acceptance speech – he has just been elected Prime Minister of the United Kingdom and he is keen to portray himself as a champion of the people, to distance himself from the calamities of the recent past and put a positive spin on future prospects: 'No one can deny we stood on the brink. This election was a rare opportunity for the British people to reclaim mastery over their fate.' Then follows the scene introducing the chorus: the employees of the wedding boutique whose gossip begins to fill in the backstory. Only after all this do we eventually meet the sisters. It could be argued that the intention is to promote the importance of Creon at Antigone's expense, but, in light of the last intervening scene, lengthy as it is and involving only minor characters, it could equally be seen as augmenting the already emerging traces of family intrigue while building anticipation for Antigone's long-delayed appearance.

Findlay opts for a more unusual way of opening the play that is both daring and imaginative. It takes place inside the underground facility where Creon and his people gather around a monitor; the screen is seen by them but not by the audience. With no words spoken, we can only judge by their reactions what is taking place, but what they convey is that they are watching a fight: there is a period of considerable tension before the side they are supporting seems to triumph as we briefly read victory in their response, but this is followed almost instantly by a development that does not please them. What they have witnessed leaves them in troubled and contemplative silence. Informed spectators will assume that they have seen the death of Polynices quickly followed by the death of Eteocles. The effects of this approach are multilayered: for those aware of the background it is a subtly played reminder, but for those unaware – just as with Rodosthenous – there are hints of a tragedy yet to be explained. In addition, it also observes the ancient Greek theatrical convention of keeping violence off-stage, but it achieves this in an innovative manner which foregrounds the modern setting of the production.

Romer's approach is radically different. The location is identified in the script as a 'street in downtown Thebes' (Williams 2014: 3), but the director creates this using only sound (traffic noises) and light (reflections of car headlamps) in the dimly lit space. The dishevelled figure who shuffles on to the stage and lies down we will only later identify as Creo. Another as yet unidentified figure – it is Esme – enters and removes her own coat to cover the prone body sprawled centre-stage. We must wait right to the end of the play to comprehend this scene fully, to discover that what we were seeing was Creo's future: this is how he will end up and the job of the rest of the play therefore is to show us how he got there. We are allowed no time at the start to contemplate the significance of this tableau because a rapid shift of scene takes us next to the execution of Orrin (Polyneikes), whom we witness being beaten to death (fig. 11): an early signal from the director – as with Rodosthenous – that the ancient Greek convention that keeps violence off-stage is to be disregarded. Tig places her jacket over the body, but Creo's men immediately remove it again. The only words heard so far are the desperate cries of Tig being dragged away from her brother. The next scene is the first with any real dialogue: we are now in a room in the nightclub and Creo's soldiers are awaiting the

FIGURE 11 *Pilot Theatre's production of* Antigone. *Photo Robert Day*

arrival of their leader. The scene that follows this is the equivalent of the one that opens Sophocles' play: the sisters discuss the fate of their unhonoured brother, Tig outraged and resentful, Esme more guarded. Again the postponement of their scene could be interpreted as shifting the spotlight from Tig to Creo, and in this case the impression that we are watching Creo's tragedy is also reinforced by the replicated focus on him at the beginning and the end of the play. But, as will be argued later in relation to Esme, the ending carries additional significance beyond the fate of Creo.

Van Hove chooses to follow his translation more closely and is the only one of these four not to displace the sisters' opening scene. Juliette Binoche as Antigone is the star of this production but it is played very much as an ensemble piece and the director's motivation is more likely to be found in serving his stripped-down approach or in his respect for Sophocles than in showcasing his star.

The chorus: New solutions to a perennial problem

Of all aspects of ancient Greek theatre, it is probably the chorus that presents the director with the biggest challenge. Originally, the chorus would have some specific role to play, sometimes even a direct impact on the action; the leader would deliver spoken lines, but the group as a whole would at times chant rhythmically (recitative) and would also sing and dance in the performance of the choral odes (stasima) that separated one act from the next.[7] There was a need for the chorus to act in unison, but also on occasion to provide a variety of responses to events unfolding in front of them. Much of this does not fit easily into a modern production, particularly if the acting is naturalistic in style. As a result, many directors omit the song and dance and the chanting – in fact, none of the productions under discussion includes these elements – but it can still be a struggle to conjure a group of people who fit naturally into the action. Goldhill believes that more modern performances 'fail because of the chorus than for any other reason' (Goldhill 2007: 45), so decisions made in this area may be crucial to the success of the production.

The old men who made up the Sophoclean chorus for this play, although they were Kreon's subjects, had more of the feel of independent citizens of the democratic Athens contemporaneous to the original audience. They might have feared Kreon but they were not servile. In many current adaptations the chorus is made up of people in Kreon's employ. Placing the chorus in the service of Kreon risks compromising that potentially independent voice. This can have the effect of further isolating Antigone, elevating her position as the lone voice speaking out against tyranny, but it might also deprive the play of a vehicle of impartial criticism of her position. Our productions have found some highly inventive and varied solutions to the problem of what to do with the chorus.

Findlay's chorus is made up of a disparate group of people. They are employees chosen to facilitate the continuance of government from Creon's underground headquarters, so some are senior military and intelligence figures, but others, as Findlay herself has explained, are there to 'clean the bathrooms and make the sandwiches'.[8] This allows for the chorus' lines to be distributed according to the status and personality of the individual, resulting in the expression of diverse opinions and varying degrees of loyalty to the man in control.

Romer follows the Williams translation in making the chorus into members of Creo's gang. In a climate of gangland culture, criticizing the boss is an especially dangerous undertaking, so it is all the more effective when any subordinate dares to do that. It is noticeable early on that one of Creo's henchmen is less willing and more questioning than the others and he provides throughout – both in conversation with his fellow soldiers and in confrontation with Creo – an ethical commentary on his boss's actions. A seismic shift in opinions follows Tyrese's visit: after listening to the old prophet, it is the other – until now obedient – soldiers advising Creo to heed the warning and all are now doubting the wisdom of their boss's decisions.

The chorus in the Rodosthenous production is an interesting variation. From the evidence that survives, it seems that Sophocles' usual practice was to supply a chorus of the same gender as the play's protagonist; the *Antigone*, then, was unusual in reversing this norm. What Sophocles achieved by that decision was to deny Antigone a source of natural sympathizers. The male citizens were generally not unkind towards her, but were critical at times of her stance and certainly were never her confidants. The members of the Rodosthenous chorus are female and they work not for Creon but for his wife Eurydice. They are frightened of their employer but also must suffer disdain from Antigone. They are not without feeling for her, but have no taste for her rebellious ideas. These young women are not, therefore, a supply of ready allies for the heroine. Theirs is a world in which Antigone might have been expected to feel comfortable, but she clearly does not. The result, if anything, magnifies her sense of alienation.

Van Hove does not use a separate body of actors to play the chorus; instead the lines are divided among the cast members, so all – with the exception of Kreon – take on additional roles as the need dictates.[9] Sophocles would have used just three actors (all male) to play all parts and a separate group of fifteen men as the chorus.[10] So van Hove preserves the idea of multiple roles, but his ingenious solution integrates chorus and actors. This has the potential to confuse the spectator, but what it achieves – as has been noted by Duška Radosavljević – is to turn the chorus into 'a heterogeneous collection of individuals rather than an anonymous mass' (Radosavljević 2015). It also reinforces the idea of Kreon and Antigone as representative of more widely shared points of view:

FIGURE 12 *Pilot Theatre's production of* Antigone. *Photo Robert Day*

their differences are therefore not to be explained away as purely a personality clash. This is also reinforced by the choice of actors; for instance, the sisters are not presented as teenage girls as the original audience would have expected. Mask and costume were the means by which Sophocles would have conveyed the generation gap between them and Kreon, but van Hove has assembled a cast where significant age differences are for the most part not readily apparent. This makes it difficult to dismiss views expressed as on the one hand rash and hot-headed or on the other hand staid and reactionary: parity among the actors encourages us to concentrate on the arguments rather than the characters.

The love story: Romance for Antigone?

Romantic love is not an explicit feature of Sophocles' play. Not only did Antigone and Haimon never meet on stage, but the name of her fiancé never passes the heroine's lips. As the plot develops, we become very much aware of Haimon's feelings for Antigone, but we have only Ismene's word that his love was reciprocated (Soph. *Ant.* 570). This leaves the whole question of their forthcoming marriage and Antigone's attitude towards it very much open to interpretation.

Findlay adheres to the Sophoclean strategy of maintaining a separation between the protagonist and her prospective husband: the two (while living) never appear together on stage and we never hear from Antigone of her love for Haemon. Adaptations can make more allowance for modern tastes, and Romer takes the liberty of exploring this relationship on stage, as does Rodosthenous. We lose much of the ambiguity fostered in the original but the reward is perhaps a more satisfying insight into the motivations and feelings of the characters.

In particular, Romer presents a conflicted Tig who really does not wish to die for the sake of her principles: she seems always on the brink of giving in and would prefer to escape Creo's stifling world and find a new life with Eamon (Haimon) elsewhere. So when Eamon successfully rescues her from Creo's soldiers, it would seem there is nothing to stop them absconding together. At this point in the script, Williams imagines a road accident: Creo has finally come to make amends, but the lovers are unaware of his change of heart and, panicked by his approach, they run into the road (Williams 2014: 72). However, even though it detracts from the catastrophe overtaking Creo, Romer removes his direct involvement: the lovers simply decide against living life on the run. Instead, they end their lives together; the impression given by the screech of car tyres and cacophony of collision is that they have thrown themselves onto the motorway. This suicidal act returns us a little closer to the Sophoclean plot, but their togetherness intensifies the Romeo and Juliet subtext.

With the Rodosthenous production, the sexual potentialities are more complicated. While Haemon does love Antigone, as with Sophocles we are not so sure of Antigone's feelings for him. In this version, however, there are numerous directorial touches suggestive of what is bubbling under the surface and threatening to erupt at any moment. These undercurrents derive from the incestuous history of the house of Oedipus. When one of the shop assistants comments that this family attracts trouble, then adds 'and each other' it has the effect of sensitizing the audience to the behaviour of all of them. Does Antigone touch her dead brother's body just a little too lovingly? Are the passionate hugs between Eurydice and her son Haemon maybe not quite appropriate? What about the sisterly feelings that prompt Ismene to climb into bed beside Antigone? But most disturbing is the development of the relationship between Antigone and Creon. Early on there is a singularly uncomfortable scene where Creon insists that Antigone be fitted for her wedding dress in front of him: a clear moment of theatrical voyeurism. A major aspect is the power relationship between them: this scene follows her defiance over Polynices' body and he hopes perhaps to intimidate his niece through the vulnerability induced by watching her strip to her underwear. But, when Antigone later accuses him of longing to take Haemon's place beside her, we have witnessed the conduct that has led her to entertain that notion. There are of course precedents for the exploration of this idea; for example, Ziter (Mee and Foley 2011: 301) comments on the 'disturbing sensuality to Kreon's manhandling of Antigone' in Jihad Saad's 2005 adaptation titled *Antigone's Emigration*.

The character of Antigone is frequently represented as completely unbending, obsessed with her one goal of burying her brother. This requires the omission of a disputed speech in Sophocles' work

(Soph. *Ant.* 904–20), which has the effect of completely unravelling her former certainty.[11] In the Rodosthenous production, the spirit of that speech is honoured when Antigone gives in to Haemon's pleas and makes a public apology for her rebellious action. It wins Antigone her freedom but proves a fatal blow to her union with Haemon. Creon sarcastically refers to them as 'star-crossed lovers', but the comparison with Romeo and Juliet is only valid in the context of their public image. Antigone has told Creon: 'You know I cannot love him after his betrayal.' Haemon too recognizes this and he too inculpates Creon as the source of the poison that has ruinously infected his relationship with the woman he loves.

Without adding any words to Carson's script, van Hove engineers a shared moment between Antigone and Haimon. It happens during the staging of Antigone's burial of her brother: while the messenger relays the details of what he has witnessed, a trap door is used to bring Polyneikes' body on stage and we watch his sister carry out the burial rites. Haimon joins his beloved while she is about this task and the looks exchanged between the two are enough to convey to the audience the mutual feeling and regard that are never confirmed by Sophocles.

Ismene: The fainthearted sister reassessed

A surprising – and for me pleasing – recent trend seems to be the reimagining of Ismene.[12] Traditionally, she is viewed as the fainthearted sister who lacks the courage of her convictions: she might agree with Antigone's stance, but is unwilling to risk her own safety. This never was exactly true of the original version: the Sophoclean Ismene willingly offered her life, but the cause to which she would give her wholehearted support was not the burial of her dead brother but the defence of her living sister. She was sensible and practical rather than showily heroic, but she did not lack courage. It is refreshing, then, to see a revival of interest in her and a readiness to look at her in a new light.

Often the difference in character between the two sisters is indicated by the choice of costume. Typical is Michael Ewans' production of 1996: Antigone is in jeans with tied-back hair, while Ismene wears a dress and shawl with her long hair flowing loose.[13] Rodosthenous, then, seems to signal a departure from the conventional approach by dressing both in black, eyes hidden by their shades. Nevertheless, it soon becomes apparent that Antigone is the dominant one of the pair and Ismene's copycat look signifies the extent to which she adores and idolizes her older sister. Ismene knows that she has no real influence over Antigone, but that does not deter her from trying. Even though she would dissuade Antigone from her chosen path if she could, she never ceases to be loving and supportive. And in this version she is not forgotten; she is the only member of the family, besides Creon, left alive at the end and is magnanimous enough to offer him the comfort of her embrace. This is the spectacle with which the play ends.

Romer's production perhaps goes furthest in finding a new role for Esme. She has appeared less brave than her sister throughout the play – or maybe just less foolhardy – but what Romer recognizes is that, with Creo a broken man abandoned by his wife, only Esme remains as the uncorrupted centre of the family. After her unsuccessful pleading for her sister's life, Sophocles makes no further use of the character, but Romer looks beyond the Sophoclean ending. The ground has been prepared by Tig's own assessment of her sister: 'She's not as weak as you think' (Williams 2014: 62). However, Esme shows her strength not in fighting as Tig had imagined but in her capacity for compassion. At the end of the play, Esme's approach to the lone and pitiable figure of Creo reveals her forgiving nature and heralds a break with the patterns of the past. What is created through the utilization of this largely ignored character – usually seen as no more than a foil for Antigone – is hope for the future.

Van Hove sets the pattern for the relationship between the sisters right from the opening scene: they may bicker and disagree but it is their closeness that allows this and the scene ends in their mutual embrace. When Antigone later pleads that her death is enough, one possible motive might be to deny Ismene a share of the glory, but that is not the case here: this Antigone wants only to keep her sister safe, to let her live. Antigone's deep feeling for Ismene encourages us too to recognize her worth. It is also noteworthy that, when Kreon is offered good advice by the chorus, the Ismene actor is typically the one to deliver those lines.

Eurydike: Giving a voice to secondary characters

The part of the Sophoclean Eurydike, wife of Kreon, is limited to a brief appearance towards the very end of the play: she comes on stage to hear the news of her son's death, then she silently departs, back into the palace to kill herself. The modern adapter feels the awkwardness of introducing a new character so late in the proceedings. The tendency, then, is either to drop the part altogether or to make more of the role.[14] The directors of both our adaptations under scrutiny have opted for the latter solution.

Findlay's choice, though, is to adhere to the dictates of the translation she is utilizing, denying herself the freedom enjoyed by the adapters to favour Eurydice with additional lines. However, by allocating her desk space in the underground facility and allowing her to share moments with her husband and with the rest of his team, Findlay has vastly increased Eurydice's presence. This policy of integrating her character into the action enables emotional dividends to be reaped when we see her drastic response to the news of her son's death.

Under Rodosthenous' direction, Eurydice is both better informed and more decisive than her husband Creon and is slowly revealed as the power behind the throne. This treatment takes the characters into territory that is more Euripidean than Sophoclean: one is reminded of the ineffectual Orestes manipulated by the obsessive Elektra, or the weak and compromised Jason outmanoeuvred by the clever and determined Medea.[15] Eurydice is politically astute; for example, she criticizes Creon for using the word 'privileged' in his speech on the grounds of its use in Polynices' manifesto, which – judging by her quotations from it – she has studied in depth. The wedding boutique is run by Eurydice, and it is telling that when Creon – the newly elected Prime Minister – visits he assures the assistants that he is 'still just the boss's husband'. Where Antigone is concerned, Creon would favour leniency, but Eurydice is implacable and determined to prevent the marriage with her son by any means. Her domination now is reminiscent of Lady Macbeth, potentially winning more sympathy for Creon but equally likely to invite contempt. Were it the case that he truly believed Antigone to be in the wrong then his treatment of her would seem less reprehensible than if he is merely trying to please his wife.

In the Romer production Creo's wife is Eunice and her character is drawn with considerable complexity. Here too she is disapproving of Tig, but more willing to negotiate, more willing to intervene if that will enable her to help her son. We first meet her when she visits Tig in her temporary place of imprisonment, the club cellar. The reasonable attitude of the older woman seems at first to show up Tig's immaturity, with Eunice advising: 'You shouldn't be so angry all of the time' (Williams 2014: 38). But soon their pre-existing enmity resurfaces and the interview breaks down with nothing achieved. The problem for Eunice is that the only way she is able to envisage serving Eamon's interests lies in extricating him from this undesirable relationship with Tig. Her objections relate to Tig's incestuous family history. Throughout the action there are many insults from various characters levelled at Tig that allude to her parents' incestuous and disastrous marriage. Given the exacerbating factor that the lovers are first cousins, Eunice's concerns are not without grounds, but that is not to justify her attitude towards the innocent girl. Romer grants all characters a fair hearing and elicits performances from his actors that make it hard to side completely with any one of them.

As with Findlay, van Hove does not add or redistribute lines in order to expand the part of Eurydike, but the actor's participation in the chorus is sufficient in itself to dissipate any feeling of oddness concerning the late introduction of the character.

The bodies: Staging death and dying

In Sophocles' time, convention decreed that a messenger should report the unseen acts of violence such as murder, but often this was supplemented by having the bodies of the victims brought on stage to allow the audience to see the result. Thus, when Kreon returns to the stage having failed to prevent the suicides of both Antigone and Haimon, the body of his son is brought back too. Eurydike's body was also displayed. What happened to Antigone's body is not clear. This is because no stage directions were included in the texts as they have come down to us, so in the absence of a spoken reference to it we cannot be sure. Some argue (see e.g. Brown 1987: 224) that since her body is not mentioned we must assume it was not there, that the ending concentrates on Kreon's tragedy and Antigone's lifeless presence would be a distraction. However, that is to overlook the fact that his treatment of Antigone is the root cause of Kreon's downfall and her body would serve as a silent reminder of this. The possibilities for modern productions multiply as the opportunity exists to bring not only the bodies on stage but the slaughter too. As these choices dictate the nature of the final impressions with which the spectators are left, they are some of the most important that the director will make.

Findlay has Creon carry the body of his son back into the bunker. The body of Antigone too is wheeled in. This is also the scene of Eurydice's suicide, evidenced by the blood spattered over the glass dividing wall. Creon, now broken, is trapped in a role he no longer wishes to fulfil. As Eero Laine has noted, Creon's punishment mirrors that which was meted out to Antigone: he is 'buried alive in his bunker and [in] his position as the living embodiment of the state' (Laine 2012). The presence of Antigone's body, then, serves to highlight the complementarity of their fates.

As discussed above, Romer has Orrin killed on stage, but his dead body remains only long enough for Tig to attempt to cover it with her jacket. This gesture, however, is significant in the way it repeats the action of Esme at the very start. When at the end we find ourselves back in that moment with Creo and Esme, it is apparent that Esme cares for her family as much as Tig. The difference is that Esme extends that care to the living.

In addition to Orrin, and in keeping with his greater emphasis on the love story, Romer features the deaths of Tig and Eamon. The scene showing their joint suicide has a surreal feel facilitated by the doom-laden music accompanying their slow-motion fall. A short blackout is followed by Creo's discovery of the bodies. His grief is not reserved for Eamon alone, but encompasses the two of them. He has learned a lesson, but the calamity is a typically Sophoclean one in that this new understanding has come too late.

Rodosthenous retains all three acts of suicide from Sophocles' version but in each case brings the deed itself on stage. The spillage of all this blood takes place at Antigone and Haemon's wedding feast, hence vividly setting the seal upon their doomed romance. The last fifteen minutes of the production contain no dialogue: in the role of what Pavis has termed a 'choreographer of silence', the director 'works with silence and non-verbal signs, be they visual or musical' (Pavis 2012: 289). As the violence is acted out against a sombre musical soundtrack – Kanchelli's Viola Concerto *Mourned by the Wind* – the movements of the whole cast, wedding guests and all, are carefully orchestrated in this macabre dance of death, the use of lighting adding to the dreamlike feel of it. First, Antigone slits her own throat with the same knife that was used to cut the wedding cake. Like a chain reaction, there follows Haemon's death, then Eurydice's. What this accomplishes is to surround Creon with death in a very graphic way. We have seen his reliance on his wife's shrewd advice and we have witnessed his power-play with Antigone, but only now does Creon recognize the true cost of his political ambition: the life of his son. It is the directorial handling of the whole sequence that brings home to the audience the enormity of that tragedy for Creon.

The only bodies displayed on stage by van Hove are those of Polyneikes and Antigone and both are brought on in the same way: by use of the trap door. This serves to relate the two of them in death most closely to each other. Kreon does not bring Haimon's body back with him, but when seated on the sofa in front of the stage, Kreon is briefly joined by the actor playing Haimon, who allows his head to be cradled. Played in this way, the fourth wall is breached intensifying the emotional impact experienced by the audience. The treatment of Eurydike is comparatively low key: she leaves on stage a garment, which metonymically substitutes for her body. The final image, though, is of an abject Kreon on stage with the dead body of Antigone projected on to the backdrop. The juxtaposition of the two adversaries brings home their similarity to each other: both are stubborn and emotionally volatile, and through their inability to contemplate compromise both end up losing everything.

Conclusions

There is so much more that could be discussed: costume, delivery, light, sound, and much else besides would undoubtedly have benefited from more sustained analysis. Moreover, the play has a vast political legacy that affects so many interpretations of it. The focus here, however, has been on the director's art, particularly in relation to the portrayal of family dynamics. I have tried to concentrate on the director's more significant choices and to cast a little light over some less well-trodden ground.

Romer, by means of the set design and the naturalistic dialogue, achieves a gritty, menacing feel of the streets. The realism is punctured, however, at intensely dramatic moments by heightened use of sound effects and lighting. The most obvious such moment is the joint suicide of Tig and Eamon (fig. 12) and it works to suggest almost a kind of romantic idealism, granting individuals the power to transcend their surroundings, until we are brought back to earth by the sight of their now lifeless bodies.

The setting of the wedding boutique and the culminating scene of the wedding indicate Rodosthenous' interest in the interpersonal relations of his characters, albeit against a political backdrop. This world of power and privilege provides a neat contrast to Romer's seedier side of life.

Findlay's radical revisiting of Taylor's script spectacularly illustrates the power of a well-chosen setting to breathe new life into an existing translation. The claustrophobic intensity of Creon's bunker creates a pressure-cooker atmosphere, which, given the state of high alert that would still exist in the immediate aftermath of an internecine war, serves to magnify suspicions and antagonisms among the already overwrought family members. It also provides at the end a perfect visual metaphor for the trap into which Creon has descended. In the hands of such a talented director, a translation can provide just as much opportunity for inventiveness as an adaptation.

Van Hove is alone in refusing to anchor his production in a specific time and place. He thereby sacrifices the advantages of giving the audience a ready route to understanding and identifying with the characters, but in the way he frames the action he uses a recognizably Brechtian device eliciting among the spectators a sense of alienation in order to engage them on a more cerebral level.[16] This production is all about detachment, depersonalization and minimalism, but the director's judicious use of heightened emotion – especially in the performances of Antigone and Kreon – prevent it from becoming just an academic exercise. The presentation brings understanding of what is at stake and the characterization of the leads gives the audience a reason to care. His sparse set design and interesting use of video projection make for a memorable experience, his singular sense of theatricality complementing Carson's sensitive new text.

Romer's framing device – the repeated scene of Creo and Esme that begins and ends the play – does most to draw attention to Creo's tragedy. Whereas the other characters exercise some level of control over their destiny, Creo's downfall comes about as a result of his own erroneous choices. These brief, dialogue-free scenes plus the killing of Orrin reflect the more sustained use of choreographed silence employed by Rodosthenous in his production: the brothers' fight at the beginning and the wedding scene at the end. In both cases, the silence contrasts with the extensive dialogue – the banter among friends, the bickering of siblings and the confrontational clashes between enemies – that these adaptations use liberally as ways of examining the tangled web of intra-familial relations. The dialogue-free space at the close fosters a mood of meditative silence to reflect on what has been witnessed.

These productions show that there is still a place for the chorus as long as the director is willing to be flexible and exercise some imagination. Sometimes it will be appropriate to include song and dance elements, but often it is enough just to preserve the idea of a group of people who can comment on the action and respond to the arguments of a protagonist. Romer's employees of Creo flesh out the workings of the gangland culture and Rodosthenous' employees of Eurydice relate in an interesting way to Sophocles' original chorus while providing essential colouring and important information by means of their gossip. Findlay has carefully distributed the lines among the government employees who make up her chorus so as to characterize each according to the role allocated, from cleaner to intelligence officer. Van Hove, exceptionally, has moved in the opposite direction and virtually anonymized his chorus. We do not need to know who they are or why they are there: their largely dispassionate reflections serve to prompt our own in response.

A welcome trend is the increasing exploration of the minor characters, often facilitating a more nuanced understanding of the extended family network. The Hegelian influence has tended to lead too easily to a reduction of the work's complexities into a binary opposition represented by the two leading characters. For

Hegel, it was family in the person of Antigone versus state represented by Kreon, but many variations have since been proffered.[17] It is most welcome, therefore, to encounter the multiplicity of meanings unleashed by inviting the other characters into the spotlight. The adapters tend to exercise more licence, since use of a translation implies a decision to adhere more closely to Sophocles' original work. Both Romer and Rodosthenous bring new light to the frequently dismissed character of Ismene and new life to the underused character of Eurydike.

So finally, we return to the question of whether the bodies should be brought on stage. What these versions illustrate is that the actual decision is immaterial as long as the director has thought through the possibilities and has chosen the approach that best delivers for the purposes of that production. Rodosthenous makes use of the triple-death scenario at the end to bring his production to a dramatic climax while simultaneously bringing the surviving two family members together. The bodies resulting from Romer's double suicide strike a sobering end-note to the Romeo and Juliet romance, but his final scene too brings Creo and Esme together. For Findlay, the bodies in the bunker remove any chance of solace for the distraught Creon, who is physically and psychologically entombed there with them. And van Hove has judiciously chosen just two bodies to display – Polyneikes' as the cause of the feud and Antigone's the result of it, the mirroring demonstrating their special relationship. Each of these versions in its own way brings a new focus on family matters. The potential for variation is endless, all of which explains why Antigone and the rest of her dysfunctional family are still with us after two-and-a-half-thousand years and show no signs yet of terminal decline.

Bibliography

Billington, M. (2015) 'Juliette Binoche Stars in Puzzling, Profound Take on Sophocles', *Guardian*, 6 March. Online at www.theguardian. com/stage/2015/mar/06/antigone-review-unusual-puzzling-profound-sophocles-reimagining (accessed 31 July 2016).

Blundell, S. (1995) *Women in Ancient Greece*. London: British Museum Press.

Brown, A. L. (ed.) (1987) *Sophocles: Antigone*. Warminster: Aris & Phillips.

Carson, A. (trans.) (2015) *Sophokles: Antigone*. London: Oberon.

Chanter, T. (2010) 'The Performative Politics and Rebirth of Antigone in Ancient Greece and Modern South Africa'. In F. Söderbäck (ed.), *Feminist Readings of Antigone*. Albany: State University of New York Press, 83–98.

Coveney, M. (2015) 'Reviews: *Antigone*' (Barbican Theatre), *What's On Stage*, 6 March. Online at www.whatsonstage.com/london-theatre/reviews/antigone-barbican-juliette-binoche_37311.html (accessed 31 July 2016).

Easterling, P. E. (1987) 'Women in Tragic Space'. *Bulletin of the Institute of Classical Studies* 34: 15–26.

Erincin, S. (2011) 'Performing Rebellion: *Eurydice's Cry* in Turkey'. In E. B. Mee and H. P. Foley (eds), *Antigone on the Contemporary World Stage*. Oxford: Oxford University Press, 171–83.

Goldhill, S. (2007) *How to Stage Greek Tragedy Today*. Chicago: University of Chicago Press.

Honig, B. (2013) *Antigone Interrupted*. Cambridge: Cambridge University Press.

Laine, E. (2012) '*Antigone* at the National Theatre, London'. *Western European Stages* 24: 85–6, 95.

Paolucci, A. and Paolucci, H. (1962) *Hegel on Tragedy*. New York: Harper & Row.

Pavis, P. (2012) *Contemporary Mise en Scène: Staging Theatre Today*. London: Routledge.

Peponi, A.-E. (2013) 'Theorizing the Chorus in Greece'. In J. Billings, F. Budelmann and F. Macintosh (eds), *Choruses, Ancient and Modern*. Oxford: Oxford University Press, 15–34.

Radosavljević, D. (2015) 'Layers of Complication'. *Exeunt*, 10 March. Online at www.exeuntmagazine.com/features/layers-of-complication/ (accessed 31 July 2016).

Sommerstein, A. H. (2002) *Greek Drama and Dramatists*. London: Routledge.

Spencer, C. (2012) '*Antigone*, National Theatre', review, *Telegraph*, 31 May. Online at www.telegraph.co.uk/culture/theatre/theatre-reviews/9303336/Antigone-National-Theatre-review.html (accessed 31 July 2016).

Taylor, D. (trans.) (2012) *Sophocles Antigone*. London: Methuen.

Torrance, I. (2007) *Aeschylus: Seven Against Thebes*. London: Duckworth.

Treu, M. (2011) 'Never Too Late: *Antigone* in a German Second World War Cemetery on the Italian Apennines'. In E. B. Mee and H. P. Foley (eds), *Antigone on the Contemporary World Stage*. Oxford: Oxford University Press, 307–23.

Trueman, M. (2015) 'London Theater Review: *Antigone* Starring Juliette Binoche', *Variety*, 6 March. Online at www.variety. com/2015/legit/reviews/antigone-review-juliette-binoche-barbican-london-1201447863/ (accessed 31 July 2016).

White, J. J. (2004) *Bertolt Brecht's Dramatic Theory*. Rochester NY: Camden House.

Williams, R. (2014) *Antigone*. London: Bloomsbury Methuen.

Ziter, E. (2011) 'No Grave in the Earth: *Antigone's Emigration* and Arab Connections'. In E. B. Mee and H. P. Foley (eds), *Antigone on the Contemporary World Stage*. Oxford: Oxford University Press, 289–306.

Exodus, Ἔξοδος: In search of a contemporary catharsis

Greek tragedy has helped shape our understanding of life, trauma, violence, war, life and death. It is the 'mother' of many contemporary theatrical narratives and it still manages to inform, educate, entertain, engage, shock and transform its audiences. This volume has consciously avoided an in-depth analytical discussions of the existing Greek tragedies, but celebrated the ways these tragedies have been adapted by visionary directors within a Western and non-Western context. By doing so, it has allowed us access to view the new work afresh, by absorbing the narrative in a fully embodied spectatorial experience.

Directors are now more eager to incorporate technological and posthuman representations to portray the characters. CREW's *O_REX Oedipus* (2007) and *Antigone* (2012) are adapted in a radical way alongside technological innovations. 'Antigone and Oedipus become a posthuman composite body, embodying the ever shifting boundary between the human and the inhuman, the animate and the inanimate' (Stalpaert 2015: 19). Innovations with technology will unfold new ways of representation, audience perception and engagement, perhaps involving a new interactive element, which will engage the audience in a new dimension and at a much deeper intensity.

The violence of the Greek tragedy has infiltrated into the Roman tragedy – especially Seneca, who adapted Greek models for a less poetically minded audience and subsequently British theatre (see Shakespeare's *Titus*, which is full of Greek references from Aegisthus' father serving his brother's children to his brother, etc.). Is it perhaps time to move back to more symbolic representations of the on-stage violence? Is it time to allow the post-dramatic theatre to rediscover new narratives of the story? When we watch theatre, 'when we spectate, Roger Simon argues, we engage actively with what we see and hear, but we also work, just as actively, to manage our experience of the other's story at a safe distance from ourselves (what Kuftinec might call an enlightenment practice of empathy)' (Solga 2008: 159). Greek tragedy has been fundamental in helping us understand ourselves, and understand the others around us.

In my *Theatre as Voyeurism*, I started my discussion by stating that

> Pentheus is regarded as one of the first voyeurs on the theatrical stage. When the god Dionysus offers him the opportunity to observe – hidden – the orgiastic activities of the Bacchants in the mountains, Pentheus accepts, even if he has to deny his muscular masculinity and dress up as a woman in order to blend in and remain unnoticed. Pentheus' desire to watch the women in the mountains dancing and singing in ecstasy does not bode well for him as, in the end, he is killed and decapitated by his own mother; his guiltless visual pleasure is punished with extreme death. (2015: 1)

Thousands of years have passed since the premiere of *The Bacchae*, and our spectatorial habits have been developed since then. Are there any positive aspects to our 'voyeurism' that will allow us to get a better understanding of our world, identify our role within it, and help us manage our actions (our dreams, passions and traumas) in a more affirmative way? Perhaps this is what contemporary catharsis actually is. It would be beneficial to remind ourselves of this today, when the twenty-first century has witnessed some extreme violence of terrorism and attitudes towards cultural heritage. What can we do when we see cultural sites being destroyed? How do we respond to the portrayals in the media and the world around us? In what ways can Greek tragedy heal these outbursts of extremism?

NOTES

Introduction: The Contemporary Director in Greek Tragedy

1   For some adaptors like David Hare, stage adaptation is 'direction by proxy'. He believes that 'as you adapt, you do create a little production in your head. When you work with a great director, you notice that what they are doing is effectively tuning the play to the audience's understanding. It is like turning a lens to crisp focus' (2015).

2   See Anne Washburn's transadaptation of *Iphigenia in Aulis* for the Classic Stage Company in New York, http://www.classicstage.org/season/greekfestival/ (accessed 9 September 2016).

Chapter 1: American Directorial Perspectives: Independence Day Meets Greek Tragedy

1   See my *Euripides in Cinema* (1983), *Ancient Sun* (1992) and *The Living Art of Greek Tragedy* (2003). Many followed in this research, notably, J. Michael Walton, Edith Hall (establishing at Royal Holloway the Centre for the Reception of Greece and Rome), Fiona Macintosh and Helene P. Foley.

2   See my chapter 'Dancing Drama: Ancient Greek Theatre in Modern Shoes and Shows' in Nadine George-Graves (ed.), *The Oxford Handbook of Dance and Theatre*. Oxford: Oxford University Press.

3   Both plays will be published by Murasaki in an anthology called *The Myth Strikes Back: Medea Plays by Women* that Velina Hasu Houston and I co-edited. My *Medea, Queen of Colchester* has

already been published, with an interview, in Wetmore 2013, pp. 293–337. However, both her version and mine are also included in this collection.

4   See Wetmore 2002, 130–41.

5   Silas Jones's play was directed by L. Kenneth Richardson at the Mark Taper Forum in Los Angeles in 1995 and later went to the Arena Stage in Washington DC.

6   From a play script by Silas Jones.

7   See Wetmore 2003, pp. 187–98.

8   Wetmore 2005. I wrote about classical influences in those films, particularly the Oedipal themes. See 'A New Hope: Film as a Teaching Tool for the Classics' in Lorna Hardwick and Christopher Stray (eds), *A Companion to Classical Receptions*. Malden MA; Oxford: Blackwell, 2008, 327–41.

9   Technology (as we've seen in *Star Wars*) is another American speciality, and some of it has made its way on to the stage – see Sellars' *Persians*, above, and also my *Trojan Women* at The Old Globe, which featured a gigantic Poseidon and a Vietnam setting with catwalks of netting over which people scrambled as guns were fired and bombs exploded in stunning displays.

10 I have also seen a production of *Medea* directed by the well-known American director Les Waters, at the University of California San Diego, in which the young children smiled at the audience, stealing the show and wrecking the performance. Waters took a leave of absence in the middle of the directing cycle, so at times even directors can be overwhelmed by a cast they cannot control.

11 McDonald 2012, which covers not only his most recent work, but gives historical context and a discussion of his directorial techniques in the rehearsal room.

12 In *Arion* 15.1 (Spring–Summer 2007): 127–56.

13 He bought a house in New York, and has lived there and in California for decades. He became a member of the American Academy of Arts and Sciences in 2013 and received a lifetime Tony award in 2011.

14 Fugard 2005. The first performance was in Los Angeles, and the director, Stephen Sachs, was assisted by Fugard.

15 'Trying to Regain Childhood's Magic', Theater, *New York Times*, 11 April 2014, Arts Section, which says that the entire performance lasts about an hour. The play was set in my house in Del Mar, where the Fugards were living. The analogy of Plato's cave to represent

man's illusions is used in this text, something I suggested to him. À propos of which, his wife, Sheila, once said to me that I gave him a classical education, beyond his omnivorous reading of the texts.

16 The rush of performance before audiences was very attractive, but it has put a serious strain on Fugard's heart condition. (I will never forget driving him to Scripps Hospital in La Jolla to have stents inserted following a heart attack.) He gets very difficult just before opening night – everything must be *perfect* – so there is a terrible strain on the actors and on him, though ultimately it pays off.

17 McDonald 2000.

18 In (1962) *Hegel on Tragedy*, Anne and Henry Paolucci (eds and intro.). Westport CT: Greenwood Press, 178.

19 When this *Antigone* went on to the Delphi Festival of Greek Drama in 2000, and then to Vienna, with an all-Irish cast (DonAd, run by Donal Courtney), it began with Irish keening (shrill wailing) as the dead were surveyed, but then the first chorus was followed by a vigorous and celebratory Irish jig with the whole company performing – so the call to dance is fulfilled.

20 Ivan Talijancic is not only an actor but a director and runs his own company (WAXFACTORY) in New York.

21 *Hana* means 'flower' in Japanese: Zeami 1984.

22 Which he dedicated to the author of this chapter, Marianne McDonald.

23 'Critic's Choice: *Antigone*', review by Anne Marie Welsh and Jennifer de Poyen, *San Diego Union-Tribune*, Thursday 5 May 2005.

24 In 1993 Edward Said and I attended the opening of Peter Sellar's *The Persians* together, and the Oud player and composer, Hamza El Din, came over and made an obeisance to Edward, since he respected his work so much. An analogy was drawn between a parallel between the defeat of the Persians and the Gulf War (Robert Auletta wrote the adaptation). Howie Seago, the deaf mute who was extraordinary in Sellar's *Ajax* at the La Jolla Playhouse in 1986, played the ghost of Darius, who lectures Xerxes. (The chorus translates for him. See my Peter Sellars' *Ajax*, and Talk at Carnuntum, *Ancient Sun, Modern Light, Greek Drama on the Modern Stage* (Columbia University Press: New York, Oxford 1992), pp. 75–95). John Ortiz was the vibrant actor who brought Xerxes to life. Said described hits during the Gulf War on the news performed for the Americans as if it was a video game. He was disgusted.

25 Lee Breuer and Bob Telson (2001) 'The Gospel at Colonus: Black
    Pearls and Greek Diamonds'. In Sing Sorrow: Classics History
    and Heroines in Opera. Westport, CT; London: Greenwood Press,
    159–78.

Chapter 2: Greek Contemporary Approaches to Tragedy: Terzopoulos' Revisions of Aeschylus

1   After graduating from Costas Michailides' drama school in Athens,
    Terzopoulos left for Germany, where he formed his background
    studying next to the expressionist choreographer Ruth Berghaus,
    Brecht's actor Ekkehard Schall and, most notably, post-modern
    playwright Heiner Müller.

2   Still under the influence of his training at the Berliner Ensemble,
    Terzopoulos directs plays by Brecht (The Bread Shop, The Little
    Mahagonny and Mother Courage), but also by Sartre, Mrozek and
    Lorca. In fact, his production of Yerma (1981) marks the beginnings
    of his growing reputation as a director; quite possibly, it is the
    first of his productions to move away from an overtly Brechtian
    aesthetic.

3   The company borrows its name from God Dionysus, who
    symbolizes loss of control. Terzopoulos' work with actors is very
    much about the alternation of physical states of control (discipline)
    and release.

4   For more on Terzopoulos' work on tragedy, see Sidiropoulou 2011.
    For revisionist adaptations of Greek tragedy, see Sidiropoulou 2015.

5   While criticism of over-eager intercultural perspectives in theatre
    practice has been fierce, in Terzopoulos' work, 'the invocation of
    global humanism is not complicit with an overwhelming hegemonic
    order' (Stone Peters 1995: 202).

6   The author is responsible for the English translations of those parts
    in the Greek original for which no given translation was available.

7   A fact that can be attributed to Aeschylus' own involvement as a
    soldier in the battle of Salamis.

8   Rejecting Realism through and through, Terzopoulos claims
    disinterest in 'character,' opting instead for the evocation of mood
    well within the crux of the dramatic situation.

9   The director actually defines *avant-garde* art as 'an explosion of the root of the classical' (quoted in Kyriakou 2012).

10 The production of the first version of *The Persians* opened at the N. Kazantzakis Little Garden Theatre, in Iraklion, Crete in August 1990, and thereafter toured internationally for two years.

11 Terzopoulos often relies on non-Western physical patterns, borrowing acting techniques from the Japanese Noh and Kabuki theatres, as well as from the Indian Kathakali.

12 Drawing from a pool of traditional techniques of ecstatic transcendence (pain, motion, self-concentration) and having studied Dionysian rituals such as the fire-walking ceremonies (anastenaria) that have survived in the Northern part of Greece, Terzopoulos bases his system on the actors' physical exhaustion, which is duly accompanied by a release of tension, both mental and psychic. Clearly, this is a biodynamic method that ultimately 'deconstructs the body.' While the head and the arms become autonomous from the rest of the body, what 'is weakened is the controlling power of the ego, allowing for the id of each performer to come to the surface' (Hatzidimitriou 2007: 57).

13 After all, Terzopoulos' ambition has always been to locate the origins of speech inside the actors, by exposing them to sheer bodily exhaustion.

14 Given the static quality of the play, poetry replaces or actually produces spectacle:

    The spectator of Aeschylus – more than the spectator of any later classical tragedy, and infinitely more than the spectator of most modern drama – must learn in the first place to listen to the verbal poetry, almost with the same attention that he would give to polyphonic music. For it is in the words that the dramatic themes are usually first developed and interlaced. The eye will have its turn later. (Burian and Shapiro 2009: 20–1)

15 Both sets of props feature repeatedly in Terzopoulos' work.

16 One of the production reviews seemed particularly hostile to Terzopoulos' fresh reading:

    Probably just so he can strengthen the cause of the Greek–Turkish friendship, the director gave an erroneous reading of the tragedy. Aeschylus never wrote a tragedy of reconciliation, in the way that Terzopoulos presented Persians. The lament blended with an amane, and the Turkish actors embraced the Greeks with empathy and support. These elements are absent in

Aeschylus. (http://www.nooz.gr/page.ashx?pid=9&aid=103353 (accessed 1 September 2015), 2006, my translation)

17 In fact, the Turkish element becomes visibly pronounced in the most memorable Dervish dance of the performance, after which the performer collapses on the stage.

18 Recent scholarship has, however, contested the tragedy's authorship.

19 Not only does *Prometheus Bound* offer a pained account of human progress (social, political, intellectual), it also suggests that 'access to knowledge and freedom to learn and the harnessing of hope for social improvement are the corollary of political freedom in general and democratic freedom in particular' (Ruffell 2012: 78).

20 Part of the same *Promethiade* project that featured Terzopoulos' 2010 version of *Prometheus Bound*.

21 Dimitris Tsatsoulis speaks of a 'dialogue' taking place between the body of the performer (who is in a state of 'ecstasis') and the very ground of the earth, from which stems the energy force that renders him 'mobile in his immobility' (2008: 285).

22 See, for example, Mikis Theodorakis' composition of Odysseas Elytis' emblematic poem 'Axion Esti' (1959), sung by the Chinese performers («Πού να βρω την ψυχή μου/το τετράφυλλο δάκρυ» ['Where shall I find my soul/ the four-petal tear'], my translation).

23 There are formal white suits for the Kratos-Bia Chorus, dark grey factory uniforms for the Oceanids and generic black pants for the topless followers of Prometheus.

24 The *Promethiade* project co-featured German theatre company Rimini Protokoll's *Prometheus in Athens* and Turkish auteur Sahika Tekand's *Anti-Prometheus (forgotten in ten steps)*.

25 Efi Marinou discusses Terzopoulos' need to explore the nebulous landscape of the new era, making reference to the production's political point of view:

> Here the ocean spits out corpses, immigrants and runaways from pogroms and wars. Five Germans, five Turks and six Greeks find refuge to the 'Caucasus' of Elefsina, sharing a similar dark future. They meet in a 'transit' space, in a European three-cultural context, and their costumes have nothing in common, apart from the gaze of a strolling pauper. They enter the space, some from the fields, others from the harbor, and mix with the spectators. These are the Prometheuses from next-door, 'nouveau-poor', homeless, hostages of the current state. (2010, my translation)

26   Decreus delves further into the meaning and functionality of
'klausigelos', which he considers to be also a strategy of delaying the
action, deactivating the dimensions of time and space, and turning
the actors into shamanistic creatures. With respect to the 2010
production of *Prometheus Bound*, he actually wonders whether
tragic life has merely become 'a question of "Lächerlichkeit"'
[German for ridicule], or if sarcasm has taken over: 'Is this the
end of tragedy, a western category that accompanied our culture
for more than 2500 years and do we finally arrive in a post-tragic
landscape?' (Decreus 2014: 64).

Chapter 3: British Auteurship and the Greeks: Katie Mitchell

1   On her feminism, and how it interacts with theatre generally,
Mitchell says that all of the work she makes 'revolves around
female experience, in one form or another' ... [I]f we do stage
Hamlet or other plays with troubling gender politics, they should
be 'reframed'. 'We've got to interrogate them,' she argues.
'Otherwise it looks like we're actually presenting the gender politics
from the [n]th century as an offering on how we should interact as
men and women in society now. And if these issues aren't framed,
then it's possible that people take a license for the certain types of
sexist behaviour from this drama. So we have to be really, really
careful about how we frame these old plays, particularly when the
gender politics are so execrable ...' (Enwright 2016)

2   'Camera show' is the name that Mitchell has given to the increasing
strand of her productions using live-feed video technology. Typically,
these will feature a large screen hung over the stage showing what
resembles a fully realized cinema film, but with the performers being
filmed – live – below this screen to achieve the scenes.

3   This is a designation that could be construed as misleading in pretty
much every meaningful possible respect. At the same time, it's an
idea that communicates *something*.

4   A good study of precisely this false binary can be found in
Radosavljević (2013).

5   As directly referenced in Spencer's quoted *Telegraph* review, earlier
in 2007 the then artistic director of the National Theatre, Nicholas
Hytner, had said he thought the chief critics of Britain's daily

broadsheets were 'dead white males' who had a particular problem with female directors.

Chapter 4: Tadashi Suzuki and Yukio Ninagawa: Reinventing the Greek Classics; Reinventing Japanese Identity after Hiroshima

1   Yet, James Brandon explicitly refuses to endorse the belief that the most powerful stage interpretations of classical texts result from such a clash between text and director, arguing that traditional Asian theatre practice reveals other models of theatre performance in which the constant push and pull between text and performing codes is delicately balanced by the performer (1989: 43–4).

2   For more on the historical transformations of the Japanese collective memory of the atomic bombing of Hiroshima, see Saito 2006.

3   For more on how the twentieth century can be mapped as the century of the body as a site of resistance, see Marshall 1992: 1–5.

4   For more, see Ian Jenkins' note, curator of the exhibition 'Defining Beauty: The Body in Ancient Greek Art' at the British Museum (26 March–5 July 2015).

5   In his introduction to On Ugliness, Umberto Eco readily stresses the difficulty involved in analysing artifacts of non-Western civilizations with the Western aesthetic criteria of beauty and ugliness although this has been the commonest approach (2007: 10).

6   For an analytical description of Suzuki's The Trojan Women, see McDonald 1993: 37–64.

7   For more about the fate of the 'A-bomb maidens', see Saito 2006: 365–6.

8   The Elizabethan and Jacobean theatre also exhibited an interest in the relationship between individual and social pathology and disease. Ben Jonson's The Alchemist, for example, is set against the background of the outbreak of plague in early seventeenth-century London. Nearly two centuries later, Henrik Ibsen dramatized individual and social pathogenesis hand in hand with hereditary syphilis. For a detailed discussion of the relation between theatre and disease, see Garner 2006.

9   For more about Matsuo Taseko, see Walthall 1998.

10 For more, see Eckersall 2006.

11 For the current changing theatre production in Japan, which signals the end of *angura*, see Eckersall 2006.

Chapter 5: Directing Greek Tragedy as a Ritual: Mystagogy, Religion and Ecstasy

1   See Hall 2010, 25ff. for a discussion of the events, religious and political, preceding the dramatic contest.

2   On the association between choral performance and the worship of the gods see especially Herington 1985.

3   On the authority of the chorus's voice, see Goldhill 1996.

4   Walter Burkert's influential work on this issue is *Homo necans* (1985). See also Burkert 1966 and 2001. On the connection between tragedy and cult, see also Seaford 1994: 275–88.

5   On political retopicalizations in the late twentieth century see especially Hall 2007.

6   On the reduced chorus in contemporary productions of Greek tragedy see Foley 2003: 1–30, 4.

7   For culturally specific adaptations of Greek drama see especially Hall, Macintosh and Wrigley 2004, Goff and Simpson 2007, and Mee and Foley 2011.

8   See McConnell 2014. See Gamel (2010) 163–5.

9   It is problematic to impose characteristics of Christian martyrs on figures such as Antigone or Iphigenia, who are essentially fighting for civic rights and political goals. Not to mention that dying a virgin in ancient Greece makes you very unlucky, but not a saint. In fact, we probably should actively try to avoid using, even subconsciously, such a prism through which to interpret these roles, precisely because in the Christian West many of us have been raised with such narratives revolving around the lives of Christian saints.

10 I would like to mention briefly here a relatively recent example of ritual/religious *retopicalization*, but with a sociopolitical undertone: *Iphigenia in T...* by Polish company Gardzienice, an adaptation of *Iphigenia in Tauris* that identified Iphigenia with the Polish cult of the Black Madonna of Częstochowa, and used the rituals of this cult.

The director, Włodzimierz Staniewski, finds in the play a conflict between two opposing worlds: 'the Primitive' and 'the Civilized' … 'the God-fearing' and 'the Enlightened', 'the Commoners' and 'the Aristocracy', 'those of the third speed' and 'those of the first': http://gardzienice.org/en/IPHIGENIA-IN-T....html (accessed 2 August 2016).

11 Alexiou, Yatromanolakis and Roilos 2002.

12 Foley 1993: 101–43.

13 Dué Casey (2006) *The Captive Woman's Lament in Greek Tragedy*. Austin: University of Texas Press.

14 Corinthians 14:34 – 'the women should keep silent in the churches. For they are not permitted to speak, but should be in submission, as the Law also says' (English Standard Version).

15 See Foley 2009 for an examination of how tragedy reflects tensions in women's social and religious roles.

16 A recording of the performance in Athens can be found here: http://youtu.be/lje3sSszS7c.

17 Charalambous 2005.

18 http://www.thoc.org.cy/gr/downloads/400paragoges.pdf (accessed 1 September 2015): Constantinou 2011.

19 For the performance history of Koun's controversial *Birds* see especially Van Steen 2007.

20 Charalambous was Koun's student. Like *The Birds*, Charalambous' *Suppliants* received great acclaim once it crossed the national border.

21 Zanos 1978.

22 Varopoulou 1979.

23 Georgousopoulos 1979.

24 See also Hadjikosti 2013: 170.

25 See http://www.missing-cy.org.cy.

26 Several Cypriot productions of Greek drama inspired by the 1974 events followed Charalambous' *Suppliants*.

27 Jenny Gaitanopoulou, interview with the author in 2013.

28 Lianis 1979.

29 From an interview with the author, 2013.

30 On the production's internal rhythm see also Zanos 1978.

31 See for example reviews of Charalambous' *Oedipus' Rex* (1986) and *Hecuba* (1988) in Georgousopoulos and Gogos 2002: 355, 372.

32 The only significant ideological difference from the original, in

my opinion, was the ironic portrayal of Athena and Theseus, who discuss a war campaign to avenge the dead, as all acts of war are seen in negative light in this production.

33 For an overview of Schechner's anthropological and theatrical exploration of ritual particularly in connection with his adaptation of the *Bacchae* see Zeitlin 1994.

34 *Orghast*, a production of the International Centre for Theatre Research, written by Peter Brook and Ted Hughes and first performed in 1971 at the Festival of Arts in Shiraz-Persepolis.

35 There is no video record of *Orghast*, but for more details on the production see Hall 2007 and Smith 1972.

36 Grotowski 1991: 19, 22.

Chapter 6: La MaMa's *Trojan Women*: Forty-two Years of Suffering Rhythms from New York to Guatemala

1 I saw it at the beginning of my life in theatre, in September 1976, at the Moray House Gymnasium in Edinburgh, as part of the Edinburgh International Festival.

2 I had just completed a short run of a solo performance, *Sacred Poison*, based on Artaud's electro-shock writings, at the Edinburgh Fringe, under the auspices of Edinburgh University Theatre Company, and was in the frame of mind to recognize a performance that embodied his signals through the flames.

3 For an explanation of Odin Teatret's practice of barter, see Eugenio Barba's *The Floating Islands* (1979: 102–7). This book also includes illustrations of the company's barter with the Yanomami indigenous people in Venezuela, South America.

4 Serban makes a similar observation, considering sound to be the authentic expression of Greek tragedy, its energy like an 'animal impulse' (Serban, quoted in Blumental 1976).

5 https://www.youtube.com/watch?v=c9sWweGh03Q (accessed 9 September 2016).

6 European Centre for Theatre Practices Gardzienice was founded by Staniewski in 1977 and takes its name from the village where it is located. Staniewski is a former collaborator of Grotowski, and he is committed to anthropological theatre research in communities.

For an account of aspects of their work, see W. Staniewski with A. Hodge (2004) *Hidden Territories*. London: Routledge.

7   S. Hemming, 3 February 2006, in the *Financial Times*, quoted on Gardzienice website.

8   New York Theatre Experience, 7 April 2005, quoted on Gardzienice website.

9   https://www.youtube.com/watch?v=CKX6nZkn7gs (accessed 9 September 2016).

Chapter 7: Theater of War: Ancient Greek Drama as a Forum for Modern Military Dialogue

1   http://www.outsidethewirellc.com/about/mission (accessed 12 June 2015).

2   http://www.outsidethewirellc.com/projects/theater-of-war/programs (accessed 12 June 2015).

Chapter 8: Jan Fabre's *Prometheus Landscape II*: [De]territorialization of the Tragic and Transgressive Acts of Arson

1   The performance took place at four o'clock in the morning, 'during the "Blue Hour" in a completely blue room, "painted" blue by hundreds of ballpoint pens, an example of his new "balpen art", called from then on "Bicart" opposing traditional "Big Art"' (Decreus, 2012: 136). This sense of liminality inherent in the space/time between night and day as well as the notion of finding alternatives through which to question 'major' artistic practices, is something that I will return to later in the chapter.

2   This chapter will not delve into claims that problematize Aeschylean authorship of the work, e.g. M. Griffith, *The Authenticity of 'Prometheus Bound'* (1977), O. Taplin, *The Stagecraft of Aeschylus* (1978) and M. L. West, 'The Prometheus Trilogy' (1979) among others.

3 For the purposes of this chapter I will be using Murray's translation of the aforementioned essay in his *Mimesis, Masochism, and Mime* (1997).

4 As Paul Huvenne and Bart de Baere state, 'there is a strong continuity between Fabre's visual world and that of the old masters' (Huvenne and de Baere in Di Pietrantonio 2009: 30). Fabre admits to being influenced by Bosch and van Eyck and his work can be placed into a genealogy of artists traced back to earlier Netherlandish painters (arguably as far back as Patinir, who developed the 'world landscape' genre/format taken up by Breughel and later adopted by Bosch).

5 For Heiner Goebbels, treating the text as landscape means to open up all its layers and dimensions (rhythmical, structural, etc.) into a composition that can be experienced beyond interpretation and illustration.

6 'When I look back at my work, I realize that for the past 20 years I have been using a conciliatory language. By this I mean a merging of elements from different disciplines guided by theory and practice [...] I have allowed the subjects that I have studied over the years to influence each other. I am not an eclectic artist, I am not a multimedia artist: I have always been very aware of what is performance, what is theatre, and what is visual art' (Fabre in Amy: 2004).

7 'It is necessary to reach the point of conceiving the war machine as itself a pure form of exteriority, whereas the State apparatus constitutes the form of interiority we habitually take as a model, or according to which we are in the habit of thinking' (Deleuze and Guattari 2007: 390).

8 Look at Zavros (2008: 58) for a discussion of Deleuze's discussion of how 'anomic' phenomena (becomings) that pervade our world exist in myth but in a way that they are 'curbed'.

9 This notion of the war machine seems to be almost entrenched in the myth itself and the tragedy by extension. However, both the phallogocentric power structures that the myth sprang from and the normalization that happens in relation to major 'texts' have surreptitiously turned the rebellious act of heroism into a controlled, 'curbed' force that eventually came under and is perpetually regulated by the State apparatus.

10 I will come back to how Fabre re-imagines the structure of the tragic performance into a more rhizomatic construct.

11 For a more detailed description of this see Bogue (2003) and Zavros's PhD thesis (2008: 77).

12 The second landscape is more modest in its exploration of the
    sonoric continuum of vocal sound and language. However, it is
    flooded by the use of different accents, the use of profanities, the
    use of the whole dynamic range (from whisper to incessant yelling
    and the expression of excruciating screaming pain). It ranges from
    very poetic, philosophical text to murmurs, childish mumblings,
    giggles and stutters, and the use of microphone amplification and a
    text 'drowned' in water. Fabre plays with the physicality/materiality
    of sound to colour his landscape like he uses the lights and bodies
    of the actors. Oceanos' words are drowned in water not only in
    a metaphoric representation of the character but on a variety of
    levels. Water causes a certain variable musicality to protrude from
    an utterance that struggles to surface and always faces the limit
    of semantic obscurity. It is not only a metaphor, but a matter of
    fact, a reality that exists in the here and now, an event with whose
    unpredictability the performer deals in every single performance.

13 For a very illuminating discussion of the staging of *Prometheus
    Bound* see Ruffell (2012: 80–104).

14 Aristophanes parodies *Prometheus Bound* and the hero's
    exhibitionistic-almost tendencies in *Birds*, where Prometheus is now
    presented to constantly (and in absurd manner) avoid being seen
    (Ruffell: 103).

15 Decreus gives the very apt example of the fresco *Heaven of Delight*
    on the ceiling of the *Hall of Mirrors* in the Royal Palace in Brussels.
    The fresco that alludes to Hieronymus Bosch's *Garden of Earthly
    Delights* (1490–1510) includes the mounting of 1,600,000 jewel-
    scarab shells on the ceiling (2012: 134).

16 And Beauty is a recurring idea in his interviews. In relation to the
    particular performance in an interview to Ileana Demade for the
    Greek *Athinorama* he states that our 'faith in the power of beauty' can
    be the only way out of the economic, sociocultural and political crisis
    that Europe is undergoing (2011). We can all become Prometheus if
    we don't choose to live like victims and revolt against our dangerous
    leaders, our corrupted leaders and the 'economic egotism' of our
    times. In the words of Pandora: 'You have to choose what you will be:
    heroes or victims' (Demade 2011, my translation).

17 E.g. Epimetheus appears as the other side of desire, the one that
    admits to being 'wrong, wrong, wrong'.

18 In Brecht's *The Life of Galileo,* Galileo declares 'Unhappy the land
    that needs heroes.'

19 As Murray explains in his notes to the translation of Deleuze's essay,

'Deleuze's notion of continuous variation puns on the biological term signifying a "variation in which a series of intermediate types connects to the extremes"' (*Webster's Third New International Dictionary*) (Murray 1997: 256 – notes to the essay).

20 The continuum will again vary between concrete references to the name of their character (e.g. Athena) to more poetic clues (on either a textual or visual level, e.g. Hephaestus) and certainly depends on individual prior knowledge of not just the tragedy itself but the relevant Hesiodic myths (Pandora, Epimetheus) and Greek mythology in general (Dionysus). Epimetheus and Pandora don't appear as characters in the Aeschylean tragedy. They are connected to the myth of Prometheus by Hesiod who recounts the story twice (in *Theogony*, 527ff.; *Works and Days*, 57ff.).

21 And this of course connects to the realization that Prometheus' gift to humanity has been made redundant through institutions that normalized, policed, regulated desire – theatre being one of them. Hephaestus made us implicit and aware of it early on in the performance:

> Fire exits are marked in green a colour chosen to induce a false state of tranquillity. You feel secure, yet you are locked up inside a pyromaniac's dream. Welcome. This world is staged to receive you in comfort.
>
> Rest assured, gods and goddesses. Actions have been taken. Drills and exercises have been done.
>
> Yet perhaps it is not safety that needs to be regulated but your own still bound imagination. (Olyslaegers 2011)

22 The use of the props is also in a process of ceaseless variation. The repeated use of the axes in different parts of the performance, for example, creates a constant play within the continuum between signification and affect (they are iconic, symbolic, metonymic, metaphoric, musical, rhythmic, affective, etc.)

23 Already a 'submersion' through a mediation that inescapably simultaneously underlines the actual distance between audience and stage/'landscape'.

24 'It is through the meticulous relation with the strata that one succeeds in freeing lines of flight, causing conjugated flows to pass and escape and bringing forth continuous intensities for a BwO' (2007: 178).

25 Just like Strauss explains in his discussion of the *Mitwelt*, 'the more we absorb it, the more we lose ourselves in it' (Strauss in Bogue 2003: 118).

26 In 'The Pedestrian Gaze' Truniger explains that Aristotle had founded a school in Athens, called Peripatos, in which lessons took place while participants were walking.

> From Peripatos, a field of meanings and applications for the concept 'peripatetic' has emerged which, on the one hand, encompasses the act of being in motion without a goal and, on the other, includes the thinking associated with it. Someone who is often in motion can be described as peripatetic, as can a reader of a text that is not linearly structured, but instead works with cross-references. To follow a textual network of references and perhaps to lose oneself in the process is understood as a form of wondering. (Bolz in Truniger 2013: 123)

Chapter 9: Dionysus the Destroyer of Traditions: *The Bacchae* on Stage

1 All the productions discussed (except for those from 1908 and the 1973) I have seen on video.

2 In the Gilbert Murray Papers, New Bodleian Library, Oxford, MSS 10, 14, 15.

Chapter 10: Ariane Mnouchkine's *Les Atrides*: Uncovering a Classic

1 See Pierre Bourdieu (1979) *La Distinction: Critique sociale du jugement.* Paris: Minuit.

2 The translations from French in this chapter, unless otherwise indicated, are my own.

3 I borrow the notion of universal classics from Pascale Casanova (2008) *La République mondiale des lettres.* Paris: Le Seuil.

4 See http://www.lemonde.fr/culture/article/2014/04/25/ le-theatre-du-soleil-a-50-ans-vous-nous-avez-raconte-vos-souvenirs_4407040_3246.html (accessed 29 May 2015).

Chapter 11: Re-imagining *Antigone*: Contemporary Resonances in the Directorial Revisioning of Character, Chorus and Staging

1   In generic allusion to Sophocles' characters I follow the standard transliterated Greek spellings of names, but in making specific reference to characters in a particular translation or adaptation I observe the choices made by the writer.

2   There was an earlier version of this performed at the stage@leeds venue by twenty students from the School of Performance and Cultural Industries, University of Leeds. It was co-supervised by George Rodosthenous and Gillian Knox.

3   According to the newspaper headline read out by Eurydice.

4   There is much literature explaining and exploring Brecht's theories. One such work is White 2004.

5   At the end of Aeschylus' *Seven Against Thebes*, the character Antigone is determined to bury her brother's body, but this is believed by most scholars (e.g. Torrance 2007: 19–20) to be a later interpolation possibly added for a revival in the wake of Sophocles' success with *Antigone*.

6   Chapter 11 (113–29) of Blundell 1995 provides an excellent description of the law, customs and societal expectations that affected women in Classical Athens.

7   For more on the history and theory of the chorus, see e.g. Peponi (Billings et al. 2013: 15–34). On modern practice, see e.g. Goldhill 2007: 45–79.

8   National Theatre video, *Greek Theatre: Antigone – The Ancient Greek Chorus*. Online at www.nationaltheatre.org.uk/ video/antigone-the-ancient-greek-chorus (accessed 24 March 2015).

9   Antigone is never part of the chorus, but she does voice lines from a messenger speech.

10 For information on background and conventions governing theatrical practice with regard to tragedy in Classical Athens, see e.g. Sommerstein 2002: 4–22.

11 See Brown 1987: 199–200 for brief discussion of the issues regarding the disputed speech and further bibliography.

12 See e.g. Honig 2013: 153–6 for a favourable reassessment of Ismene. Honig also cites other modern defenders.

13 See www.youtube.com/watch?v=167R-4TUNXE (accessed 2 March 2015).

14 Şahika Tekand (see Erincin 2011) wrote and directed a version of *Antigone* for the International Istanbul Theatre Festival in 2006. His chosen title, *Eurydice's Cry*, testifies to the importance of that character for him.

15 As in, respectively, Euripides' *Elektra* and *Medea*.

16 For more explanation of the theory, see e.g. White 2004.

17 See e.g. Paolucci and Paolucci 1962 for analysis of Hegel's arguments.

INDEX